LEGENDARY LOCALS

OF

ASHLAND

OREGON

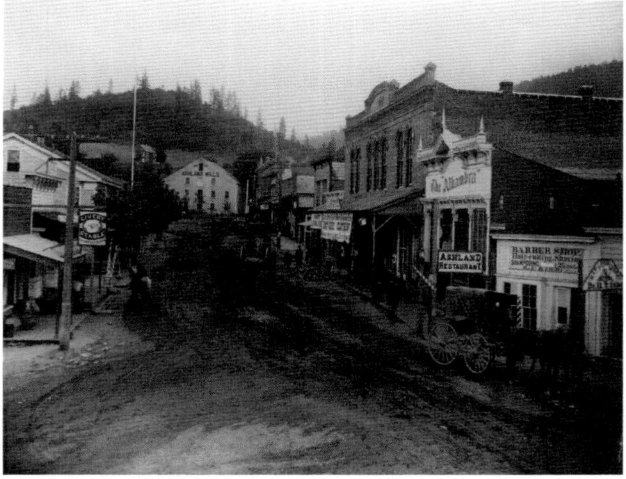

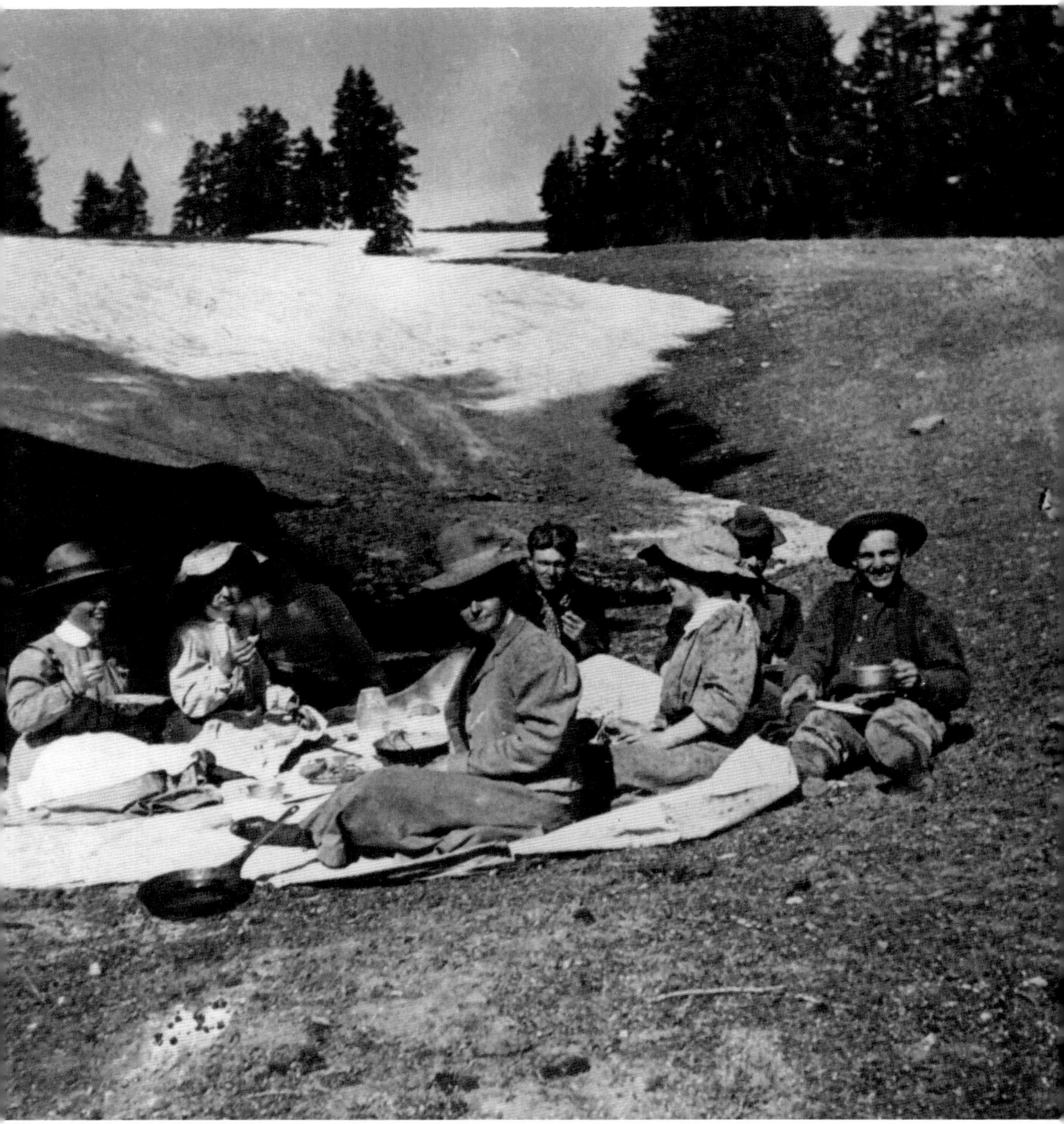

Picnic on Mount Ashland
Local picnickers eat breakfast on a sunny late spring day in 1910 near the summit of Mount Ashland. (Courtesy of Southern Oregon Historical Society, #7692.)

Page 1: Ashland Plaza 1887
Looking south onto the Ashland Plaza from near the present-day intersection of Water Street and North Main Street, the white-splashed walls of Ashland Mills—which served as the flagship building of downtown Ashland—are visible. The three-story mill stood at the front entrance lawn of Lithia Park. (Courtesy of the Southern Oregon Historical Society, #79.)

LEGENDARY LOCALS

OF

ASHLAND

OREGON

SAM WHEELER

LEGENDARY LOCALS

Copyright © 2015 by Sam Wheeler
ISBN 978-1-4671-0145-5

Legendary Locals is an imprint of Arcadia Publishing
Charleston, South Carolina

Printed in the United States of America

Library of Congress Control Number: 2013955114

For all general information, please contact Arcadia Publishing:
Telephone 843-853-2070
Fax 843-853-0044
E-mail sales@arcadiapublishing.com
For customer service and orders:
Toll-Free 1-888-313-2665

Visit us on the Internet at www.arcadiapublishing.com

Dedication
To all those who have called Ashland their home.

On the Front Cover: Clockwise from top left:
Oregon Shakespeare Festival founder Angus Bowmer and Allan Harris posing above the Elizabethan Theater (courtesy of the Oregon Shakespeare Festival; see page 54), Mount Ashland Ski School (courtesy of the Southern Oregon Historical Society, #16905), Brammo Inc. founder Craig Bramscher (courtesy of Brammo Inc.; see page 115), Twin Plunges (courtesy of the Southern Oregon Historical Society, #6514; see page 44), man and woman by balanced rock in Lithia Park (courtesy of the Southern Oregon Historical Society, #33282), Ashland High School graduate Diana Banda (courtesy of Diana Banda; see page 108), Oregon Shakespeare Festival artistic director Jerry Turner (courtesy of the Oregon Shakespeare Festival; see page 63), former F1 mechanic and Ashland resident Ana Delfosse (courtesy of Ana Delfosse; see page 70), Weisinger Family Winery founder John Weisinger (courtesy of Weisinger family; see page 69).

On the Back Cover: From left to right:
Ashland founder Abel Helman (courtesy of the Southern Oregon Historical Society, #398; see page 11), Oregon Shakespeare Festival senior scenic theater designer Richard L. Hay (courtesy of the Oregon Shakespeare Festival; see page 66).

CONTENTS

ACKNOWLEDGMENTS

The author would like to gratefully acknowledge Kay Atwood, Marjorie Lutz O'Harra, and Joe Peterson, whose concise and well-written histories of Ashland make understanding its past more feasible; Terry Skibby, whose passion for photographing Ashland and its development has helped provide an important visual understanding of its history; the Southern Oregon Historical Society, Southern Oregon University archives, and Hannon Library and the Oregon Shakespeare Festival archives for their tireless cataloging of historically relevant materials that provide a foundation for understanding Ashland history; and the *Ashland Daily Tidings* and the *Medford Mail Tribune* for their consistent documentation of life in Ashland and southern Oregon as a whole.

INTRODUCTION

Ashland, Oregon's prestige emanates from a vast array of historic and modern-day tributaries. Nearly 200 years have passed since early explorers and trappers from the Hudson's Bay Fur Company, such as Peter Skene Ogden, first laid eyes on the valley in whose southern branch Ashland is nestled. French trappers of the late 1820s began referring to the fertile trough as "la Rivière aux Coquins," or "the River of Rogues," named after the Native American tribes who thrived in the region for at least 10,000 years before settlers arrived.

It is unknown whether Scottish botanist David Douglas, whose adventures near the Umpqua River during the early 1820s are well documented, ever saw the Rogue Valley, but interpretations of his published notes suggest he may have on his way to northern California from Oregon. Ogden arrived as the first confirmed white person in the Rogue Valley on January 24, 1827. He led a party of nearly 30 people and over 100 horses and was accompanied by several Native Americans on the expedition. For the Hudson's Bay Company, present-day southern Oregon and the Rogue Valley were the last unexplored areas of North America south of the 49th parallel.

According to Ogden's journal, while he and his party were camped for a week along the Rogue River near lower Table Rock, Native Americans approached the group of explorers and trappers in peace, offering gifts, trading goods and relics, and dancing before departing without conflict.

One of the first violent disputes—or, at least one of the first recorded—between settlers and Native Americans of the Rogue Valley took place in 1837. A party of men led by trapper Ewing Young was driving about 800 head of cattle north between California and the Willamette Valley. While that party was staying overnight near the Klamath River, two of Young's men fatally shot a pair of local Native Americans who peacefully walked into their camp. As the party hurried through the Rogue Valley, its members engaged in battles with Native Americans near present-day Gold Hill. From men like Ogden and Young, word of the valley's fertile climate and land and abundance of natural resources spread quickly, but it was not until the 1851 discovery of gold in southern Oregon that wagonloads of settlers began to populate the area.

The site of Ashland's historic downtown plaza, which today plays host to colorful community gatherings, dialogues, and demonstrations, was the site of a sprawling Ikirakutsum village until the outbreak of conflict between local Native Americans and settlers in 1852. In January of that year, two groups of settlers arrived in present-day Ashland, pitching camp near Ashland's former railroad yards. The first pair, Robert B. Hargadine and Sylvester Pease, arrived on January 6. On January 8, Abel D. Helman arrived. His travel partners, Eber Emery, Jacob B. Emery, James A Cardwell, Dowd Farley, and A.M. Rogers, arrived on January 11 and also chose to remain. Coincidentally, Ashland Mills was settled directly following the discovery of gold in Rich Gulch, a tributary of Jackson Creek, near present-day Jacksonville. Helman, alongside the Emerys, immediately went to work building a water-driven sawmill along Mill Creek, now Ashland Creek, to supply miners in the area with lumber. The sawmill was the first in Jackson County, and was established by the Oregon Territorial Legislature the day after the arrival of Helman's party.

By 1854, most of the Rogue Valley's Native American population had been forced onto the inadequately supplied and disease-stricken Table Rock Reservation, which, despite military protection from nearby Fort Lane, was the target of several violent attacks carried out by bands of murderous settlers. Conflict between a steady stream of gold-hungry settlers and tribes in the valley, which included Athapaskan Rogue River and Takelma Native Americans, did not cease until 1856, when US Army forces in the area grew large enough to quell any resistance from local tribes. Less than a year after the conclusion of the

Rogue River Wars, fought in southwestern Oregon between 1855 and 1856, the vast majority of Native Americans who survived the conflict had been forcibly removed by the government to the site of today's Siletz Reservation of the Confederated Tribes of Siletz Indians, or to Oregon's Yamhill Valley, the site of today's Grand Ronde Indian Reservation of the Confederated Tribes of Grand Ronde.

In 1855, the first group of Native Americans to be forcibly removed from the Table Rock Reservation was marched about 180 miles to Port Orford, on the Oregon coast, where they were shipped by boat most of the way to the Grand Ronde Reservation. Near the end of the war, a second group was marched, again by military escort, from the Table Rock Reservation to the Yamhill Valley. The over 300-mile march and forced removal is known as the "Oregon Trail of Tears." Also in 1956, a third group of Native Americans who camped at the Table Rock Reservation was removed and marched about 275 miles to the Siletz Reservation. By the end of 1856, Fort Lane, which was originally built to protect those living on the Table Rock Reservation but then used as a military headquarters during the war, was closed, as the majority of Native Americans who once lived in the Rouge Valley had been removed. Once the fort was abandoned, the reservation around the Table Rocks was dissolved and the land was open to settlement.

CHAPTER ONE

Shasta Indian Village to Ashland Mills

1800–1860

The Ikirakutsum of the Bear Creek Valley were the northernmost band of the Shasta Native American people. The band occupied the southern stretches of Bear Creek and its tributaries around present-day Ashland. When settlers arrived, the Ikirakutsum were led by Chief Tipsu, who called the band's village along the banks of Ashland Creek K'wakhakha. The village, stretching from the site of today's downtown plaza south into Lithia Park, was known in the Shasta language as "where the crow lights." The headman Tipsu Tyee (Chinook for "bearded chief") was killed less than a year after K'wakhakha was abandoned by the Ikirakutsum in 1852.

Chief Tipsu was killed near the Klamath River by the chief from a band of Shasta Native Americans who occupied territory near present-day Hornbrook, California, along the banks of the Klamath River. Known as Tyee Bill, the Shasta headman is reported by some sources to have killed Chief Tipsu in order to keep peace with local militiamen, many of whom were self-proclaimed "squaw hunters."

Despite southern Oregon's plaguing shadow of guerrilla warfare between Native Americans and the volunteer militia–backed military during the first half of the 1850s, the settlement of present-day Ashland slowly grew. A modest but steady stream of settlers followed the January 1852 arrival of Robert B. Hargadine, Sylvester Pease, Abel D. Helman, Eber Emery, Jacob B. Emery, James A Cardwell, Dowd Farley, and A.M. Rogers. In 1853, carried by 159 wagons, one particularly large group of settlers arrived in the Rogue Valley with about 700 men, women, and children. Several thousand cattle, sheep, and horses arrived as well. It was in April 1853 that Elizabeth Fine Hill arrived by wagon to Ashland. She is the first known white woman to live in the town.

During 1854, in addition to the town's first school opening, Helman and Eber Emery partnered with M.B. Morris to build and open Ashland Flouring Mills. The building, which stood at what is now the entrance to Lithia Park, ground the first flour in Oregon south of Roseburg. Eli K. Anderson, who went on to own the mill, grew the first wheat processed there. In October 1855, the mill also served as a fortified shelter for Ashland families, who feared violence after Native Americans massacred 20 people just north of Jacksonville.

The settlement was dubbed Ashland Mills in 1853, and two years later became a formally recognized town with the establishment of a post office, where Helman was postmaster for 27 years. It is unclear whether Ashland Mills was named after Ashland County, Ohio, where Helman was born, or Ashland, Kentucky, which was the home of politician Henry Clay, a former senator, congressman, secretary of state, Whig Party founder, and three-time failed presidential candidate who was greatly admired among the first settlers of Ashland Mills. The town dropped the "Mills" in 1871 and was known from then on as simply Ashland.

In order to promote the growth of the town in 1855, Helman sectioned off 12 lots outside the front door of the flour mill he helped found. The area was reserved for business establishments and became known as "the plaza." By 1860, Ashland Mills was the hub of the Rogue Valley. Jacksonville was where the gold was, but the means to remove it were produced and available in nearby Ashland Mills. Where the Ikirakutsum village existed just eight years earlier, several painted milled-lumber homes and other structures now stuck out from the hillsides and creek banks. A blacksmith shop, meat market, cabinet shop, and wagon shop had sprouted up in the plaza area sectioned off by Helman five short years earlier.

Being situated beneath the Siskiyou Pass, the town was also the first stop in Oregon for travelers from San Francisco headed north and the last stop for southbound travelers about to embark on the daunting mountain pass. Taking advantage of Ashland's location along the main route in 1859, Eber Emery started building Ashland House, a bed-and-breakfast-style business for travelers moving between Oregon and California. He went on to manage the business for several years after opening its doors in 1860.

Ashland Mills had a population of about 50 when Oregon became a state on February 14, 1859. Once statehood was achieved, the California-Oregon Stage Company began running a transit line for passengers between San Francisco and Portland, operating on a newly constructed road over the Siskiyou Mountains that brought passengers through Ashland Mills. The town's first public school was built in 1860. The wood-framed building cost $596 and was located near the intersection of Gresham and East Main Streets. Furthering Ashland's connection to life beyond the Rogue Valley, the transcontinental telegraph line was extended to Ashland Mills from San Francisco three years later.

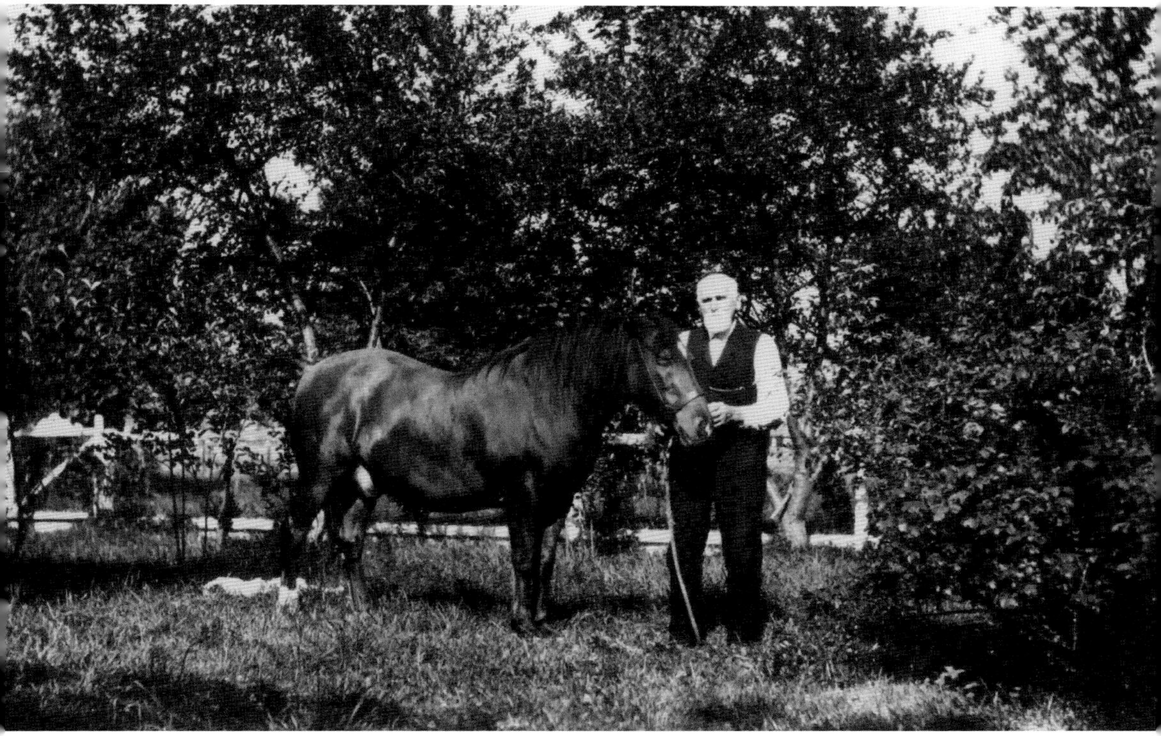

Abel Helman

Abel Helman set out west from Ohio in 1850. He was 26 and hungry for a shot at striking California gold. Luckless as a wandering and sometimes starving prospector, in 1851 he began to explore opportunities in shipping supplies to miners. After purchasing a pack mule and a horse, he moved through western Oregon territory in an effort to bring valuable supplies back to miners in northern California from the Willamette Valley. Helman's party camped near present-day Ashland on its way north and passed through the Rogue Valley again on its return to present-day Yreka with a delivery of valuable supplies. Soon after his return, Helman rejoined his Ohioan mining partner, Eber Emery, on the North Fork of the Salmon River, where the pair had established claims and placer mines. Emery and Helman were lousy miners but talented carpenters. They decided to abandon their claims and head back to Yreka, known then as Shasta Butte City, and easily found work that suited their talents. It was from there, in the summer of 1851, that the pair learned of a temporary peace treaty between exploring miners and Native Americans in the Rogue Valley. They descended the northern slope of the Siskiyou Mountains above Bear Creek in January of the following year and staked out their land claims at present-day Ashland. Helman and Emery went on to stake the first Donation Land Claims on January 11, the day before Jackson County was established by the Oregon Territorial Legislature. In addition to the town itself, Helman went on to co-found the mill that supplied the materials to construct Ashland. In 1853, he was elected to make the return trip to Ohio and bring back his and Emery's families. Helman also had a hand in the construction and opening of Ashland Flouring Mills, established a dozen lots for the development of the site of Ashland's present-day downtown plaza, and became the town's first postmaster. Helman fought in the Rogue River Wars of 1855 and 1856 and also served as captain of the Oregon militia in Ashland. Helman was born on April 10, 1824, and died on March 5, 1910. He is the namesake of Helman Elementary School. (Courtesy of the Southern Oregon Historical Society, #398.)

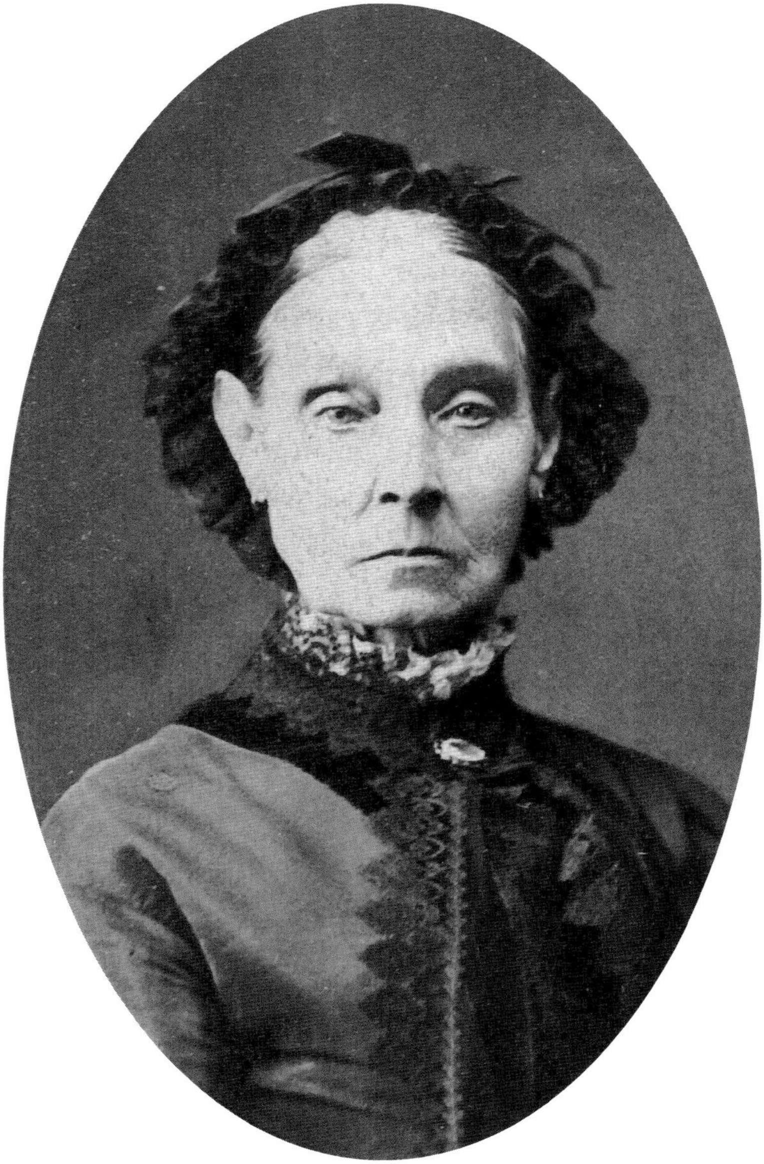

Elizabeth Fine Hill

Elizabeth Hill arrived by wagon in April 1853 as the first woman in Ashland. Married to Isaac Hill, she settled with him in a one-room cabin on a plot of land now covered by Emigrant Lake. Elizabeth and Isaac raised their son, Cicero, and their three daughters, Mary, Haseltine, and Martha, in the cabin. The year of the Hills' arrival, the family established what was known as Kingsbury Cemetery and Soda Springs Cemetery. Around the Hills' land claim, a town known as Klamath Junction developed over time. As a last stop at the base of the Greensprings wagon road, the town went on to support a few homes, a garage, a pair of service stations, and a dance hall. When what was left of the failed settlement was submerged with the expansion of Emigrant Lake in 1960, those buried in the cemetery were moved to present-day Hill Dunn Family Cemetery on the bank of the lake. (Courtesy of the Southern Oregon Historical Society, #19876.)

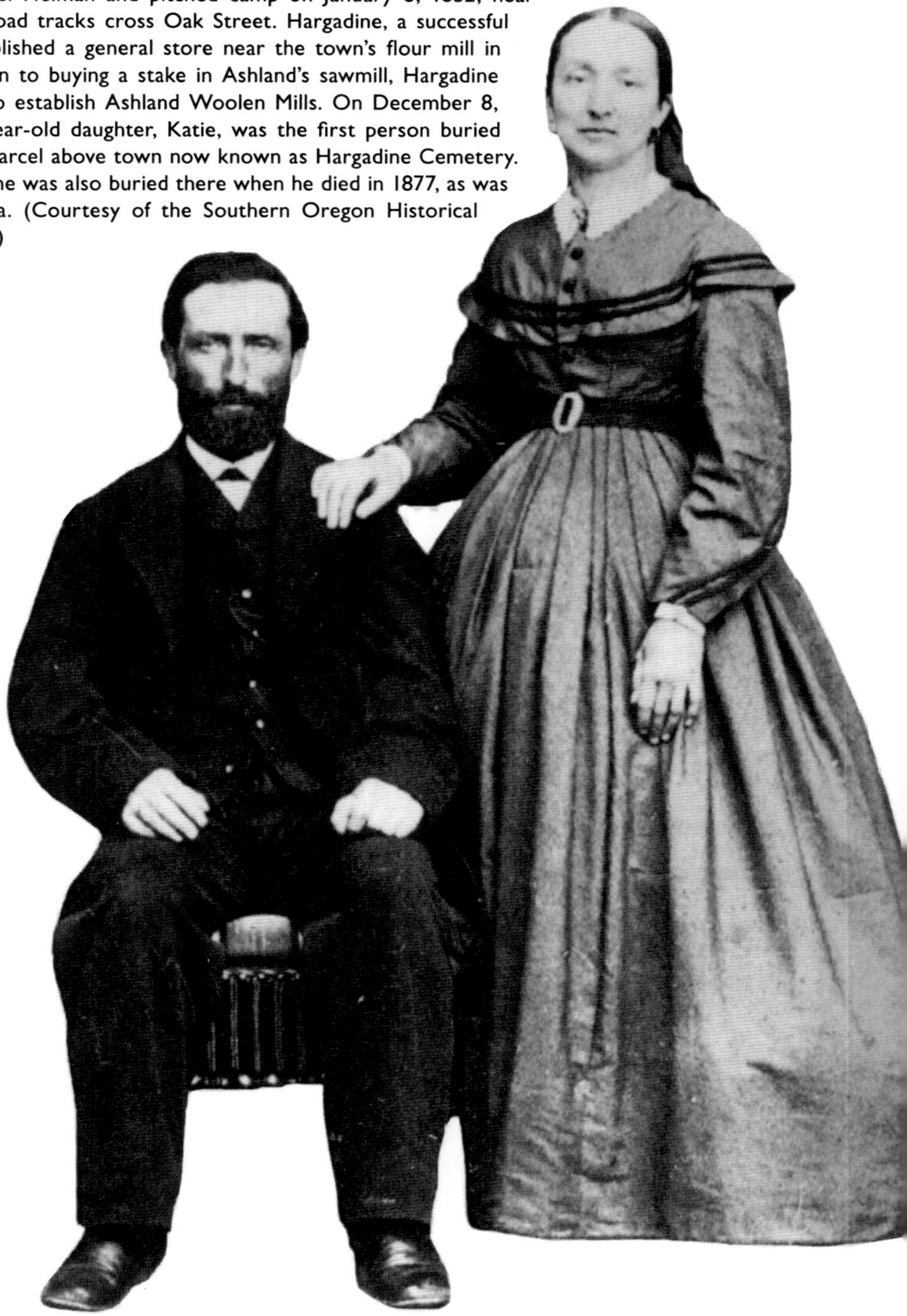

Robert B. Hargadine and Wife Martha Hargadine
Robert Hargadine, the first white settler to arrive in the Ashland area, filed the second Donation Land Claim in Ashland Mills. He and his partner, Sylvester Pease, actually arrived to the area a few days before Abel Helman and pitched camp on January 8, 1852, near where the railroad tracks cross Oak Street. Hargadine, a successful merchant, established a general store near the town's flour mill in 1856. In addition to buying a stake in Ashland's sawmill, Hargadine went on to help establish Ashland Woolen Mills. On December 8, 1867, his one-year-old daughter, Katie, was the first person buried on a one-acre parcel above town now known as Hargadine Cemetery. Robert Hargadine was also buried there when he died in 1877, as was his wife, Martha. (Courtesy of the Southern Oregon Historical Society, #10911.)

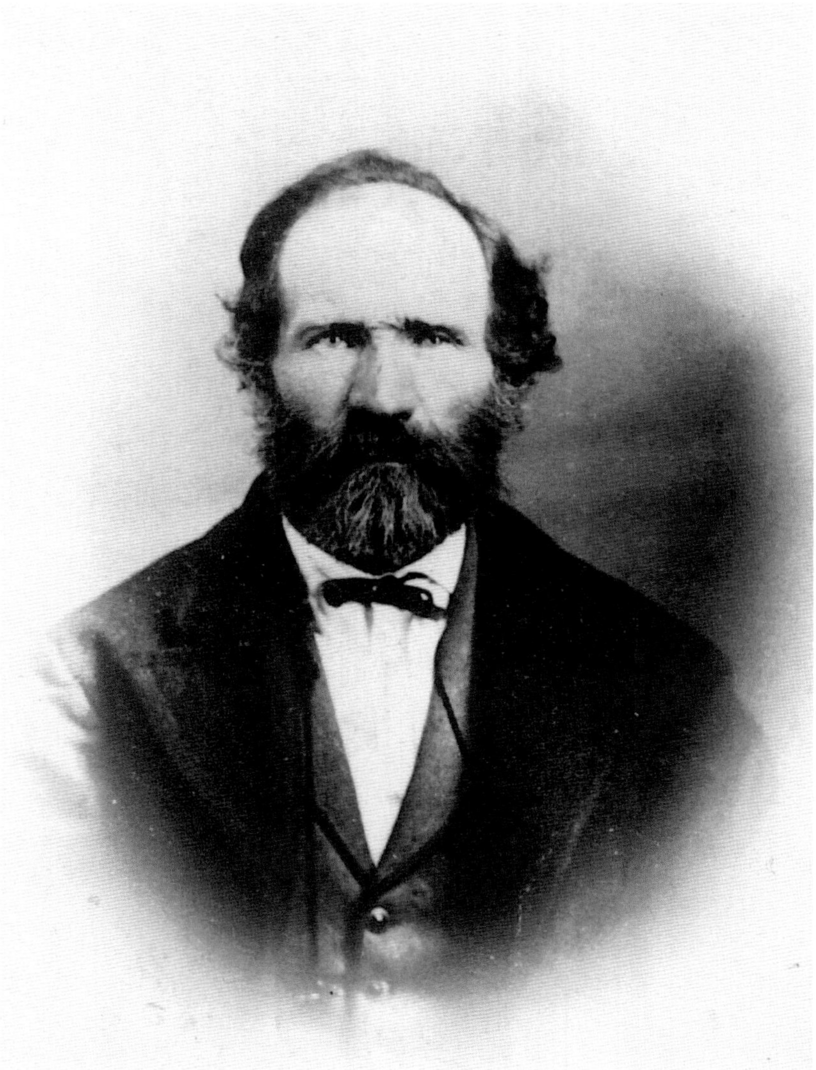

Eber Emery

In addition to accompanying Abel Helman on a gold-seeking venture from Ohio to California in 1851, Emery went on to help settle Ashland, lent a hand in building the town's first sawmill, and, in 1854, opened the town's first flour mill. The main room of Emery's home served as the site of Ashland's first schoolhouse, with classes beginning in October 1854. In 1859, Emery started building Ashland House, an inn for travelers between Oregon and California. He went on to manage the stopover for several years after opening its doors in 1860. Ashland House's accommodating atmosphere appealed to worn-out travelers fresh off or about to face the daunting stage road over Siskiyou Pass. The building was torn down in 1960. Always mindful of continuing the development of the city he helped found, in 1876, Emery sold the land of present-day Ashland Historic Cemetery, where Abel Helman and many other first-generation settlers are buried, to Ashland's school district. Following its sale from Emery, the property was annexed by the town trustees, and plans were established for a long-lasting cemetery. The cemetery was listed in the National Register of Historic Places in 1994. (Courtesy of the Southern Oregon Historical Society, #11261.)

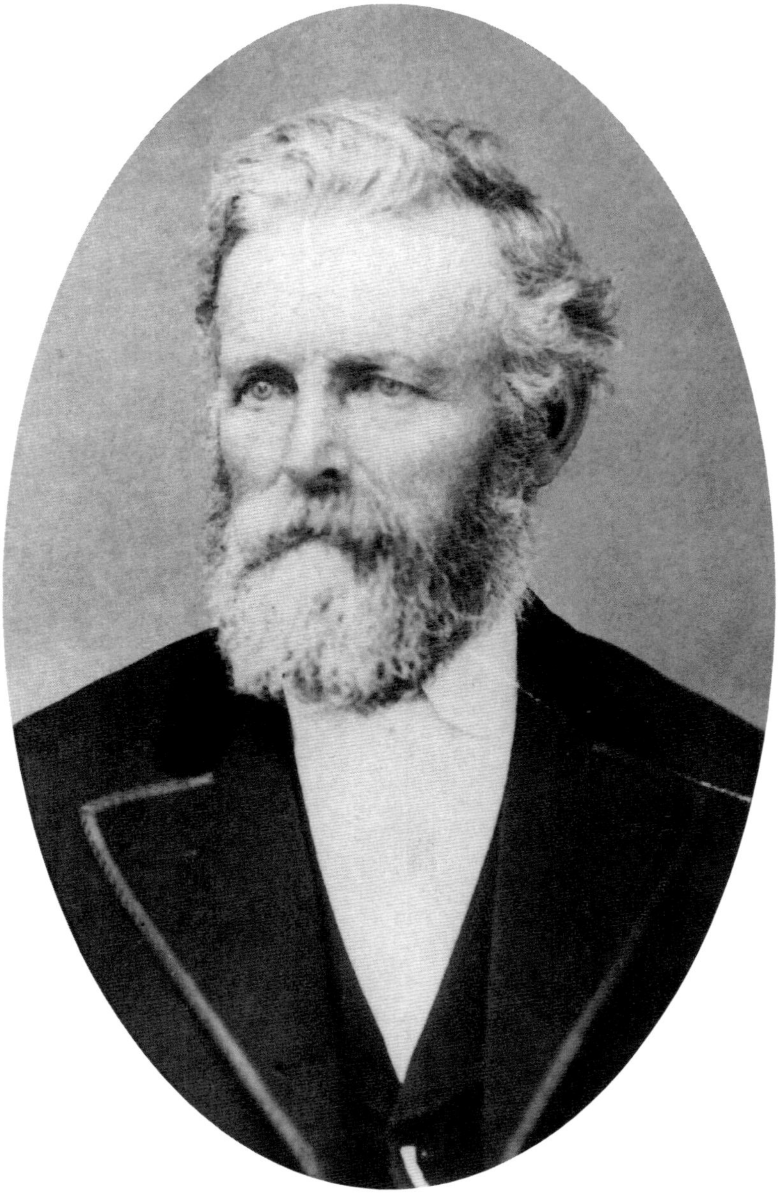

Jacob Wagner
The namesake of Wagner Butte above Ashland Creek Watershed, Jacob Wagner actually settled and built the first home where Talent, Oregon, would eventually be developed. Wagner Creek is also named after the noteworthy settler. Wagner's Ashland connection is linked to none other than Abel Helman, whose name was written across the land title covering the parcel on which Ashland Flouring Mills stood. In 1858, Wagner bought out another Ashland man written into the title by Helman for partial ownership of the mill and moved to Ashland to run it. For some time, it was the only mill grinding flour south of Roseburg, and served settlers across the entire Rogue Valley. Wagner had a hand in the mill's ownership and operations from 1858 through 1884. (Courtesy of the Southern Oregon Historical Society, #1068.)

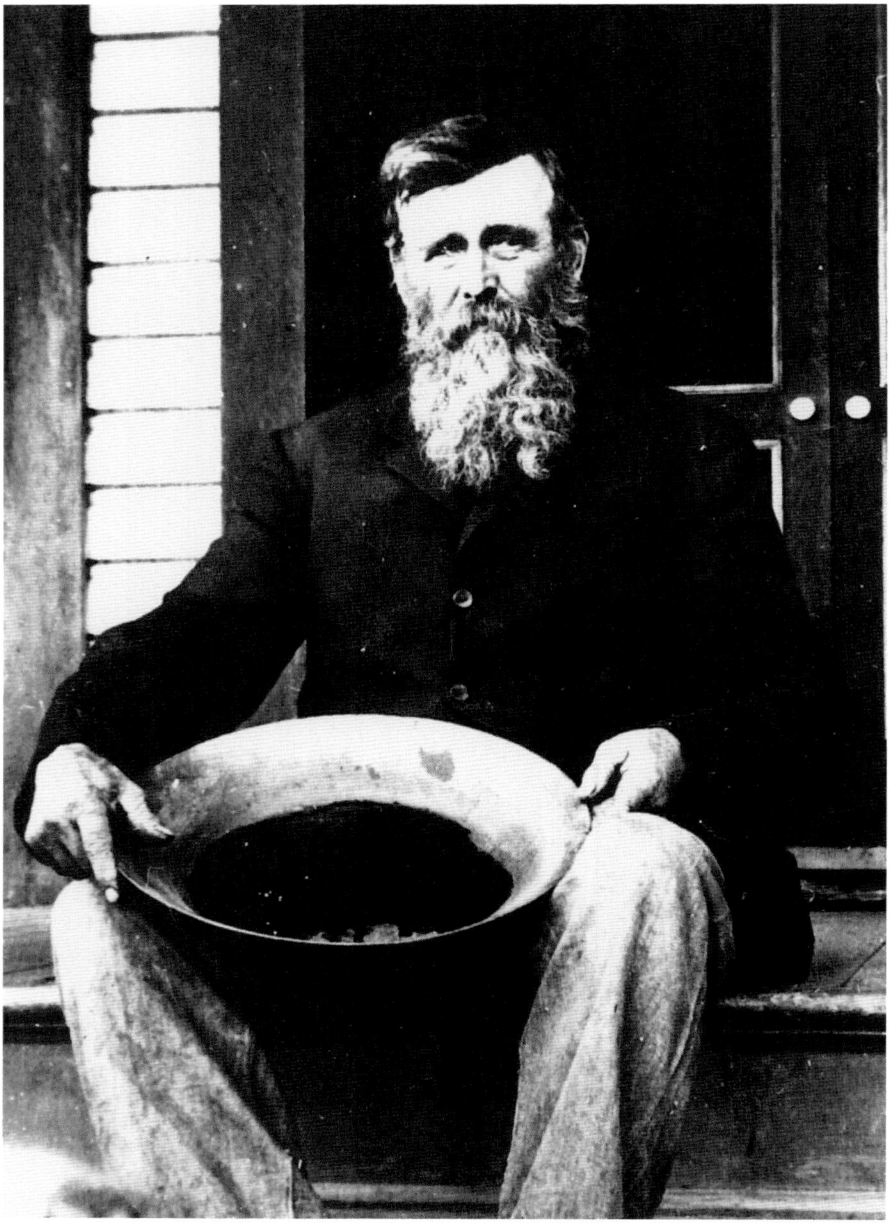

Eli K. Anderson

One of the first settlers of Ashland, Eli K. Anderson passed away on March 13, 1912, as the town's oldest living settler. One of his most notable accomplishments as an Ashlander was his major contribution to the discovery of gold in the hills above town in 1891. Anderson co-founded Ashland Mine that year, a 250-foot-deep tunnel that followed a lucrative quartz vein. The initial pulling from the mine resulted in three bricks of gold valued at $3,340. Anderson also helped found and partly owned Ashland's flour mill and operated its well-known woolen mill for several years. When Ashland Woolen Mills was destroyed by a fire in 1900, Anderson was its foremost owner and well known as an influential citizen of southern Oregon. (Courtesy of the Southern Oregon Historical Society, #6740.)

Orlando Coolidge

Orlando Coolidge arrived to the Ashland area with his wife, Mary Jane Foss Coolidge, in 1862. He purchased a large farm and, upon recognizing the Rogue Valley's exceptional growing season, converted the acreage into a successful fruit and nut orchard by 1869. It was the first orchard in Jackson County, and is still known for its high-quality fruit production. Continuing his nursery business, Coolidge and his wife moved to Ashland in 1871 and later built a home above North Main Street near downtown. The elegant house, in operation today as the Coolidge House Bed and Breakfast, was surrounded by about 35 acres of the Coolidges' productive orchard land. (Courtesy of the Southern Oregon Historical Society, #6758.)

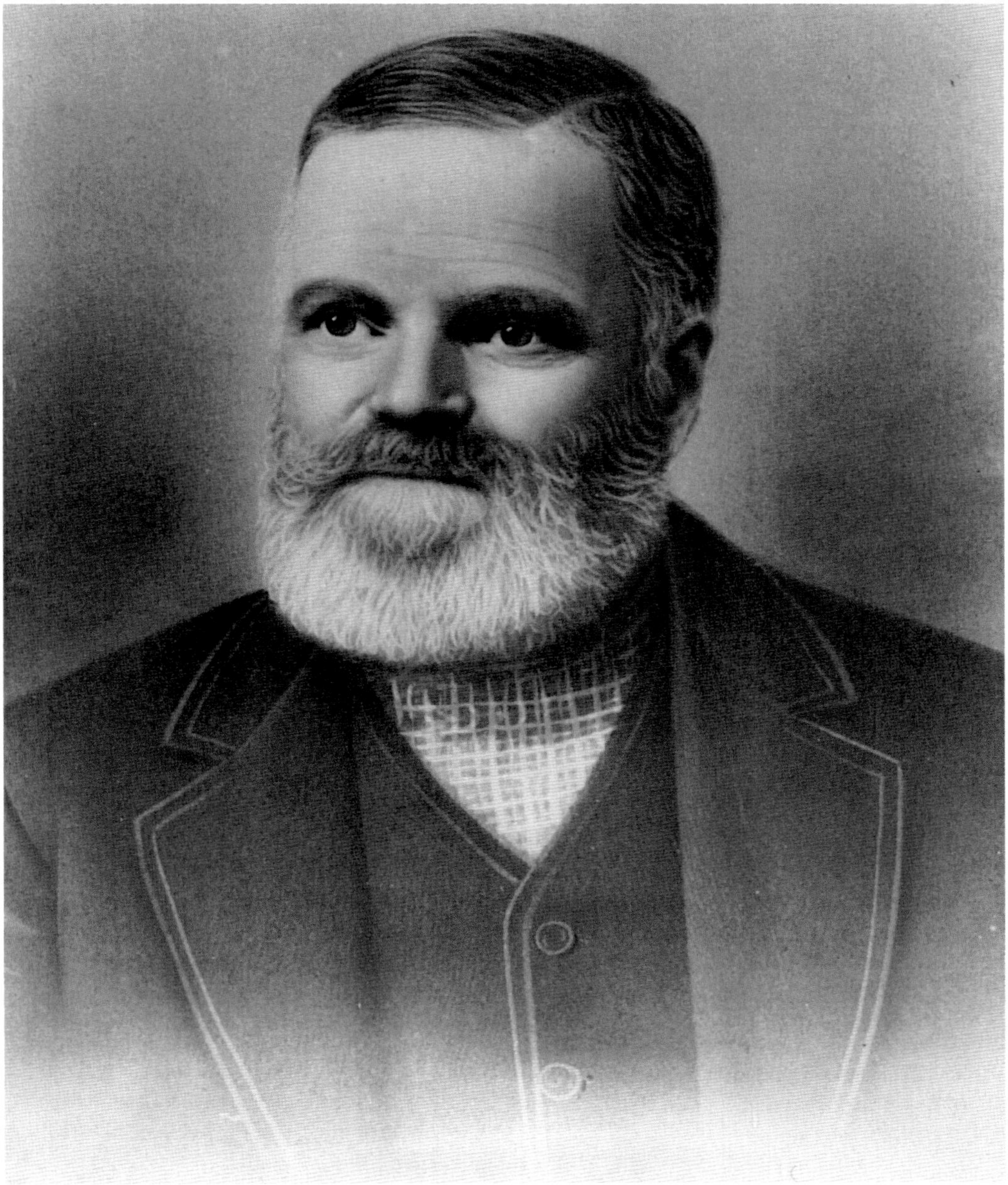

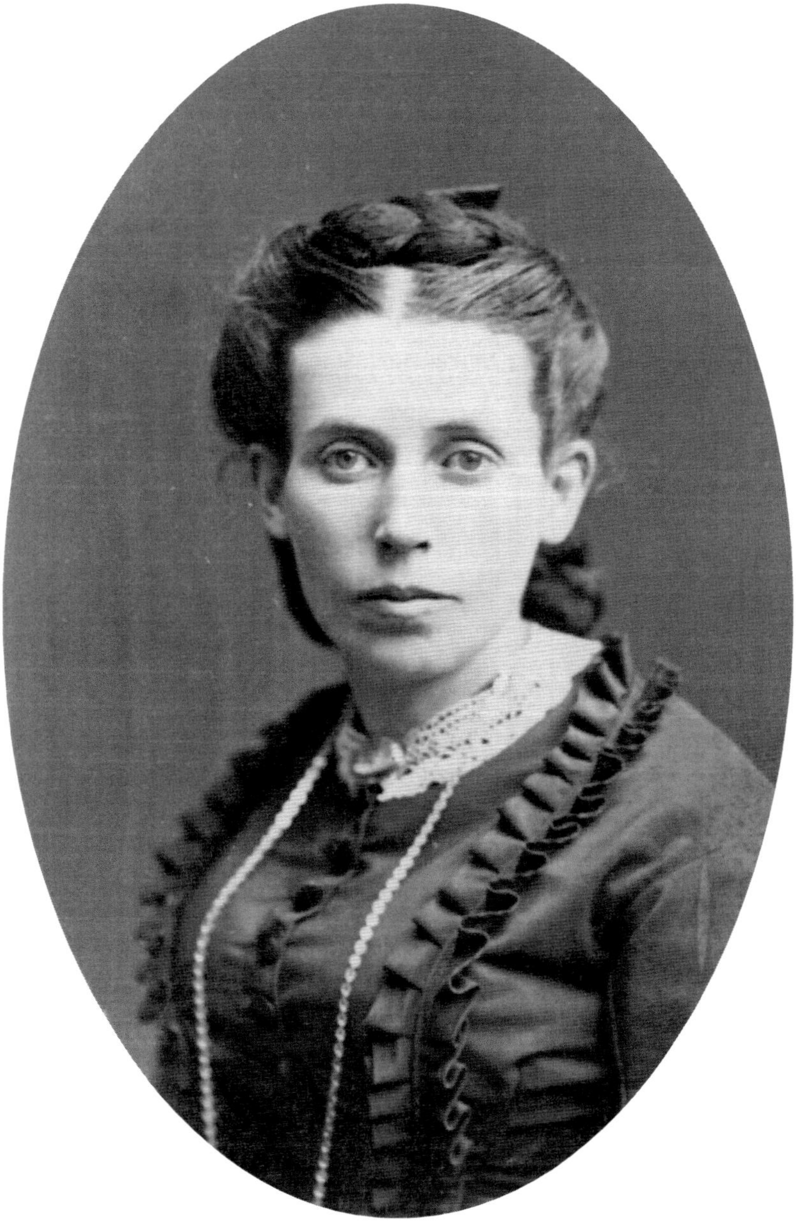

Mary Elizabeth "Lizzie" Anderson

The younger sister of Eli Anderson, Lizzie Anderson was Ashland's first teacher. In 1854, she taught the first classes to Ashland children in the front room of Eber Emery's home. Apart from teaching Ashland's inaugural group of bright-eyed youngsters and many others thereafter, she is credited with saving the life of 15-month-old John Helman, the son of Abel Helman, who fell nearly 30 feet from the flour mill while his father was working. As the story goes, on March 4, 1855—when John fell—Abel scooped up the lifeless child before handing him over to Anderson. She quickly carried him to the bank of Ashland Creek and began pouring water over his face, bringing him back to life. (Courtesy of the Southern Oregon Historical Society, #21664.)

CHAPTER TWO

Booming Ashland

1861–1900

The outbreak of the Civil War in 1861 brought a noticeable uneasiness to Ashland Mills, which, harboring a population of about 330, was divided on the issue of slavery and whether it should expand into the nation's developing western states. Oregon's constitutional ban on black immigration between 1859 and 1927 was not something the majority of Ashlanders were upset about. The town has by no means always been characterized as the forward-thinking community it is known as today. That, of course, had no effect on its early prosperity, and Ashland Mills ascended into a 40-year boom of significant growth.

Gold fever in Jacksonville began to fizzle out in the early 1860s. As the town's surrounding drainages and mines were picked clean of worthwhile gold, many prospectors turned their attention to the Rogue River for gold or other means of work altogether. Nonetheless, industry in Ashland Mills thrived with the expansion of agriculture throughout the Rogue Valley. The construction of Ashland Woolen Mills in 1867 near the present intersection of Water and B Streets added another invaluable manufacturing asset to the region. The additional mill furthered the prominence of Ashland Mills as the area's economic hub. The town also boasted a meat market, cabinet shop, lumber mill, blacksmith shop, and, among other businesses, a marble mill, which utilized stone pulled from a quarry beneath present-day Emigrant Lake. A Methodist Episcopal church was organized in July 1864, and that group went on to have an influence on the introduction of higher education to Ashland Mills. Following an 1869 Methodist Episcopal gathering, it was suggested that the town was well suited for a college.

Throughout the 1870s, Ashland was Oregon's fastest-growing community south of Portland, firmly establishing itself as Jackson County's economic, political, and cultural hub despite Jacksonville being the county seat. During the following two decades, agricultural development in the Rogue Valley, including the introduction of fruit orchards, continued to benefit Ashland significantly, and its population swelled. By the time the city was incorporated on October 13, 1874, US census estimates and other sources put its population above 400. Organized religion prospered in Ashland during the 1870s, leading to the construction of Baptist and Presbyterian churches, along with the development of plans to build a Catholic church. Another step in the town's coming of age was the establishment of the *Ashland Daily Tidings*, whose first edition rolled off the press on June 17, 1876. The newspaper was founded by former *Jacksonville Sentinel* editor James Sutton. The same year, Capt. J.M. McCall, the city of Ashland's treasurer, was elected on the People's ticket as a representative in the state legislature. The People's Party adhered to an anti-elitist, populist political doctrine.

A fire in 1879 destroyed many of the businesses on Ashland's plaza, but even that did little to slow the progress of significant growth and prosperity into the 1880s. Nearly 900 residents called Ashland home by the end of 1880. In 1885, present-day Ashland Fire and Rescue was established after the city created an official committee for fire protection. The committee led to more efficient means of fire protection than the "bucket brigade," which was what had been used to battle fires since 1859.

The most significant stride of the 1880s in Ashland was the arrival of a railroad. Early in the decade, train tracks stretching north from San Francisco and south from Portland were poised to meet in Ashland under the direction of Southern Pacific Railroad. Unfettered by the daunting climb over the

Siskiyou Mountains, the railroad from Portland reached Ashland first. The first locomotive choo-chooed through town on May 4, 1884. The track from California did not reach Ashland until about three years later. A golden spike to commemorate the connection of Southern Pacific's Portland–San Francisco line was driven in Ashland on December 17, 1887. The conjoining of tracks in Ashland was nationally significant, as it established the linking of railroads around the border of the contiguous United States. Charles Crocker, a Southern Pacific executive, pounded in the golden spike.

The arrival of rail traffic in the Rogue Valley bolstered local economies, especially Ashland's, which hinged on wool, timber, fruit, and other agricultural products. Conversely, the arrival of the railroad led to Ashland's slow decline from its decades-long position as Jackson County's economic hub. After a decision by railroad surveyors in 1883 led to the railroad's bypassing Jacksonville and streaking straight through the heart of the Rogue Valley toward Ashland, a depot site was staked out near the center of the valley floor. The small community that sprouted up around the site developed into Medford, which was incorporated by 1885.

But it was a slow decline for Ashland from the Rogue Valley's economic spotlight, and with a bolstered significance lent by the arrival of the railroad, the town grew rapidly from the 1880s through World War I. The town boasted free public education at two local schools, dental services, insurance and real estate offices, and five saloons. In 1884, Ashland Woolen Mills was producing about 16,000 pounds of wool each month, and in 1899, about 75,000 boxes of fruit from the Ashland area's numerous thriving orchards filled train cars leaving the Rogue Valley.

In 1888, the city used $3,000 to grade Ashland's streets and improve drainage. The streets, and the plaza especially, were known for becoming a muddy, slippery mess in the wet months. Culverts were installed, along with one-and-a-half miles of wooden sidewalks. The Ashland Electric Power and Light Company was established in 1888 and used hydropower harnessed from Ashland Creek to light the city's streets and homes. Ashland established an electric rate schedule a year later, which was the first of its kind in southern Oregon. Also in 1888, prominent local orchard owners Henry and Harriet Carter deeded a large cleared swath of land through the middle of their orchards to the city of Ashland. The family envisioned the land becoming a grand avenue for Ashland, but at the time, it led nowhere. Instead, much of the city's traffic passed through East Main Street. Locals raced horses on the open strip, but the Carter family's dreams of grandeur did not go down in vain; their grand avenue to nowhere is now known as Siskiyou Boulevard.

By the end of the 1880s, Ashland's population had swelled to 1,784, and the city owned over 200 acres of land. Ashland dug straight into the 1890s and struck gold. Local entrepreneur E.K. Anderson, who established Ashland's flour mill and operated its well-known woolen mill, founded Ashland Mine in 1891 along with William Hackett.

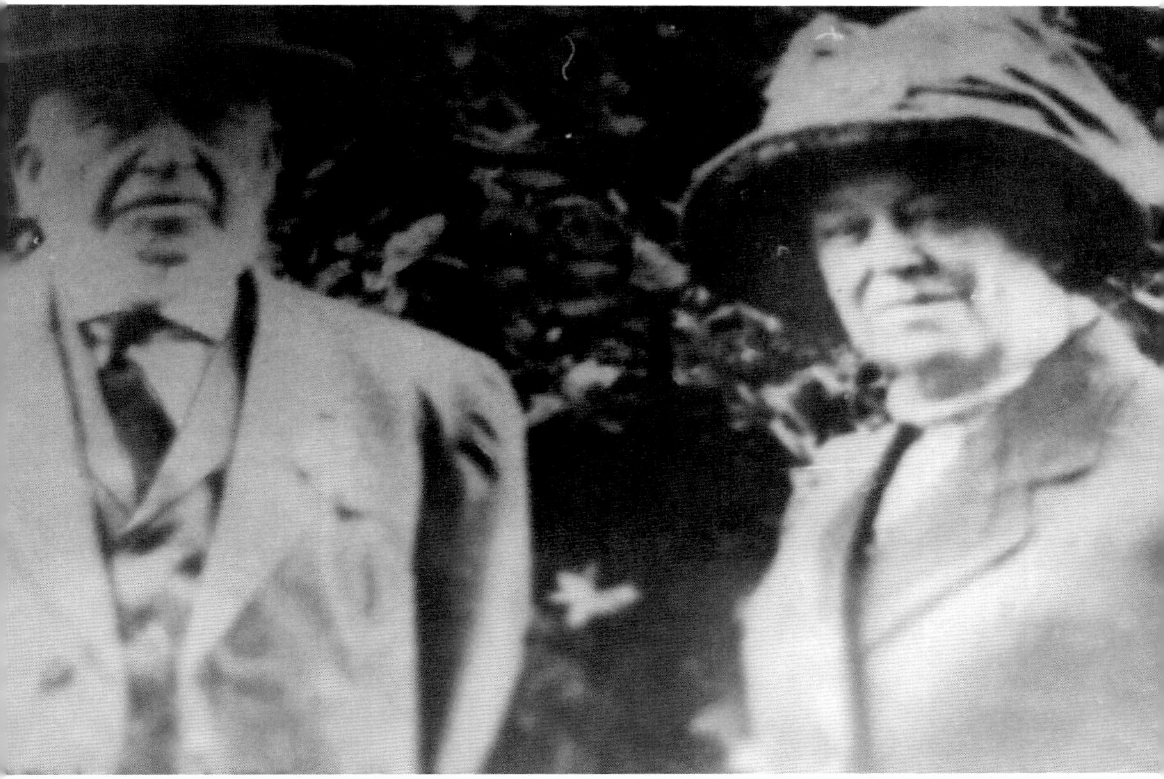

Rev. Joseph Henry Skidmore and Wife
Following an 1869 Methodist Episcopal conference in Ashland during which it was decided that the quaint southern Oregon town would make a logical location for a college, the Rev. Joseph Henry Skidmore was the first person to act on the conference's ambition. In 1872, Skidmore completed the carpentry work on an unfinished Ashland building and began a short-lived college, of which he was the president. Due to lack of finances, Skidmore's endeavor failed within the first two years, and in 1878, the Methodist Episcopal Church assumed control of the institution and arranged for it to be reopened. It was feeble beginnings for the college, but nonetheless, the school developed into what is known today as Southern Oregon University. (This photograph is part of the Southern Oregon University Archives and made available courtesy of Southern Oregon University Hannon Library.)

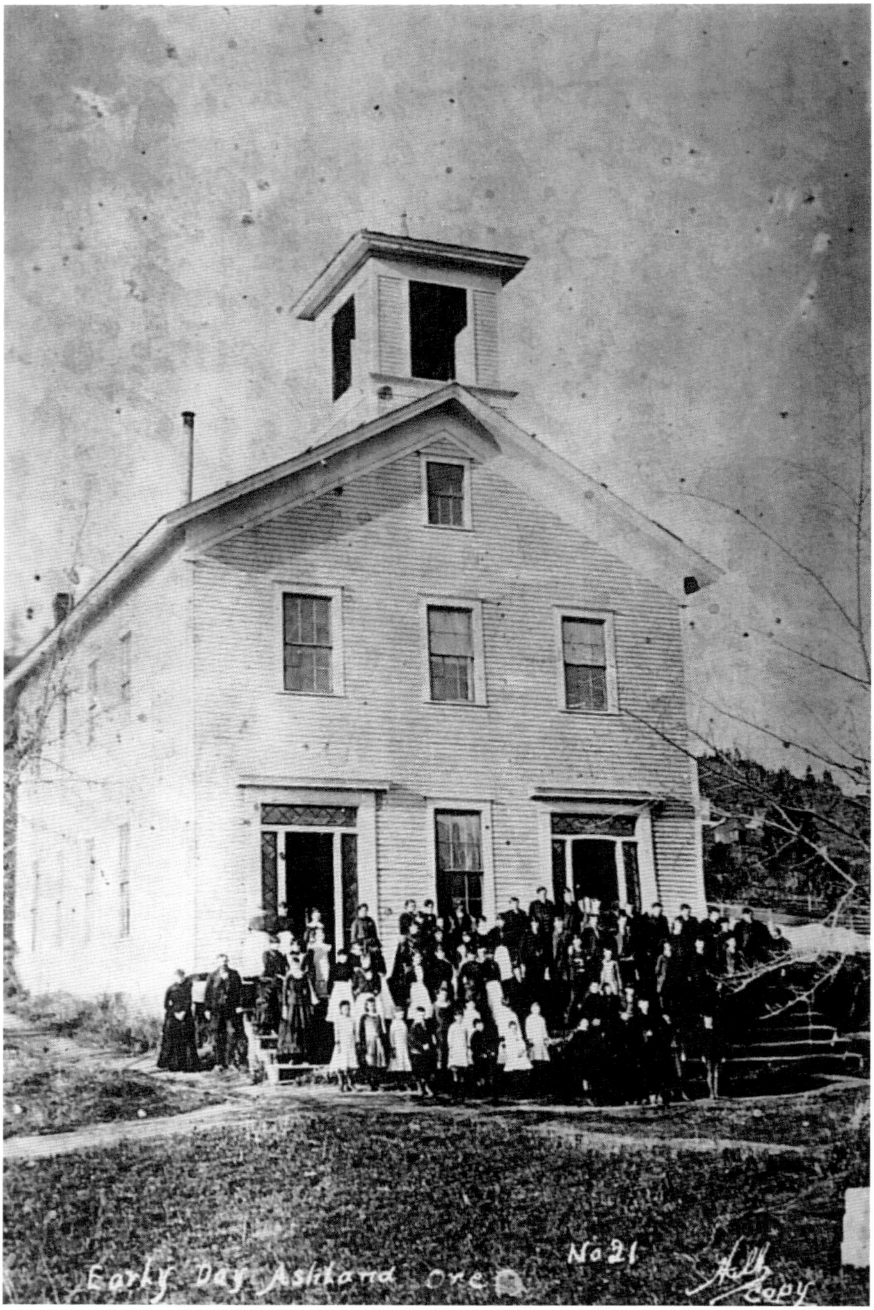

Skidmore Academy

Two years before the city was incorporated, Rev. Joseph Henry Skidmore opened Ashland Academy, whose name was changed to Ashland College in 1878, and then to Ashland College and Normal School two years later. The school was established to train teachers. In 1882, it had 42 enrolled students and was located on North Main Street where the former George A. Briscoe School now stands. (Courtesy of the Southern Oregon Historical Society.)

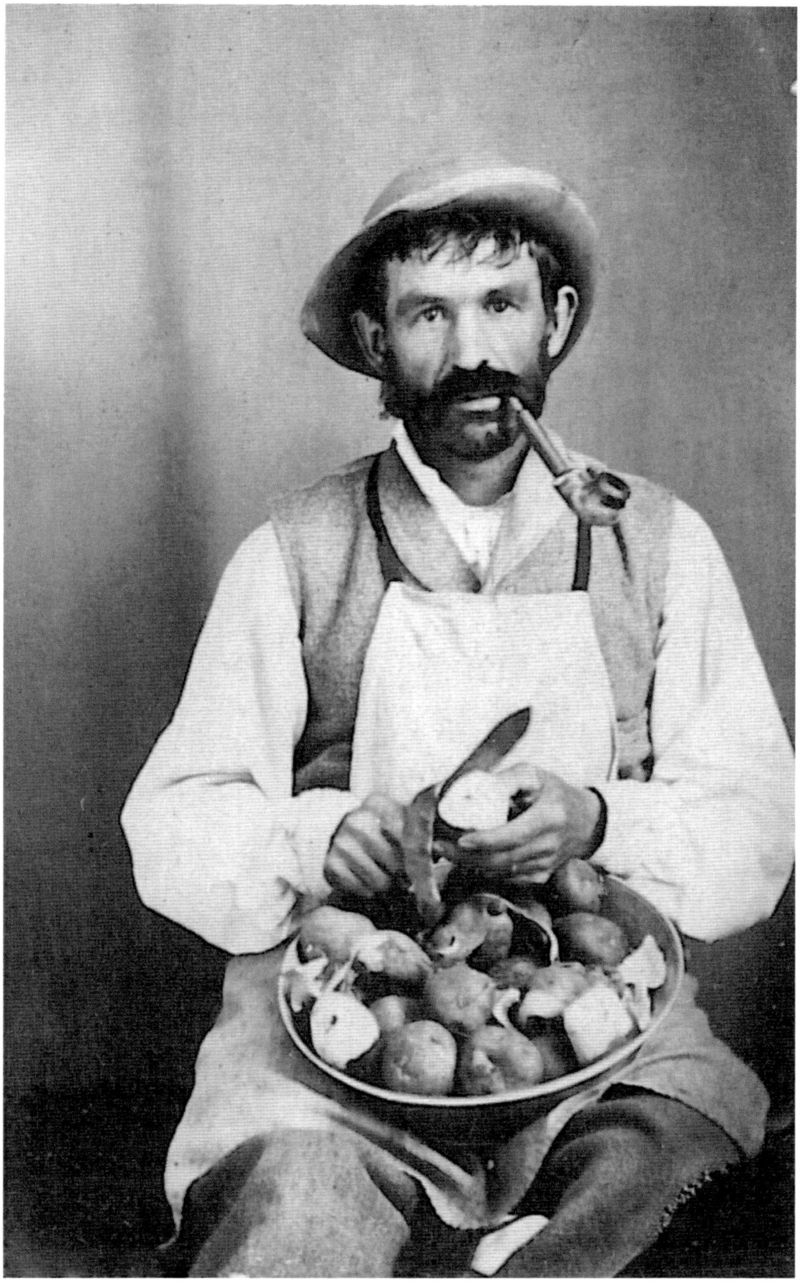

James Sutton

Former *Jacksonville Sentinel* editor James Sutton founded the *Ashland Daily Tidings* on June 17, 1876, when the first edition of the newspaper came off the press. Sutton also operated an iron foundry in Ashland. He promised that the *Tidings* editorials would be "independent and fearless," and he lived up to his promise. Sutton also coined the name "Crater Lake" in reports published on August 21 and 28, 1869, in his Jacksonville newspaper known then as the *Oregon Sentinel*. Sutton died in Ashland on October 21, 1878, at the age of 49. (Courtesy of the Southern Oregon Historical Society, #496.)

Rev. M.G. Royal

Following the Methodist Episcopal Church assuming control of Ashland's college founded by Skidmore, the institution closed within a year, suffering again from a lack of finances. It was not until the Oregon Conference redeemed the institution in 1882 and named Rev. M.G. Royal as its president that the college enjoyed some stability. Royal, a Rogue Valley pioneer and Methodist minister, served as the president of Ashland Academy, also known as Ashland College, from 1882 through 1886. The college was recognized as an official normal school by the Oregon legislature in Royal's first year as president. Known officially as Ashland College and Normal School, the school boasted four teachers and 42 students. The primary mission of the school at that time was to train teachers. (Courtesy of the Southern Oregon Historical Society, #27239.)

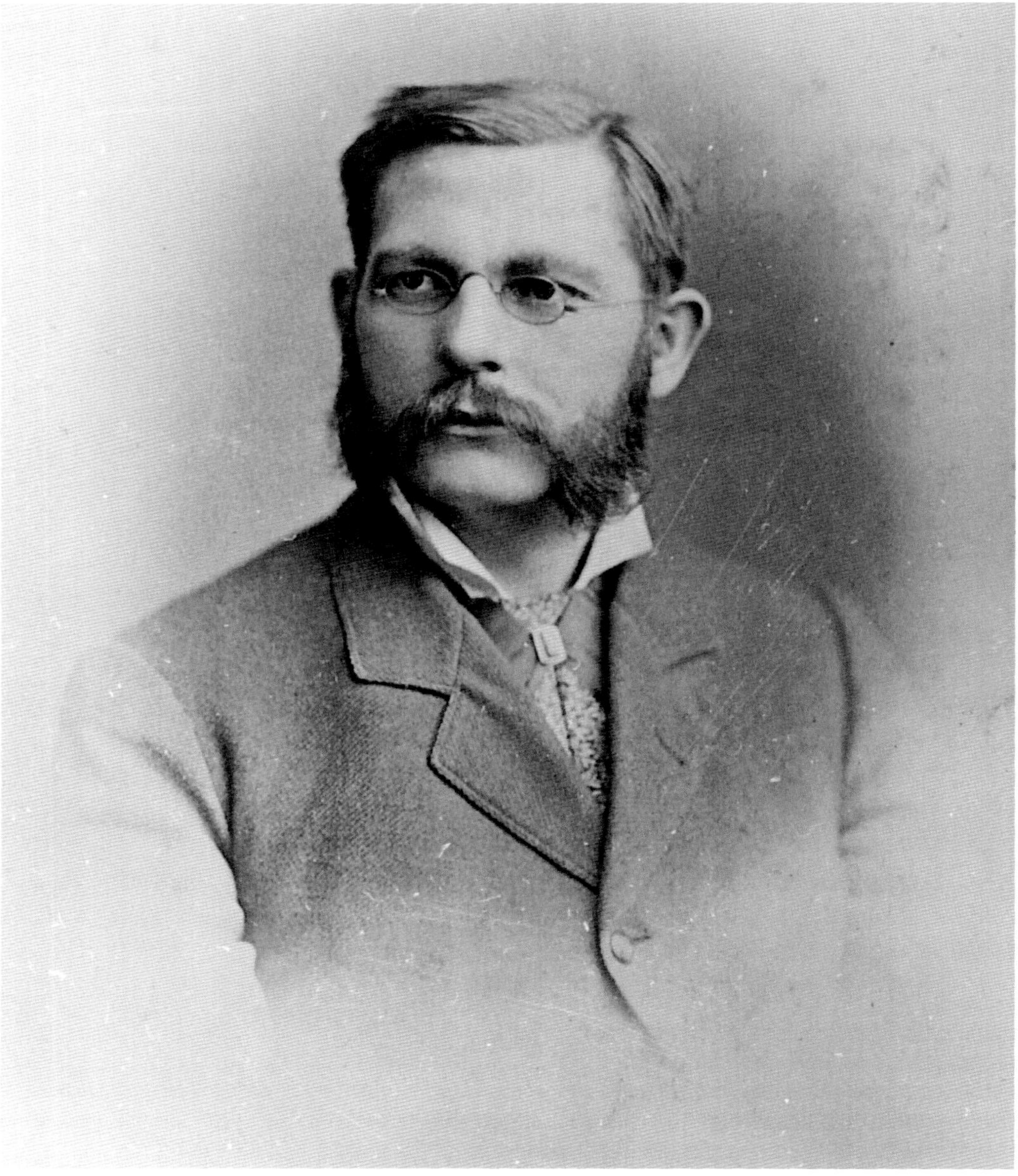

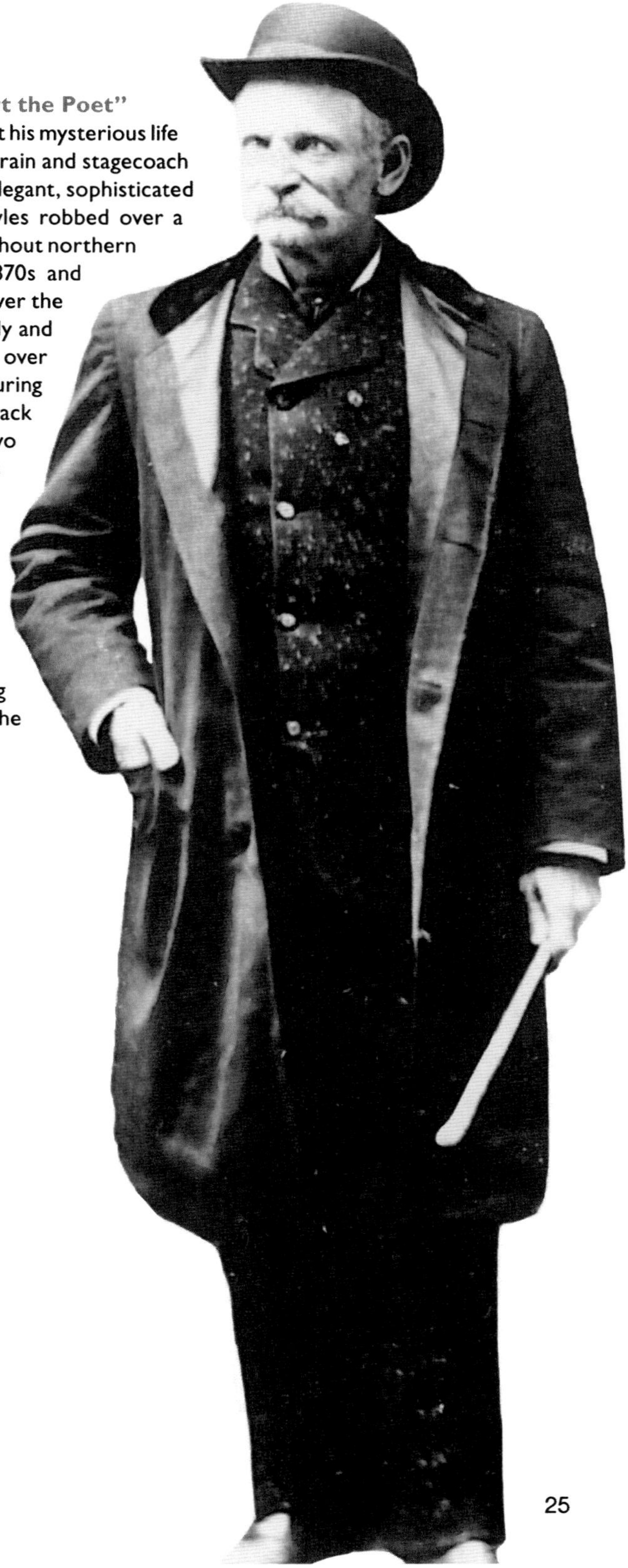

Charles Earl Bowles, a.k.a. "Black Bart the Poet"
According to an in-depth historical saga about his mysterious life as a northern California–southern Oregon train and stagecoach robber, Bowles was known as much for his elegant, sophisticated style as his train and wagon stickups. Bowles robbed over a dozen trains on Southern Pacific lines throughout northern California and southern Oregon in the 1870s and 1880s, frequently while they were passing over the Siskiyou Pass, where the trains moved slowly and were far from law enforcement. He robbed over a dozen more stagecoaches in the area during the same span. Bowles became known as Black Bart the Poet following his placement of two short poems at a pair of California robberies he carried out in the summers of 1877 and 1878. He signed the short verses "Black Bart the Po-8." Never firing a shot or killing anyone in his robberies, the English-born Bowles robbed his last train in 1883 and spent the following six years in San Quentin State Prison. About a month after his release in January 1888, he went missing and was never seen again. (Courtesy of the Southern Oregon Historical Society, #264.)

Grant Helman

With the help of his father, Abel Helman, Grant Helman opened the Helman Baths in 1886 and continued developing the site through the turn of the 20th century. Formerly a muddy, warm, bubbling spring surrounded by Abel Helman's cow pasture, the site of the bathhouse—just off present-day Otis Street—was well known to Native Americans of the Bear Creek Valley before settlers began frequenting the sulfurous springs for soaking purposes. Grant Helman saw an opportunity in the springs, which were regarded as medicinal, healing waters. He opened the bathhouse initially with three soaking rooms and went on to add a swimming pool, where many Ashlanders learned to swim. The popular attraction, which went on to be managed, expanded, and owned by Grant's brother Otis Helman, closed in 1956. Pictured here with a baritone horn, Grant, who was missing a portion of his right arm, also played in Ashland's city band. (Courtesy of the Southern Oregon Historical Society, #23520.)

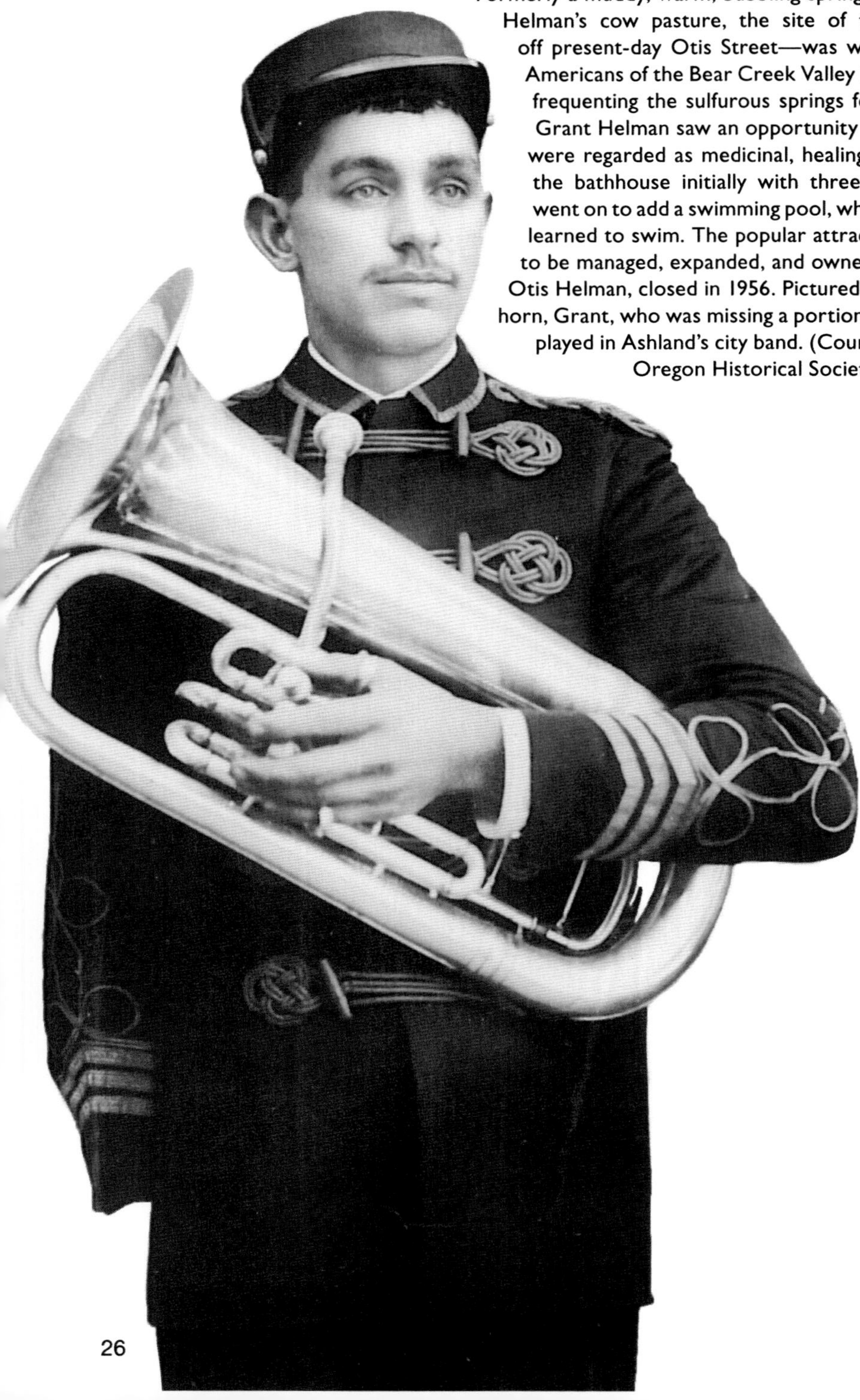

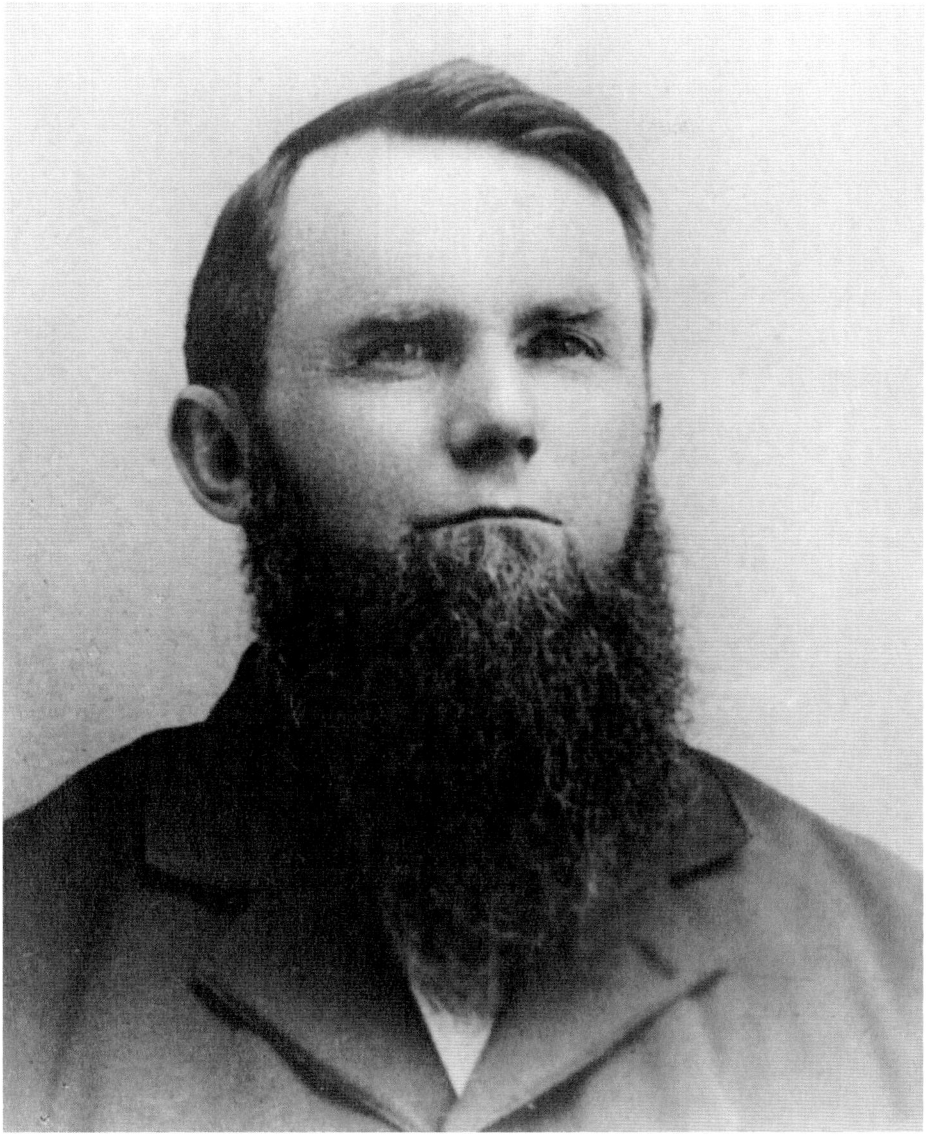

Professor Thomas VanScoy
Before arriving in Ashland to oversee and teach at Ashland's college in 1895, W.T. VanScoy—as he is commonly referred to in historical texts—served as the dean at Portland University. As dean there, VanScoy reached out and even met with the Ashland community and offered financial support on behalf of Portland University for Ashland's struggling normal school. Following the leadership shown by VanScoy, the Ashland community went on to raise $12,000 in support of the local college. Unfortunately, the Portland institution went belly up financially and was unable to make any monetary contribution. VanScoy became president of the Ashland college, and with the locally raised funds, Southern Oregon State Normal School was able to open in a new building. The school was endowed by the state in 1899 and enjoyed funding from the legislature over the course of the next few years. (This photograph is part of the Southern Oregon University Archives and made available courtesy of Southern Oregon University Hannon Library.)

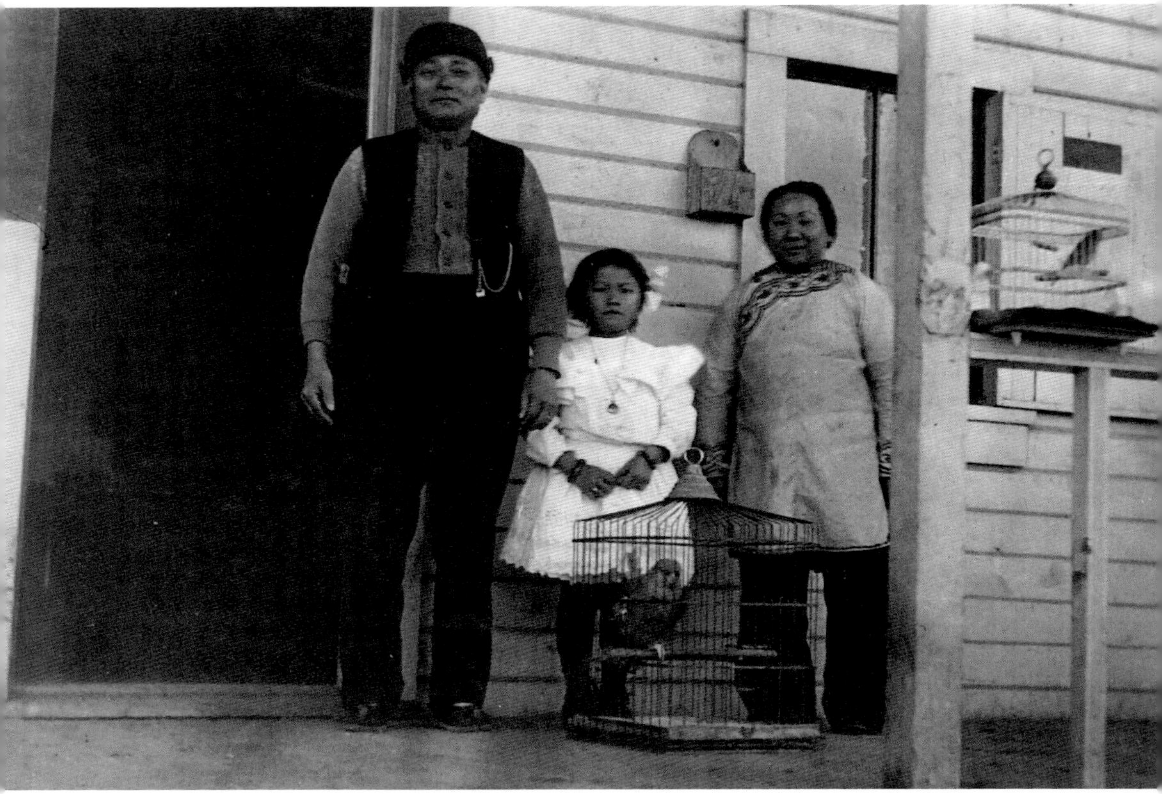

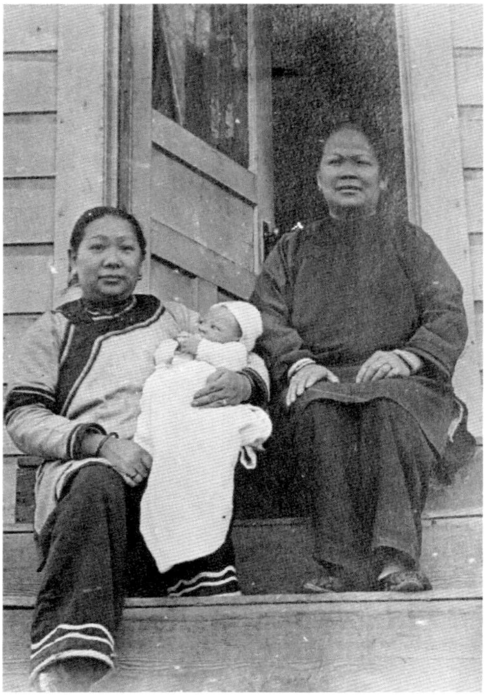

Wah Chung and Family

Of the about 4,000 laborers who helped bring Southern Pacific's railroad over the Siskiyou Mountains into Ashland, over half were Chinese. Wah Chung served for the railroad company as a labor agent for over 40 years and helped bring many of those Chinese workers to the Ashland area. Wah Chung, pictured above with his daughter Jenny and wife, known only as Mrs. Wah Chung, owned a two-story Chinese grocery store on the corner of Second and A Streets in Ashland's Railroad District. The Wah Chung family lived in a home next door to the small store, and, along with about 250 other Chinese, stayed in Ashland following the completion of the railroad in 1887. Pictured at left are women of the Wah Chung family in Ashland. (Both, courtesy of the Southern Oregon Historical Society, #1150, #14333.)

Otis Helman

Classically trained at the Chicago School of Music, Otis Helman had already made a name for himself in Ashland by 1890 when he was named director of the Ashland Brass Band. Helman, who also led a dance band that played around Ashland for about two decades, was well known for his musical talents, which rubbed off on the members of the Ashland Brass Band. The band went on to evolve into the Ashland City Band, which is still an annual Fourth of July parade staple and the popular feature of summer evening concerts at Lithia Park's Butler Band Shell. Helman also succeeded his brother Grant in the ownership and maintenance of the Helman Baths. He went on to build a public park and baseball field there. Helman is pictured here on the left at the Helman Baths. (Courtesy of the Southern Oregon Historical Society, #20968.)

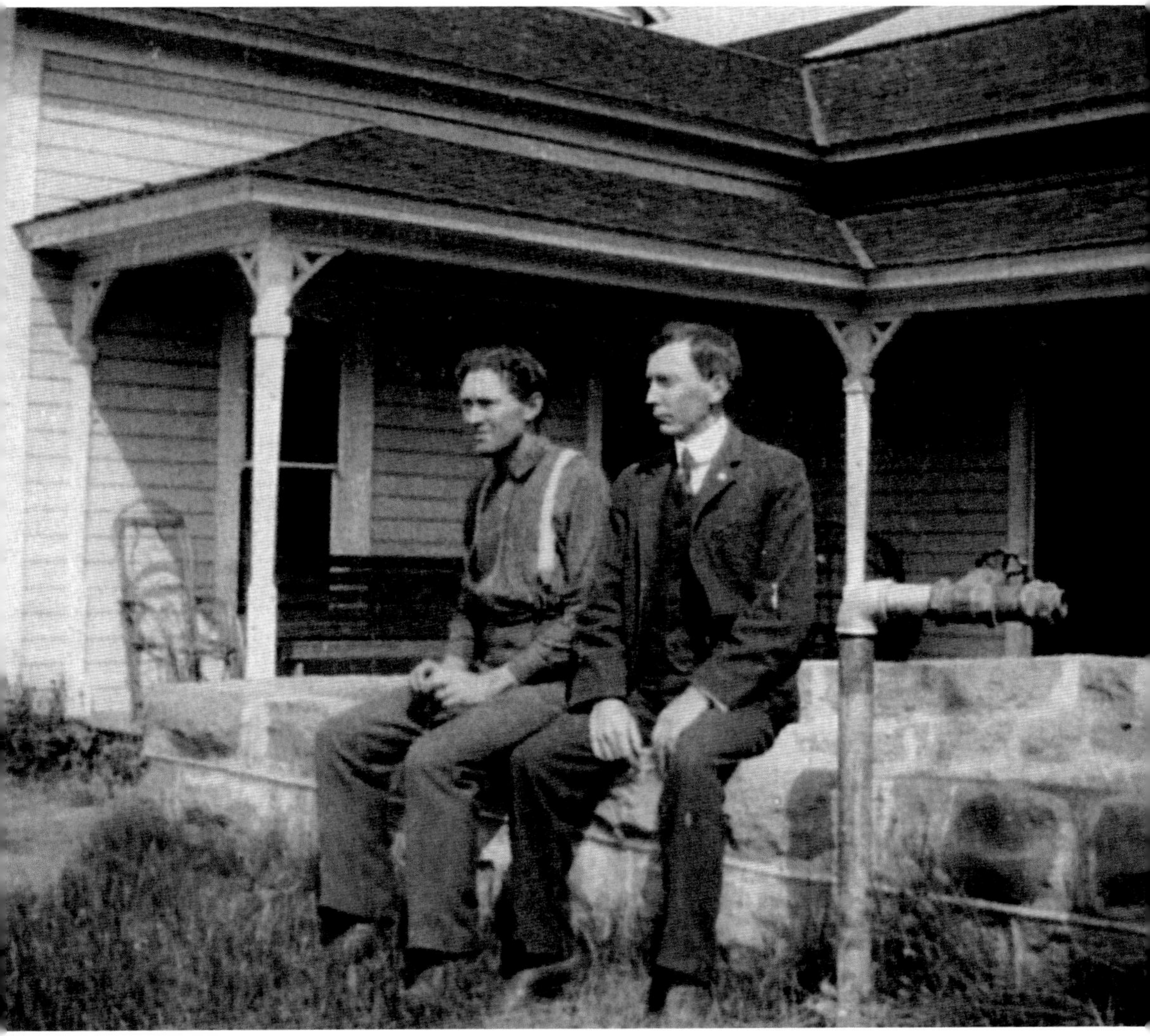

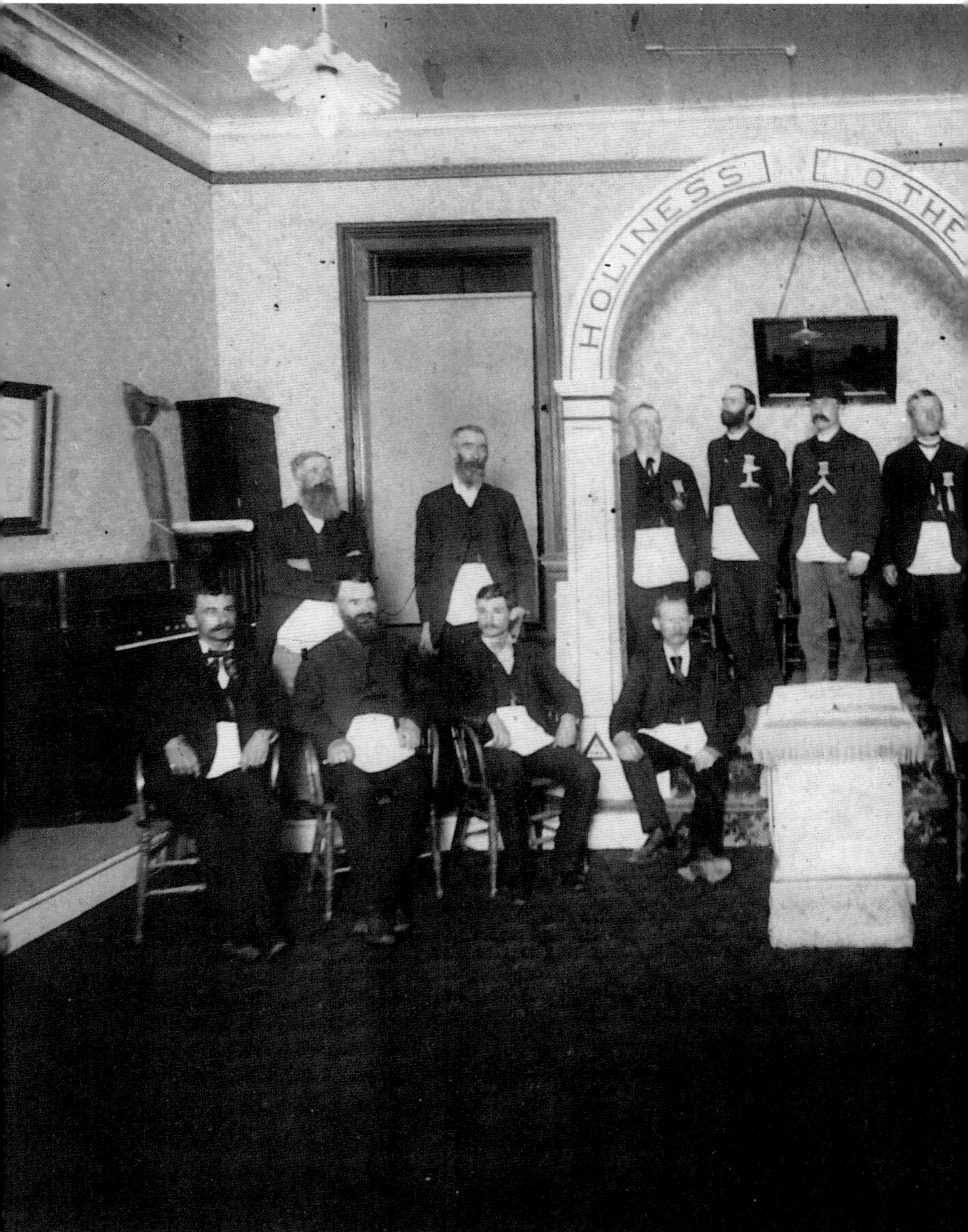
HOLINESS
TO THE

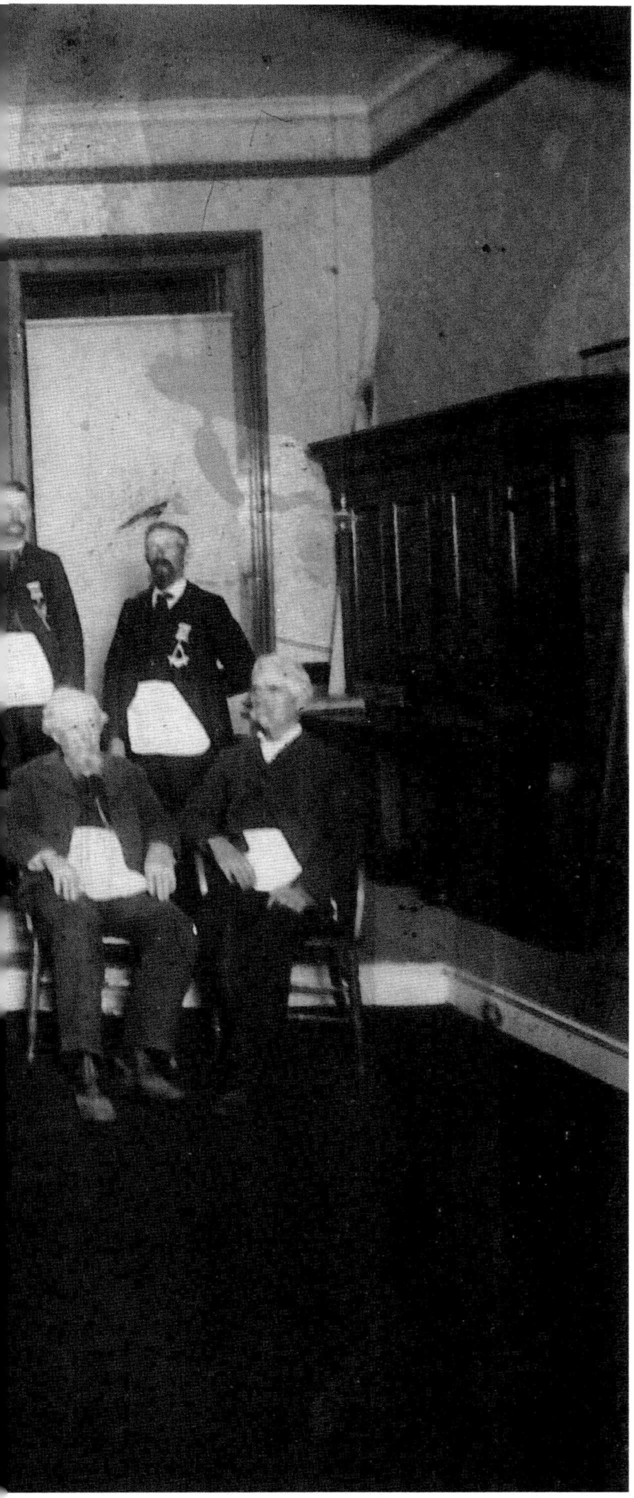

Prof. P.A. Getz
A Pennsylvania native passionate about education, Professor Getz was not in Ashland long, but he left a studious mark. He was named principal of Ashland's public schools in 1889, and went on to establish Ashland High School in 1890 while enjoying a steady stream of funding from a community tax levy. The high school served as Ashland's third school and a permanent institution of education for the community during a time when its college shuddered frequently due to a lack of funding. Pictured here with a group local Masonic Lodge officers in 1895, Getz is standing fourth from the left in the back row. (Courtesy of the Southern Oregon Historical Society, #9798.)

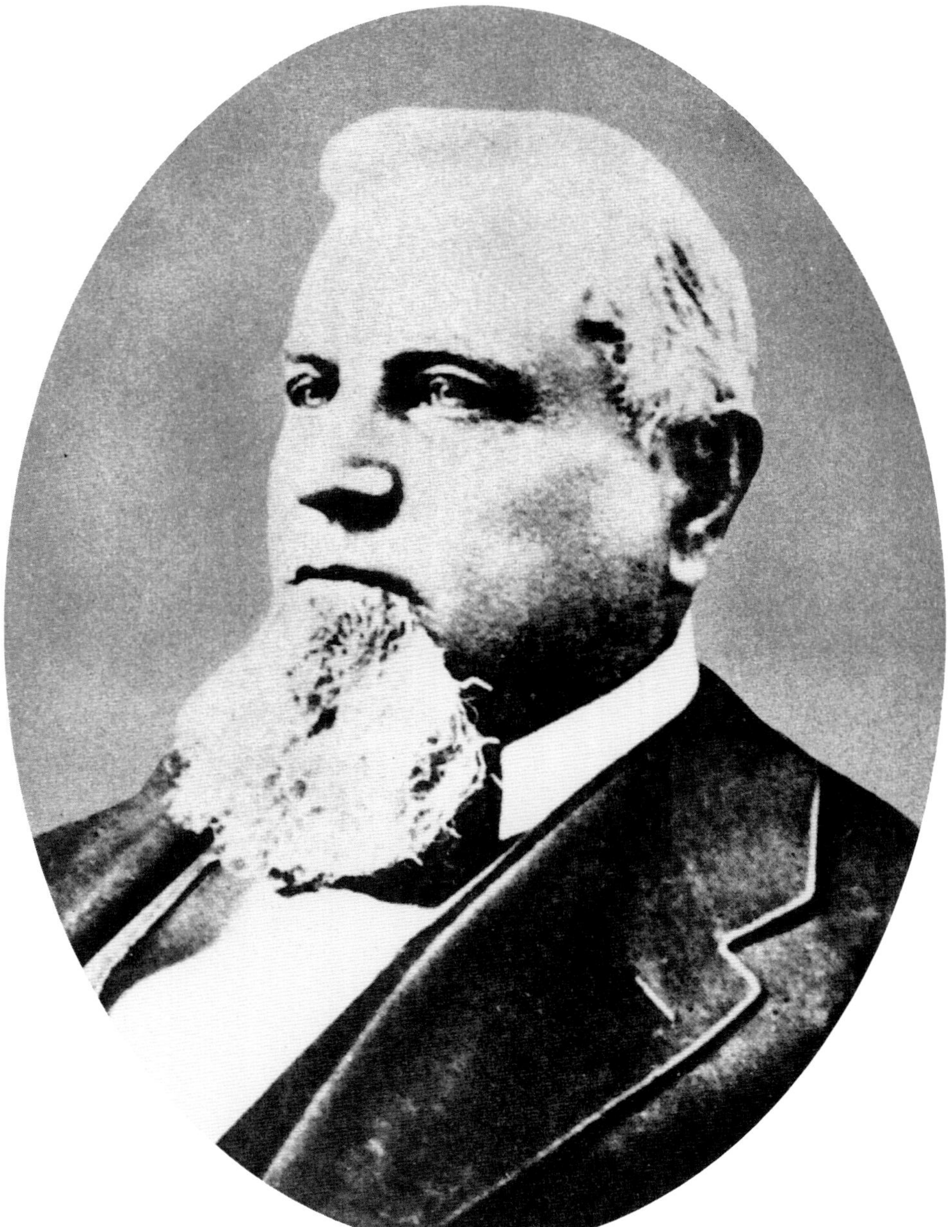

Charles Crocker

Charles Crocker never had much to do with Ashland, and Ashland never had much to do with him; however, the man helped put this town on the map. It was on December 17, 1887, that Crocker, a Southern Pacific Railroad executive, hammered home the golden spike to commemorate the connection of the railroad company's Portland–San Francisco line over the Siskiyou Mountains. Although there were other "golden spike" ceremonies on the line, the conjoining of tracks in Ashland established the linking of railroads around the borders of the contiguous United States. (Courtesy of the Southern Oregon Historical Society, #5127.)

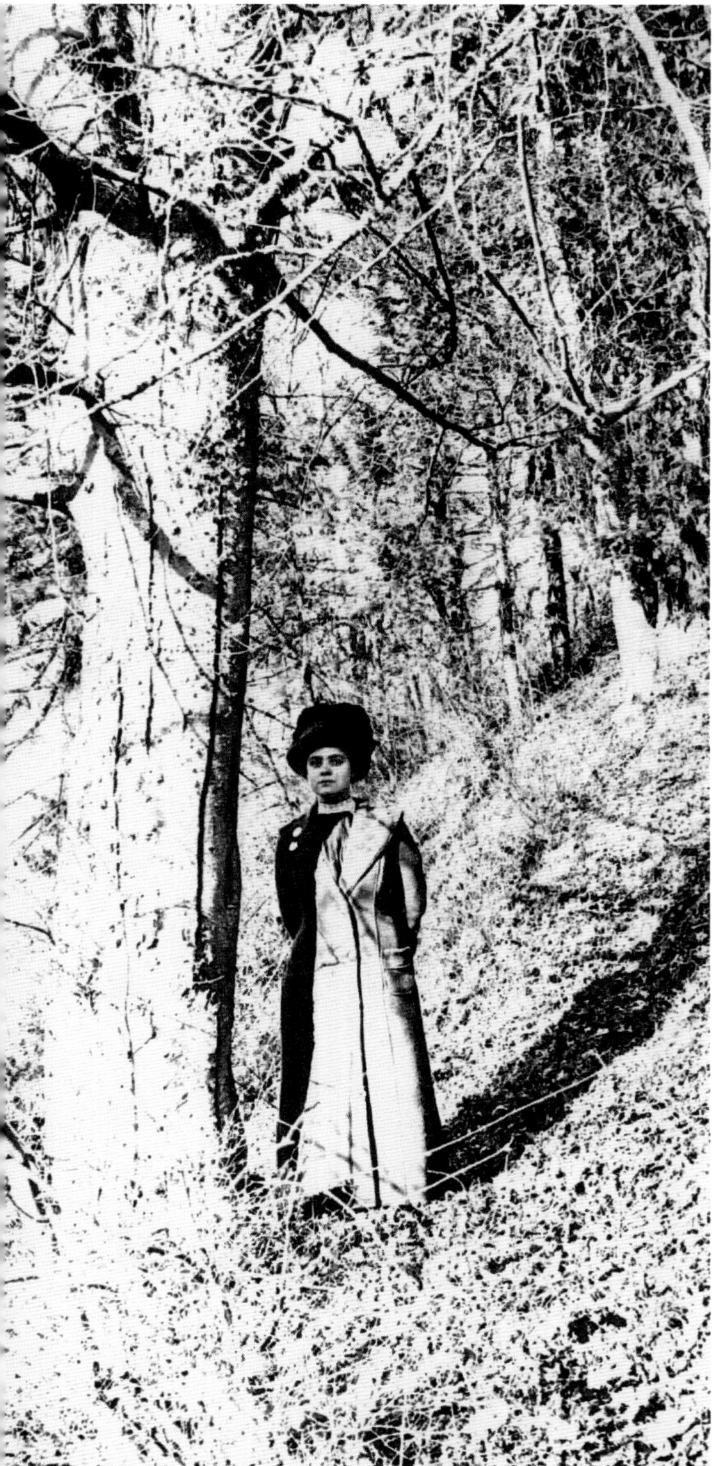

Almeda Helman-Coder
The granddaughter of Ashland's founder Abel Helman, Almeda Helman-Coder lived over 100 years. Born on February 4, 1891, she passed away on March 28, 1994. Compared to the settlers who came before Almeda, her privileged and well-educated life, enabled by her grandfather's success, is indicative of the lifestyle second-generation Ashlanders were able to enjoy. The comforts that Ashlanders like Almeda were able to take advantage of no doubt led to the town's progression from any old Oregon city to what Ashland is today. Almeda frequented Chautauqua programs in her adolescence and watched Ashland mature into much of what it is today. Her oral histories of Ashland paint a clear picture of its progress, and she always said Abel could have never imagined what a town Ashland would become. (Courtesy of the Southern Oregon Historical Society, #8301.)

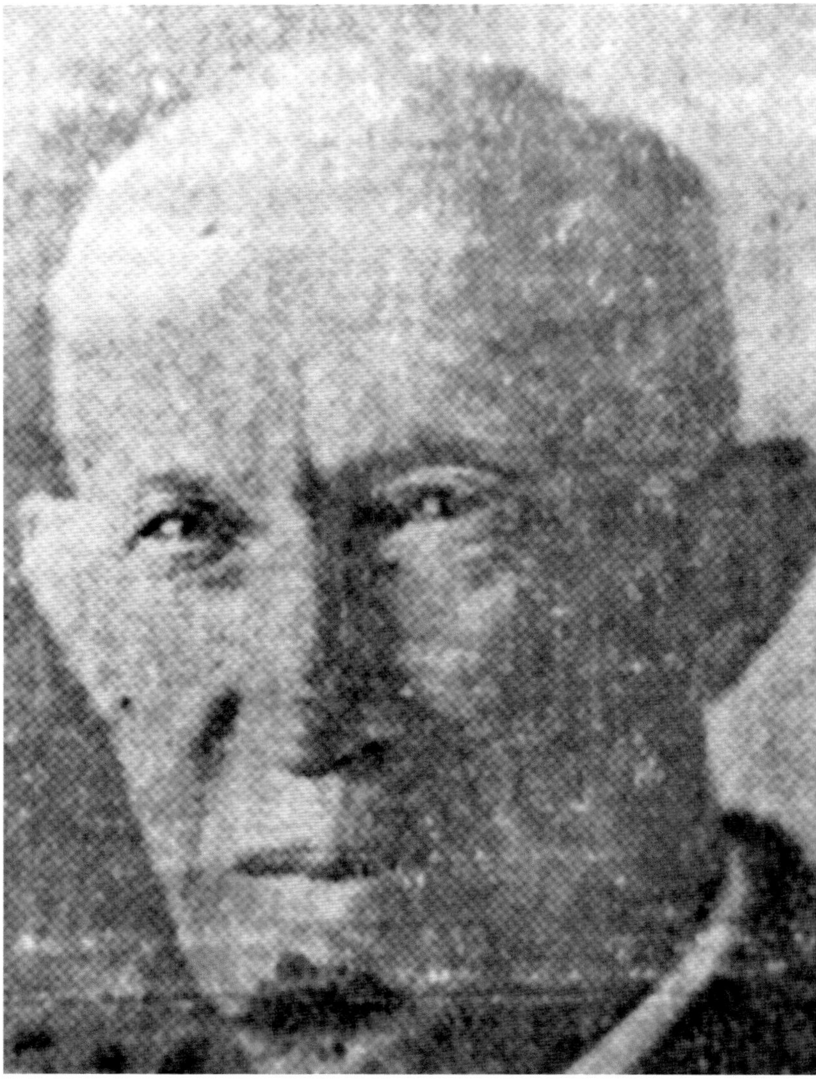

George F. Billings (ABOVE AND OPPOSITE PAGE)
Pictured above in a 1931 issue of the *Ashland Daily Tidings*, Billings was one of Ashland's most prominent individuals. While serving on the local public school board, Billings also handed out the diplomas to Ashland High School's first graduating class in 1891. The following year, when the idea of hosting an annual Chautauqua assembly in southern Oregon was first discussed, Billings led the way in convincing decision makers that Ashland was the best location southern Oregon had to offer for the cultural event. He went on to serve as president of Ashland's Chautauqua Association for 22 years. The culture brought to Ashland by the presence of the Chautauqua programs no doubt pushed the town in a direction of appreciation for the arts. Billings died in 1933 and is buried at Hargadine Cemetery. The remains of the Chautauqua building, pictured opposite under expansion in 1917, today serve as the outer walls of the Oregon Shakespeare Festival's Elizabethan Theater stage. The Shakespeare Festival also started on a rebuilt stage inside the walls of the building. Also pictured are patrons of Ashland's Chautauqua show camping in present-day Lithia Park. (Above, courtesy of Southern Oregon Historical Society, #6962; opposite, both courtesy of the Oregon Shakespeare Festival.)

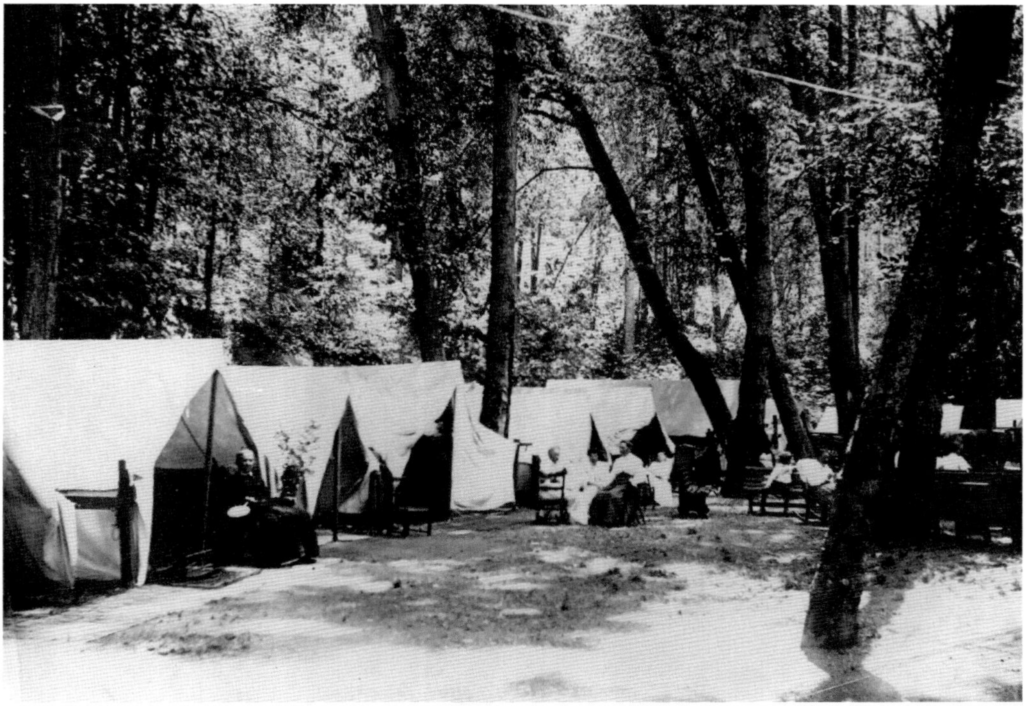

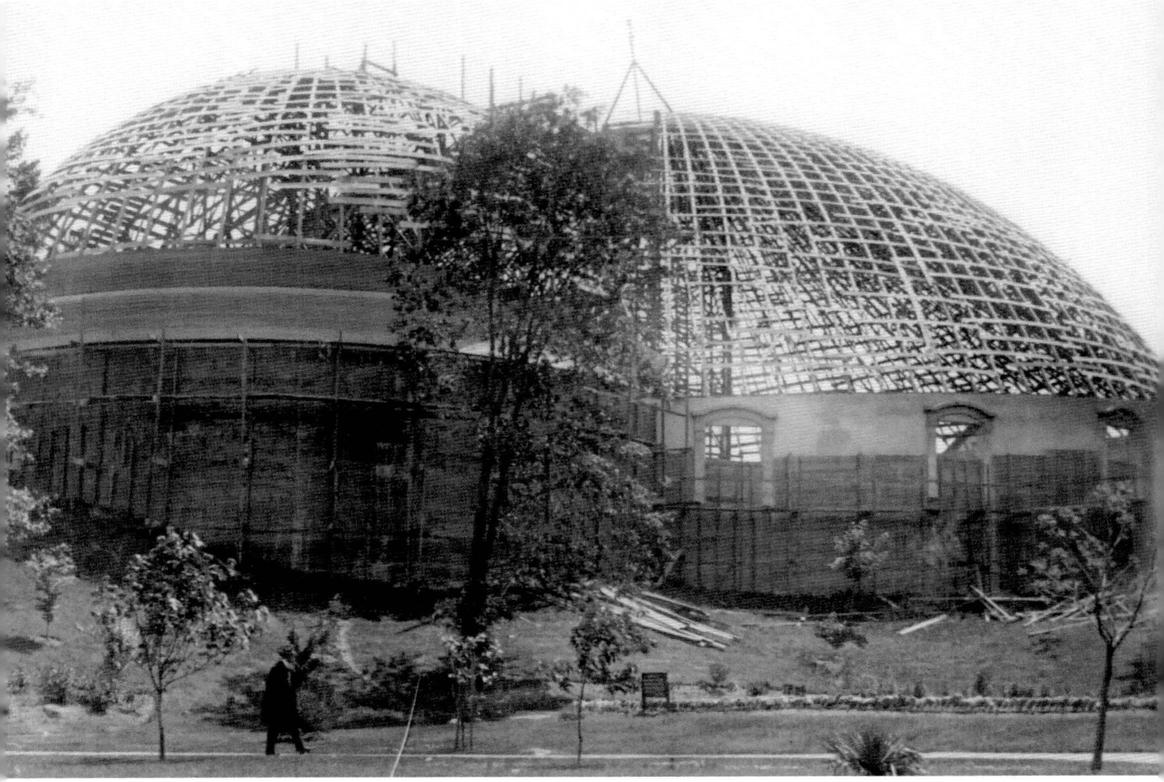

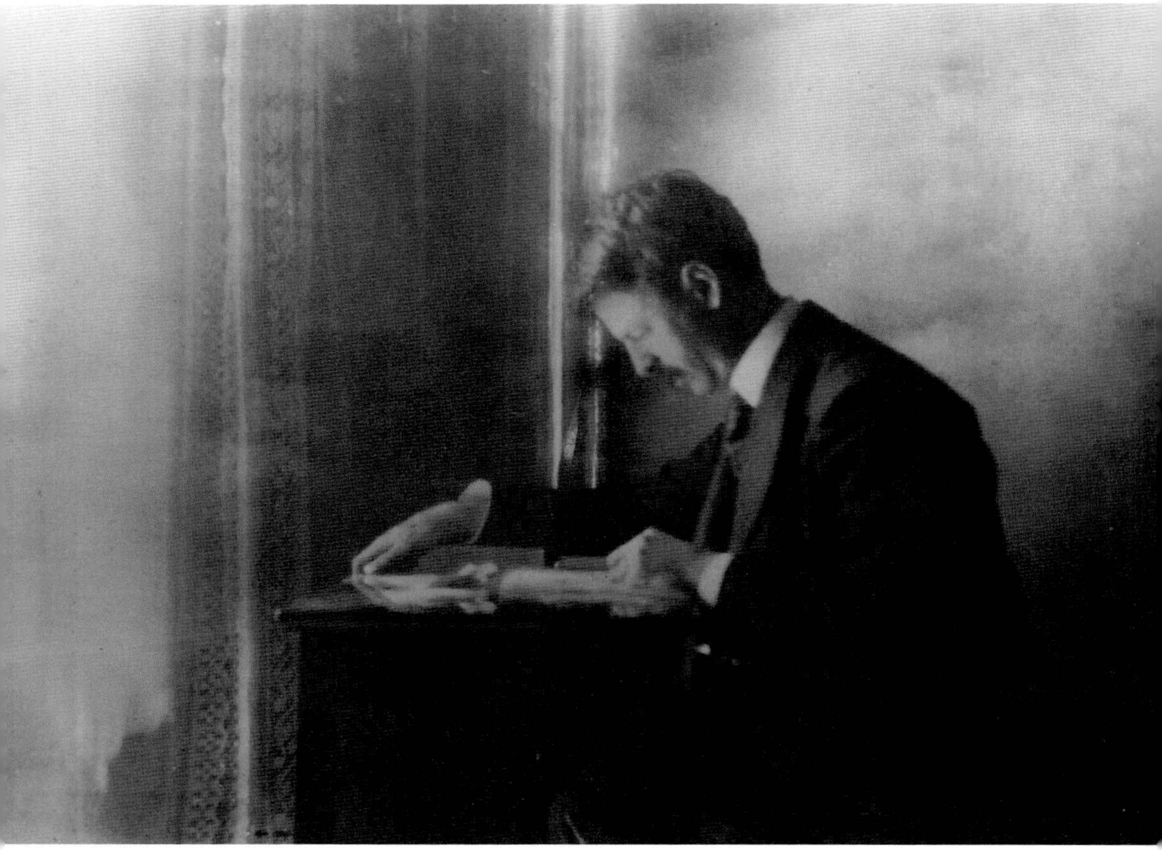

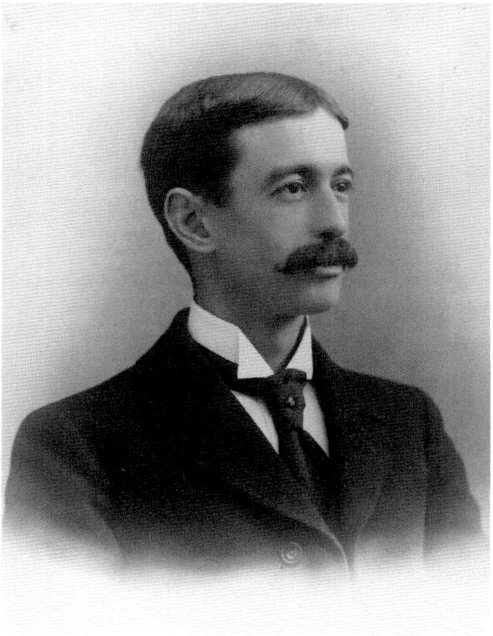

Frank C. Clark

Franklin Chamberlin Clark, who headed west from his hometown of Greene, New York, in 1896 to study architecture, was Ashland's and the Rogue Valley's premier architect during most of the first half of the 20th century. In Ashland, his most notable designs include the Ashland Masonic Lodge Building. Built in 1909, the building now houses the lodge of the Ashland Benevolent & Protective Order of Elks. Clark also designed the 1904 Chappell-Swedenburg House, known now as the Southern Oregon University's Plunkett Center. Though his design was not used, Clark put forth an initial rendering of Ashland's public library that helped the project achieve funding. In addition to several private Ashland homes and others throughout the Rogue Valley, Clark designed Ashland's Granite City Hospital, which was constructed in 1910 and was later known as Ashland General Hospital. (Both, courtesy of the Southern Oregon Historical Society, #5183, #2134.)

CHAPTER THREE

Shaping Prosperity

1901–1980

In 1892, Ashland was promoted by local leaders to play host for the national Chautauqua movement, a presentation of entertainment and education programs for the public. That year, the Southern Oregon Chautauqua Assembly was founded following a Methodist camp meeting near Central Point, where the idea of hosting an assembly in southern Oregon was first discussed.

At the turn of the 20th century, there were about 3,000 people living in Ashland, and it was still the largest city in Jackson County. Local timber, livestock, and farming industries acted as the backbone of the county's thriving economy, and Ashland was leading the way. Ashland also expanded intellectually and artistically around this time. In 1895, Ashland College and Normal School was reopened as Southern Oregon State Normal School, and its state funds were reinstated in 1899.

The beginnings of what would eventually become Lithia Park were spurred in 1908 by the local Woman's Civic Improvement Club. A city vote was passed on December 17, 1908, to demolish the mostly abandoned Ashland Flouring Mills building and make way for a park entrance, set aside acreage and tax dollars for future park development, and appoint a committee for oversight. Within a year, the former mill building was torn down, a park board was formed, and 45 acres were purchased by the city and set aside above the existing Chautauqua Park.

Ashlanders were especially patriotic and supportive of the World War I effort. The United States joined the dispute in April 1917, and Ashland citizens dove straight into subscribing to Liberty Loans in support of the Allied cause against Germany. Citizens adhered to wheatless and meatless days, those too old to join the fight resumed a working lifestyle, and Ashland women joined local labor efforts. The first group of Ashland men deployed for the theater of war in January 1918, and by November, the war was over.

Ashland continued to thrive during and after World War I, and by the mid-1920s, its population had swelled to 4,283. Pushed by ease of access via railroad and a paved and widened Pacific Highway over the Siskiyous, tourism to the Rogue Valley was increasing steadily during the 1920s.

In 1926, Churchill Hall was constructed, named after the college's first president, Julius A. Churchill. It was the school's all-encompassing building and served 258 enrolled students as well as administrators and staff. In 1932, the state board governing the normal school in Ashland renamed it Southern Oregon Normal School, and the school was renamed again in 1939 to Southern Oregon College of Education. That name held until 1956, when the institution took on its eighth name: Southern Oregon College. Again, in 1975, it was renamed Southern Oregon State College, a name it held until 1997, when it settled, at least for now, on Southern Oregon University.

Ashland's fall from grace as a railroad hub came in 1927, when the Southern Pacific Railroad Company opened the Natron cutoff route. The new line, designed to avoid daunting Siskiyou Summit, departed the company's existing north-south rail line near Weed, California, and headed to Klamath Falls before reconnecting to the main line in Eugene. Ashland as a whole—especially the businesses in the town's railroad district—was hit hard economically by the sharp drop in rail traffic and passenger services. Southern Pacific completely discontinued its passenger service to and from Ashland in 1955.

By 1931, well into the Great Depression and over a decade into the county's alcohol prohibition, which locally resulted in the tearing up of hundreds of acres of productive grape vines used to make wine, Ashland was known as "Little Chicago."

But 1931 had positive implications for Ashland as well. It was the year Angus Bowmer arrived in town to teach English composition and public speaking at Southern Oregon Normal School. It was during the preparations for Ashland's 1935 Fourth of July celebration that Bowmer convinced the city to support a three-day festival of Shakespearian plays. The production, which took place on a refurbished stage inside the concrete skeleton of Ashland's former Chautauqua building, was a stunning success, and it was agreed that it would be continued the following summer.

By the time of America's entry into World War II on December 7, 1941, about 5,000 residents called Ashland home, and about 1,200 of them served in the US armed forces during the global war. A Civilian Defense Board met in Ashland's city hall, and the city was divided into 18 preparedness zones. Air raid shelters were designated in buildings throughout town, and the Red Cross and American Legion helped train citizens for the looming possibility of a Japanese invasion of the US Pacific Coast. Needless to say, no World War II battle ever came to the Rogue Valley, and the conflict came to a complete close in 1945.

Following the war, Ashland set off into a period of significant growth. The city was long past its heyday as the hub of the Rogue Valley, but it flourished—particularly on the heels of a booming timber industry. More than a dozen sawmills, mostly family owned, operated in Ashland during the early 1950s.

The times they were a changing in Ashland at the onset of the 1960s. The war in Vietnam raged, and on Ashland's college campus, similar to other campuses around the country, it was adamantly opposed through public protest. In 1962, the city of Ashland covered an area of 2,952 acres and had a population of about 9,500. Southern Oregon College had grown into one of Ashland's largest economic contributors and the city developed a master plan for its future growth in 1966.

In 1963 and 1964, Mount Ashland Ski Lodge and Winter Sports Area was constructed in the hopes that it would extend the city's tourist season and serve as a recreation area for local winter sports enthusiasts. Mount Ashland Corporation financed the development of the area, which opened in 1964, and operated it before going bankrupt in 1970. It then passed off operating responsibility through a lease agreement to Jackson County, Oregon–Mount Ashland Winter Park and Recreation Facility Inc. During that period, it operated under management of the Southern Oregon State College Foundation. Local businessman Dick Hicks purchased the ski area in 1977 and built the Windsor chairlift before selling it to Harbor Properties of Seattle in 1983. The Seattle-based corporation installed lights to enable night skiing and built the Sonnet and Comer chair lifts. Ten years later, after Harbor decided its investments were not being met with adequate financial returns, it announced a plan to close the area and remove its equipment. The community of Ashland was aghast. Rogue Valley residents, through the organization of Ashland leaders, raised $1.6 million, including a $500,000 grant from the Oregon Economic Development fund, and the City of Ashland became the ski area's owner and holder of a US Forest Service permit enabling its existence. The ski area was subsequently leased to the Mount Ashland Association for $1 a year through 2017.

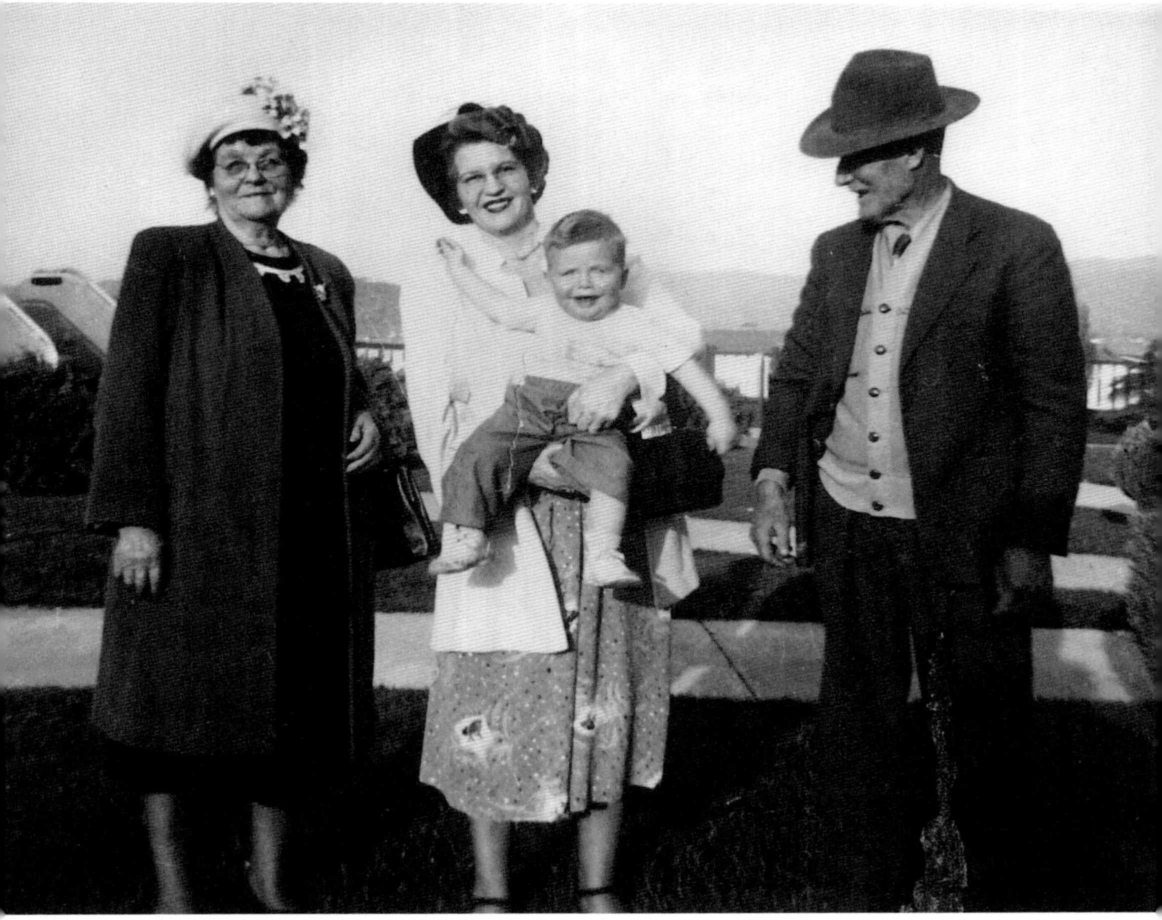

Walter M. Blair and Family
The granite man Walter M. Blair began developing one of Ashland's most successful and renowned businesses in 1916. A report issued by the Oregon Bureau of Mines and Geology just prior to Blair opening his granite quarry described the granite outcropping as one of Oregon's finest, lauding Ashland granite as "pleasing in color and texture." Blair incorporated the operations at his quarry, located on the western ridge above Neil Creek, about eight miles southeast of Ashland, as Blair Granite Inc. in 1929, the same year he stepped down from its operations. The company's holding were transferred to Ashland Granite Quarries Inc. in 1937. (Courtesy of the Southern Oregon Historical Society, #8183.)

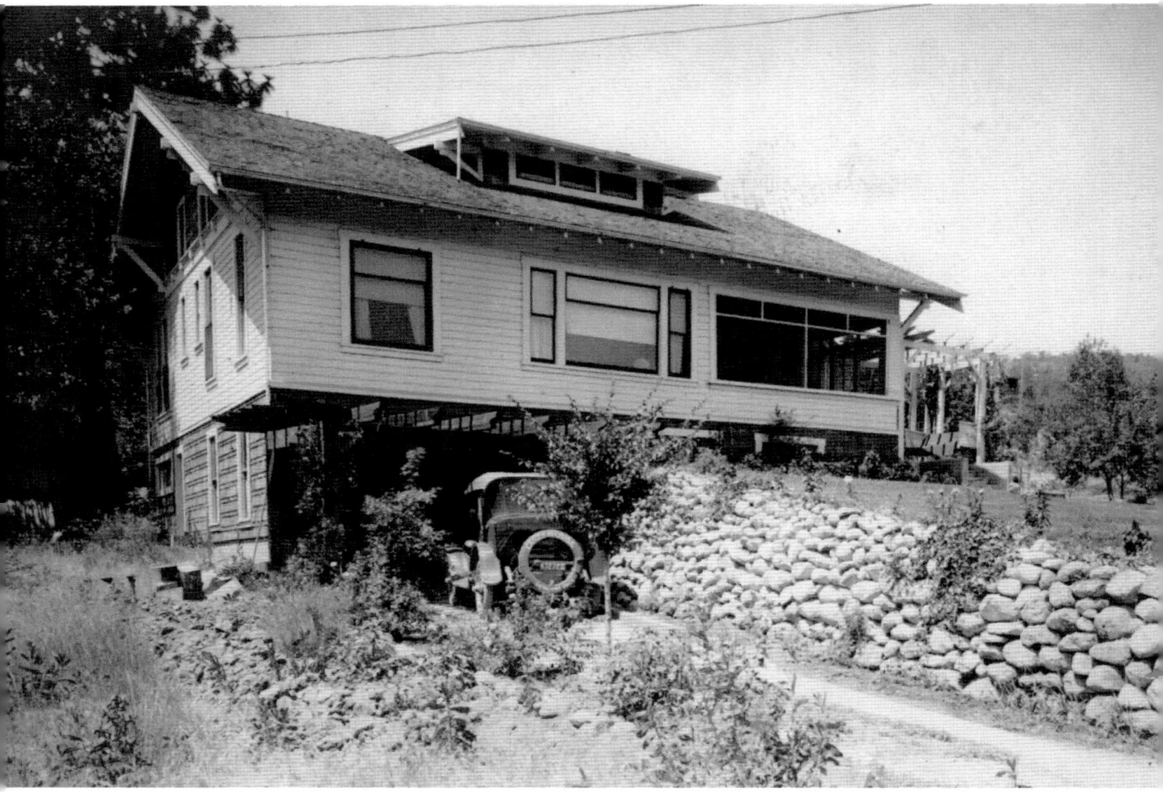

Bert Greer (OPPOSITE PAGE)

Bert Greer moved to Ashland in 1911 and bought the *Ashland Daily Tidings*. Taking note of the town's nearby mineral springs and history involving the so-called Lithia healing waters, Greer used the newspaper to spread the idea of transforming Ashland into a spa-based resort town. The idea was popular enough that meetings were held to outline a plan for piping water from a sulphur spring east of Ashland to the downtown area. In 1914, Ashland residents went on to approve a $175,000 Mineral Springs Bond, which funded the piping effort and redesign of the park. Lithia water bubbled from several fountains around town and the park, which took on most of the aspects it is known for today during its expansion and redesign, but further transformation of Ashland into a spa town never took off. It was during the campaign effort behind the Mineral Springs Bond that the phrase "Ashland grows while Lithia flows" was coined. Pictured above is a photograph of Greer's early 1900s Granite Street home in Ashland. (Both, courtesy of Terry Skibby.)

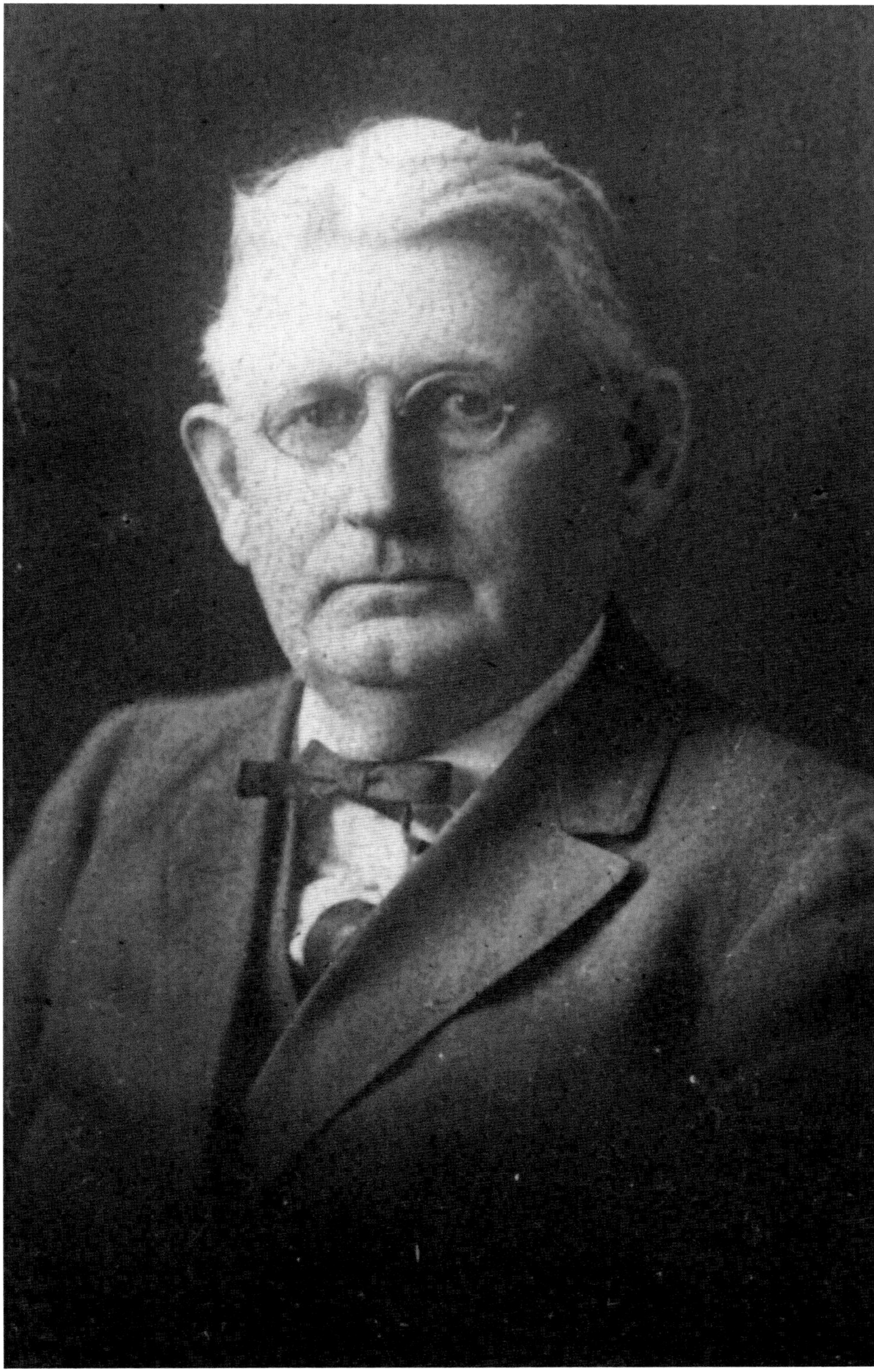

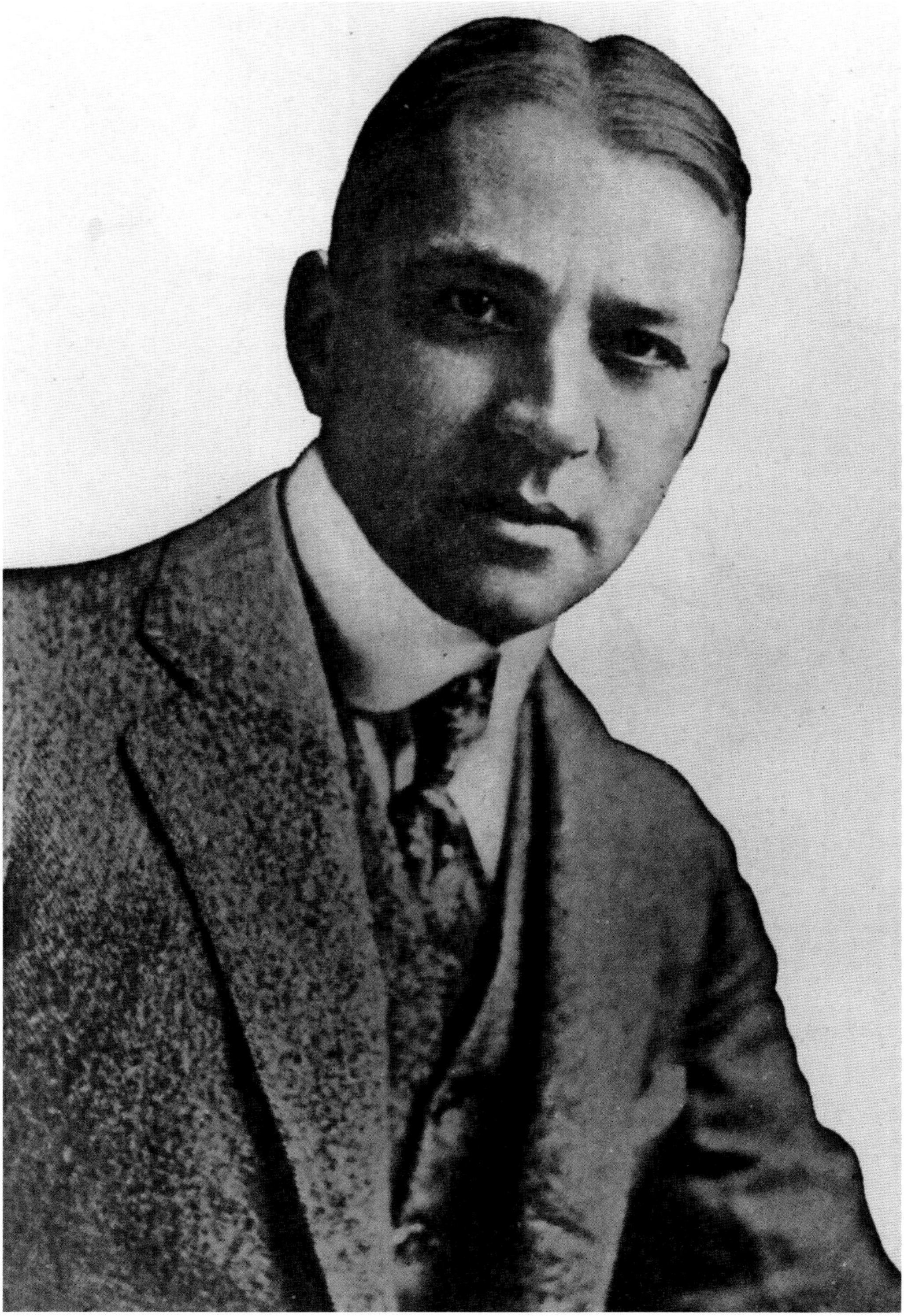

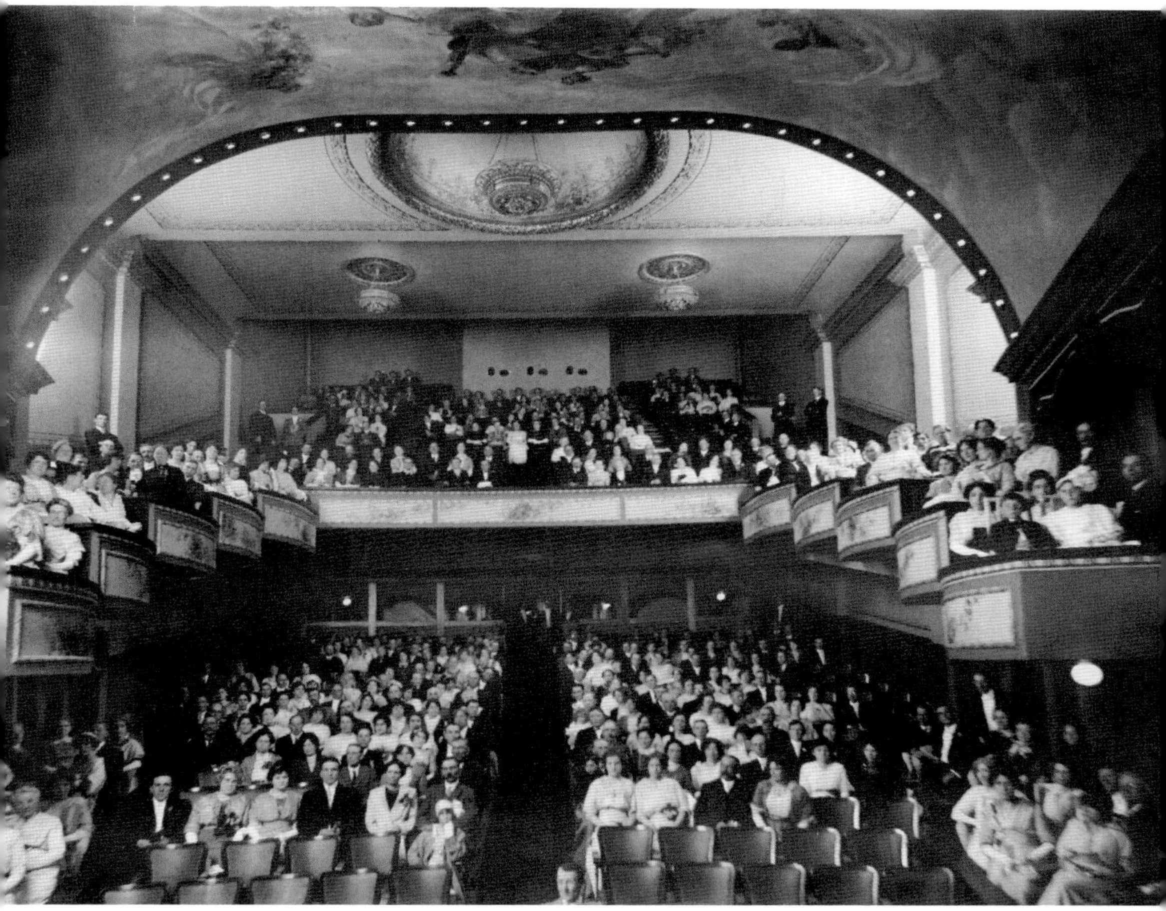

Irving E. Vining and Robert Vining (ABOVE AND OPPOSITE PAGE)
Irving Vining (opposite), a graduate of Southern Oregon State Normal School, along with his brother Robert Vining, opened the Vining Theater in Ashland in May 1914. The 800-seat theater cost the brothers about $35,000 to build and was lauded as "fireproof." In 1932, after being sold by the Vinings, the theater was renamed the Lithia Theater. It closed in 1951 but was refurbished by Oregon Shakespeare Festival founder Angus Bowmer in order to stage his winter theatrical endeavors before it burned to the ground in 1952. Pictured above is a packed house on the opening night of the Vining Theater for the opera *Faust*. (Both, courtesy of the Southern Oregon Historical Society, #5836, #4237.)

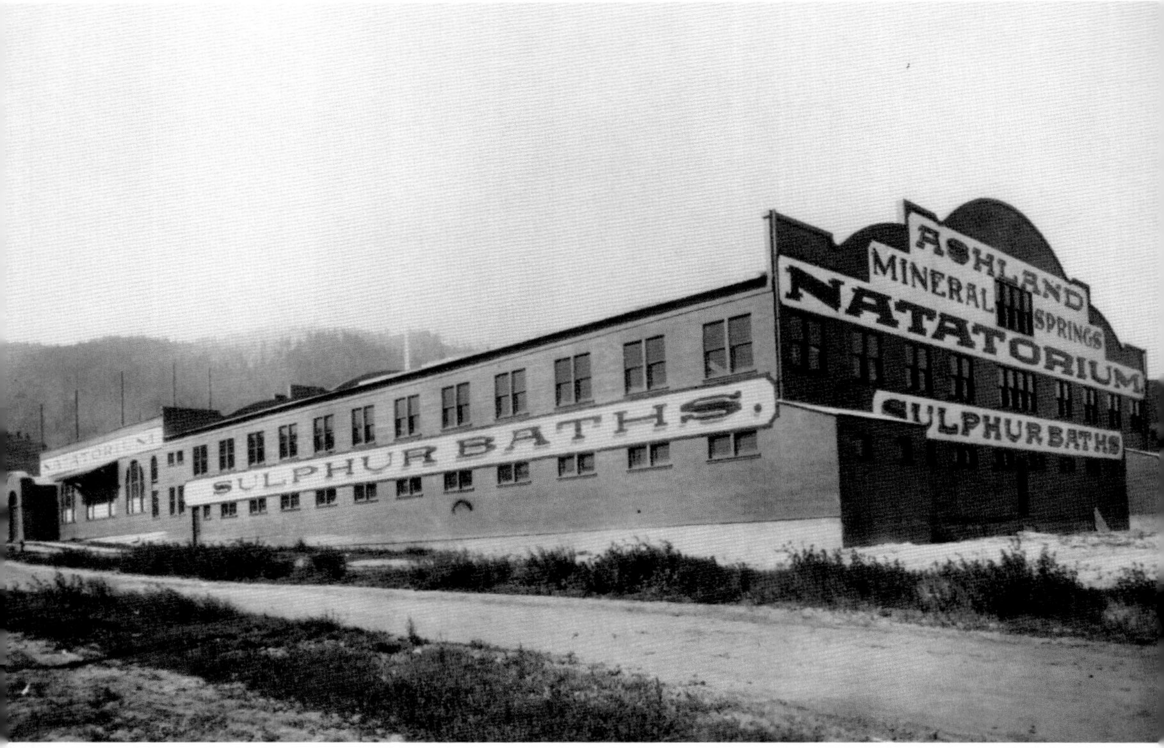

Natatorium and Twin Plunges (ABOVE AND OPPOSITE PAGE)
Ashlander E.C. Gard was the lead investor in the construction of the Ashland Mineral Springs Natatorium in 1908. Located between First and Pioneer Streets on A Street, the about 100- by 200-foot building housed two swimming pools fed by underground sulphur springs. The indoor swimming area featured spring high dives, slides, trapeze rings, and nearly 60 dressing rooms. In addition to serving locals, the facility was also built to attract visitors from outside the Ashland area. There was a hardwood-floor ballroom inside the building and enough seating for 500 people on balconies surrounding the pools. The natatorium was shuttered in 1919, and the building was torn down in the 1920s. The Twin Plunges Ashland was financed and built on the site in 1931 by Ashland lawyer William Briggs; his father, E.D Briggs; and G.S. Briggs. Twin Plunges went on to serve as the Ashland community's local swimming hole until it closed in 1977. (Both, courtesy of the Southern Oregon Historical Society, #6514, #5072.)

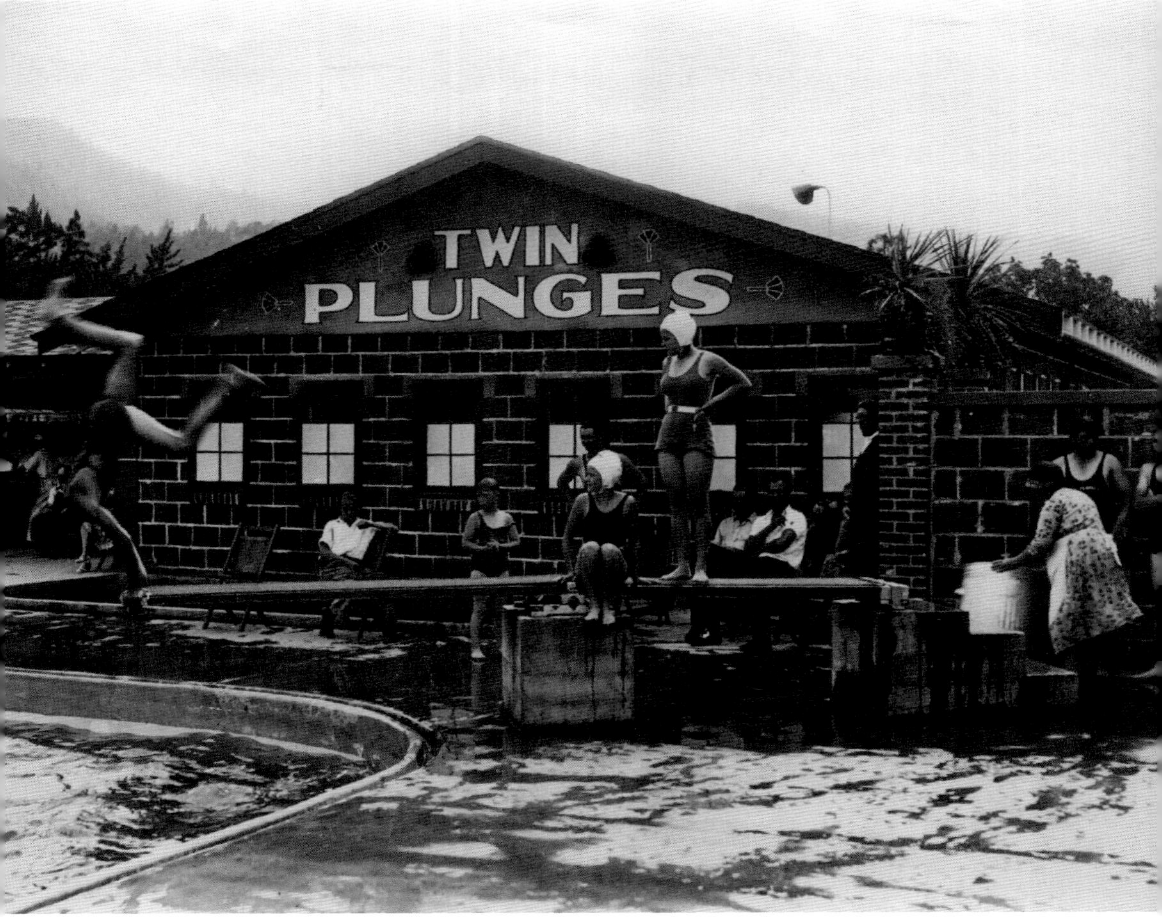
TWIN
PLUNGES

Hugh, Ray, and Roy DeAutremont (BELOW AND OPPOSITE PAGE)
When the DeAutremont brothers dynamited the mail car of the passenger-filled San Francisco Express train No. 13 of the Southern Pacific Railroad Company on October 11, 1923, they set off one of Oregon's most publicized manhunts. The train, unbeknownst to the brothers, was not filled with anything of significant monetary value that day on its way over the Siskiyou Summit. If it had been, they would not have recovered it anyway because of how badly they damaged its mail car. They killed three trainmen and US mail clerk Elvyn Dougherty in the holdup and fled without anything to show for it. Wanted posters plastered with the DeAutremonts' mug shots were circulated around the country, but the brothers fled justice for three years before being arrested and brought back to Jackson County for trial. Pictured opposite is some of the aftermath of the brothers' dynamite job on the mail car. Pictured below, standing left to right outside the Jackson County courthouse, are Ray and Roy DeAutremont. A hatless Hugh DeAutremont is also pictured opposite outside the courthouse following trial. (All, courtesy of the Southern Oregon Historical Society, #6791, #10938, #10939.)

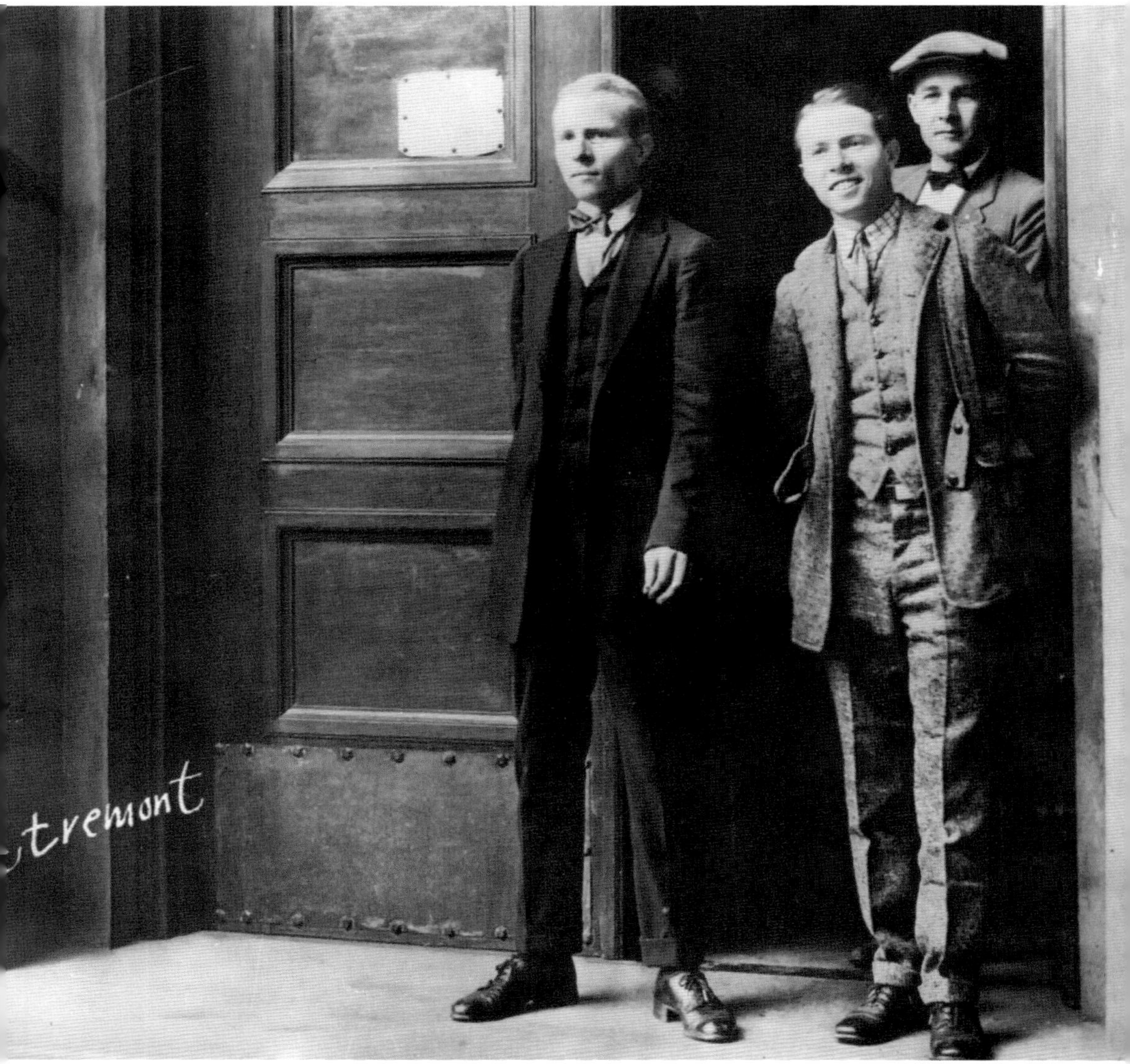

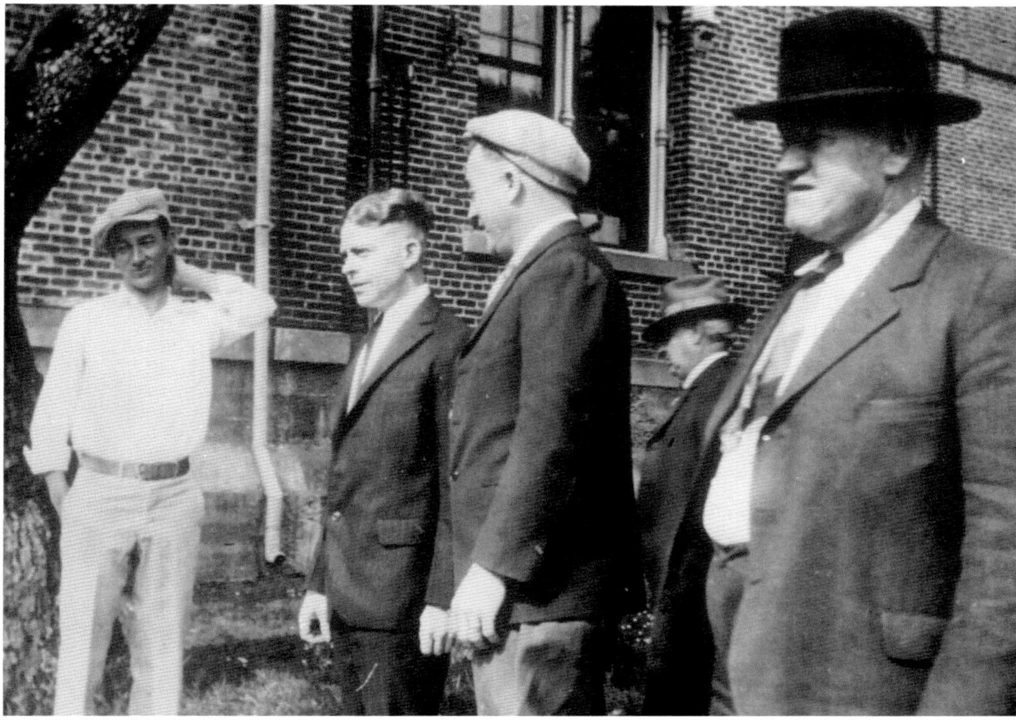

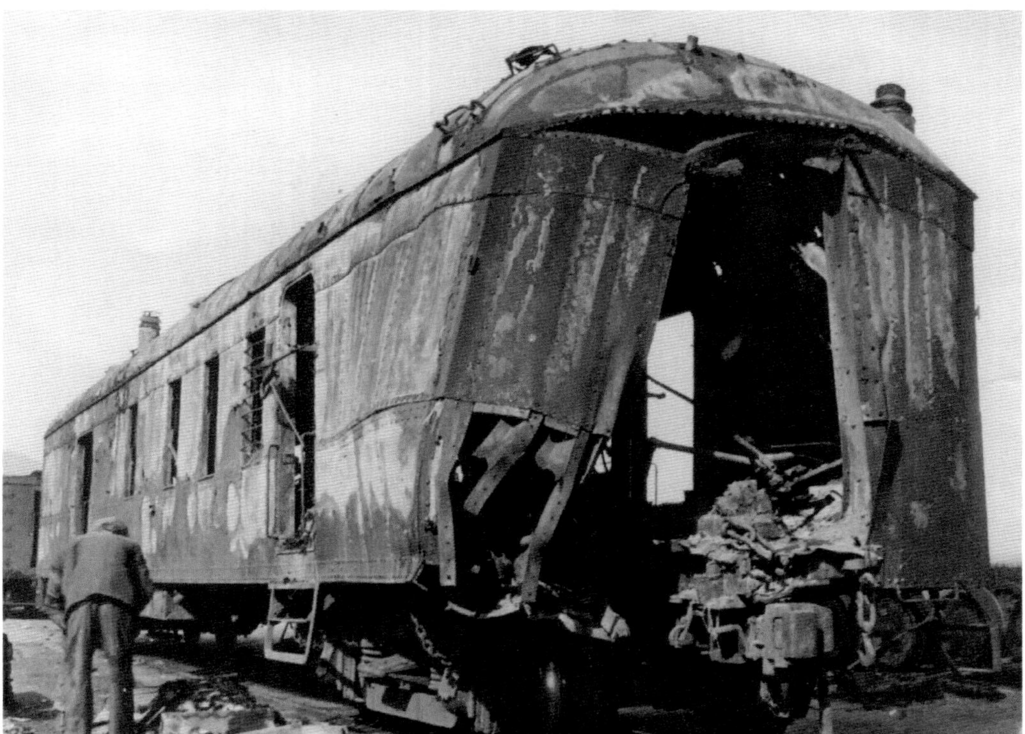

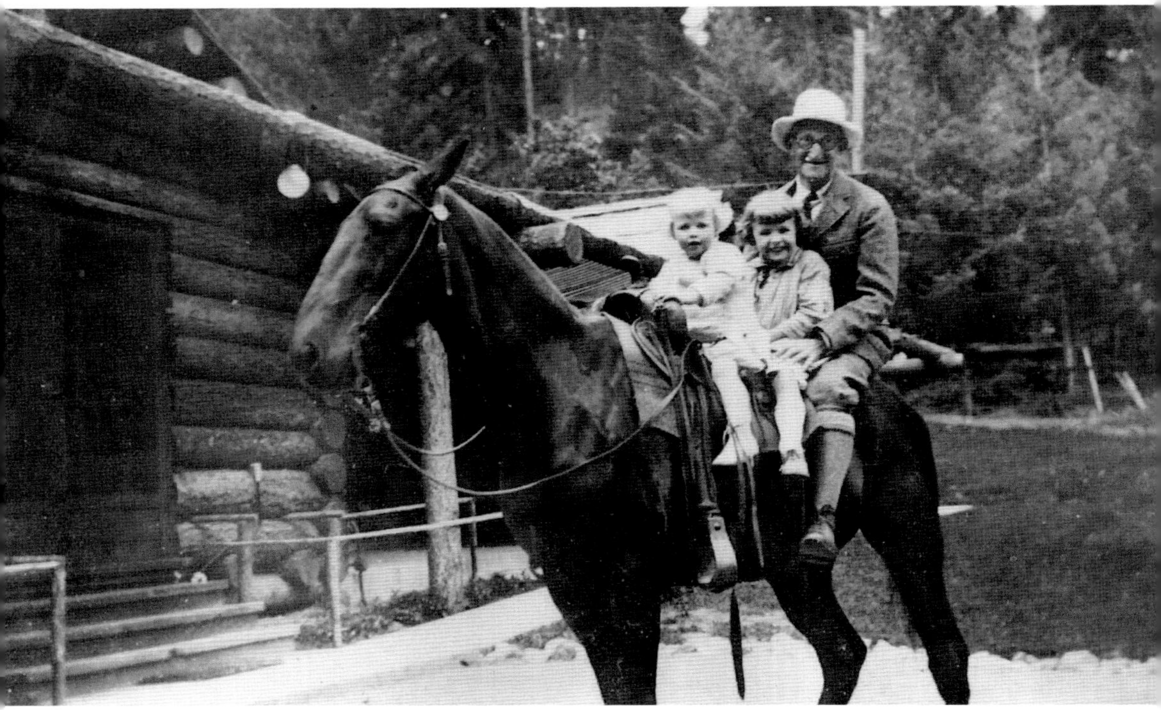

Jesse Winburn

A fiery, bold man, short in stature, Jesse Winburn only lived in Ashland for two years, 1921–1922, but made a point of leaving his mark. Winburn became wealthy in New York City after introducing subway advertising, and, impressed by Ashland's source of Lithia water, picked up where Bert Greer left off in lauding the potential Ashland had as the site of a world-renowned health and spa resort. Just as when Greer promoted the idea, Winburn's vision failed to gain momentum. He lived in a cabin above Lithia Park dubbed Sap and Salt in the Woods and was notorious and frequently fined by city officials for fishing in and grazing his cattle around Ashland's source of drinking water. He was tolerated among locals, though, because of his generosity toward the city, including the funding of parades and celebrations and the remodeling of Granite City Hospital. The city went on to name after him Winburn Way—his path between his canyon dwelling and town. Winburn is pictured here on his horse with Jeannie and Helene Salade. (Courtesy of the Southern Oregon Historical Society, #8466.)

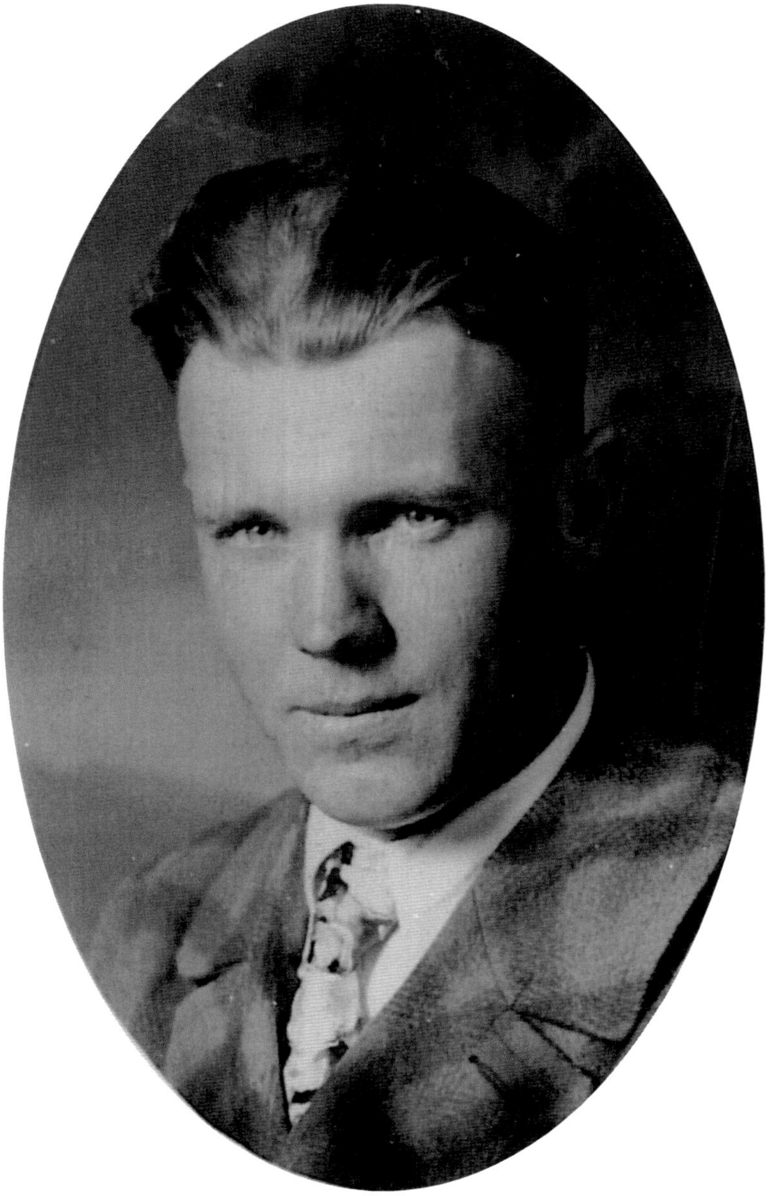

Sam Prescott

City police officer Sam Prescott was gunned down on Siskiyou Boulevard by a professional rumrunner on January 24, 1931. The rumrunner, James C. Adams, is reported by some sources to have been carrying 35 cases, about $3,000 worth, of illegal liquor when Prescott tried to apprehend him after stopping his stolen DeSoto sedan. Other sources say Adams had no liquor when he shot Prescott three times. Regardless, Adams was later convicted and executed by hanging in Salem for the crime. Prescott is one of two Ashland Police Department officers to have been murdered while on duty. The second, Victor Knott, was shot while patrolling in the Railroad District in November of the same year. Due to a sharp uptick in crime associated with Prohibition, Ashland was known as "Little Chicago" during 1931. (Courtesy of the Southern Oregon Historical Society, #2045.)

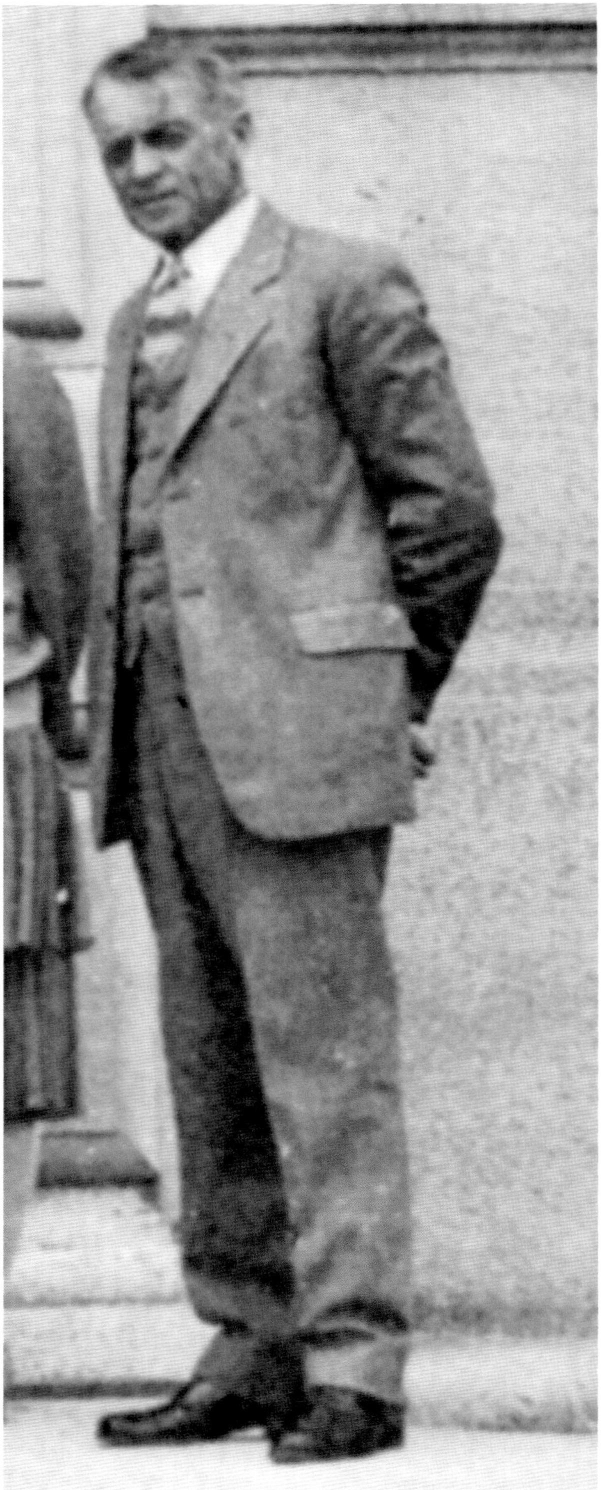

Julius Alonzo Churchill
In 1926, after serving as the superintendent of state schools in Oregon for 13 years, Churchill was appointed the first president of Southern Oregon State Normal School, now Southern Oregon University. During his first year as president, the school built and opened Churchill Hall, named for him. Today, Churchill Hall, the school's oldest building, houses most of SOU's administrative offices, including the office of the president. In 1932, Churchill transferred to become president of the State Normal School in Monmouth, Oregon, today's Western Oregon University, where he served as president until his retirement in 1939. (This photograph is part of the Southern Oregon University Archives and made available courtesy of Southern Oregon University Hannon Library.)

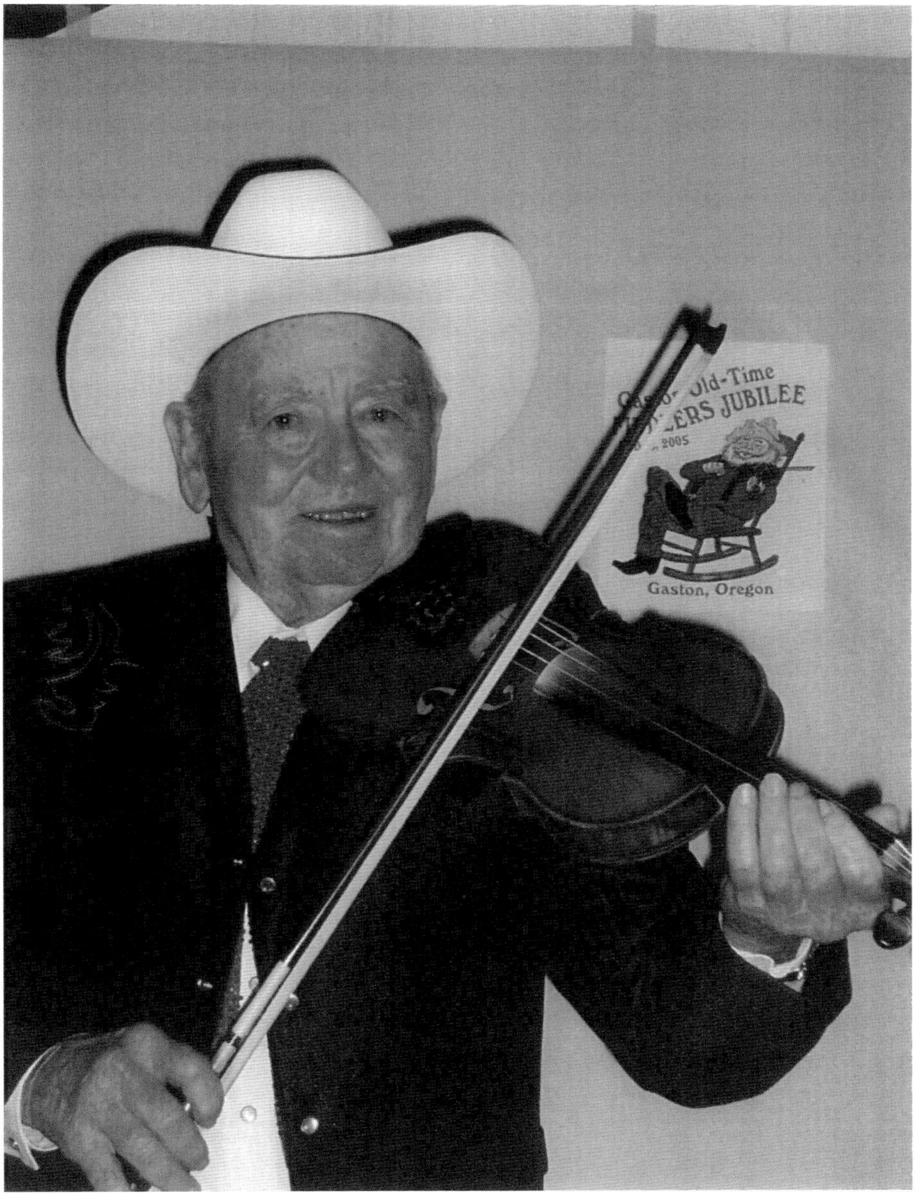

Don Juan Maddox

Named Kenneth by his mother, famous fiddler Don Maddox has spent the last 55 years as a cattle rancher on the slopes of Grizzly Peak above Ashland, but few residents know he was once a part of the most popular band in America—Maddox Brothers and Sister Rose, dubbed "America's Most Colorful Hillbilly Band." Maddox is the last surviving member of his family's band, which included his brothers, Fred, Cal, Cliff, and Henry, and their little sister, Rose. The band, which formed in 1935 as the Alabama Outlaws, is credited with laying the foundation for rockabilly music. Don was inducted into the Western Swing Hall of Fame in 2005, and at the ripe old age of 91, he can still tell the stirring story of his family's migration to California in 1933 from a life of sharecropping in Boaz, Alabama. (Courtesy of Don Maddox.)

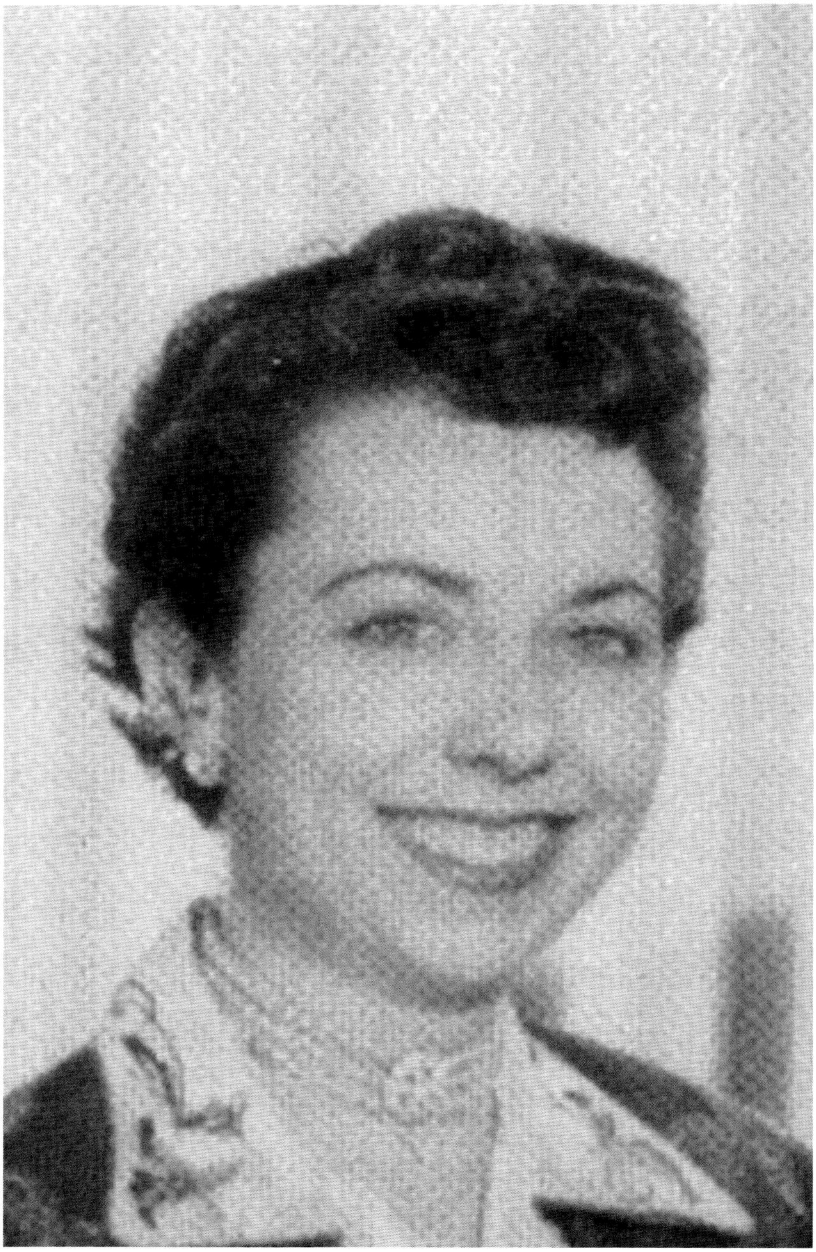

Rose Maddox

Rose Maddox, born Roselea Arbana Maddox, passed away at the age of 72 while living on her brother Don's property above Ashland on April 15, 1998. Rose was the singer and centerpiece of the family's band—Maddox Brothers and Sister Rose. Following the band's breakup in 1956, Rose went on to have some success as a solo artist with such hits in the late 1950s and early 1960s as "Gambler's Love," "Kissing My Pillow," "Sing a Little Song of Heartache," and "Bluebird, Let Me Tag Along." In 1996, she sang a rendition of Woody Guthrie's "Philadelphia Lawyer" with Johnny Cash at the Britt Festivals in Jacksonville. (Courtesy of Don Maddox.)

Dr. Elmo Stevenson

When Dr. Elmo Stevenson was appointed president of Southern Oregon College in 1946, the school was experiencing an alarming lull in enrollment brought on by the beginning of World War II and was threatened with closure. Less than 100 students were registered for classes in the fall of 1945. By the end of 1946, as veterans began to return home and take advantage of benefits associated with the Servicemen's Readjustment Act, or GI Bill, Stevenson helped foster an enrollment increase to about 500 students. Much of Stevenson's legacy at the school can be traced though a concise history written by former university professor Arthur Kreisman, who remembers Stevenson as a charismatic and sometimes authoritarian leader who insisted his male professors wear ties. In Stevenson's 23 years as president—nearly twice as long as any other president has served—he helped establish long-standing links between the school and the community through his involvement in the establishment of Jefferson Public Radio and the Rogue Valley Symphony Orchestra. Stevenson also oversaw the construction of several new buildings on campus, including the Suzanne Holmes and Cascade dorms and McNeal athletic complex. (This photograph is part of the Southern Oregon University Archives and made available courtesy of Southern Oregon University Hannon Library.)

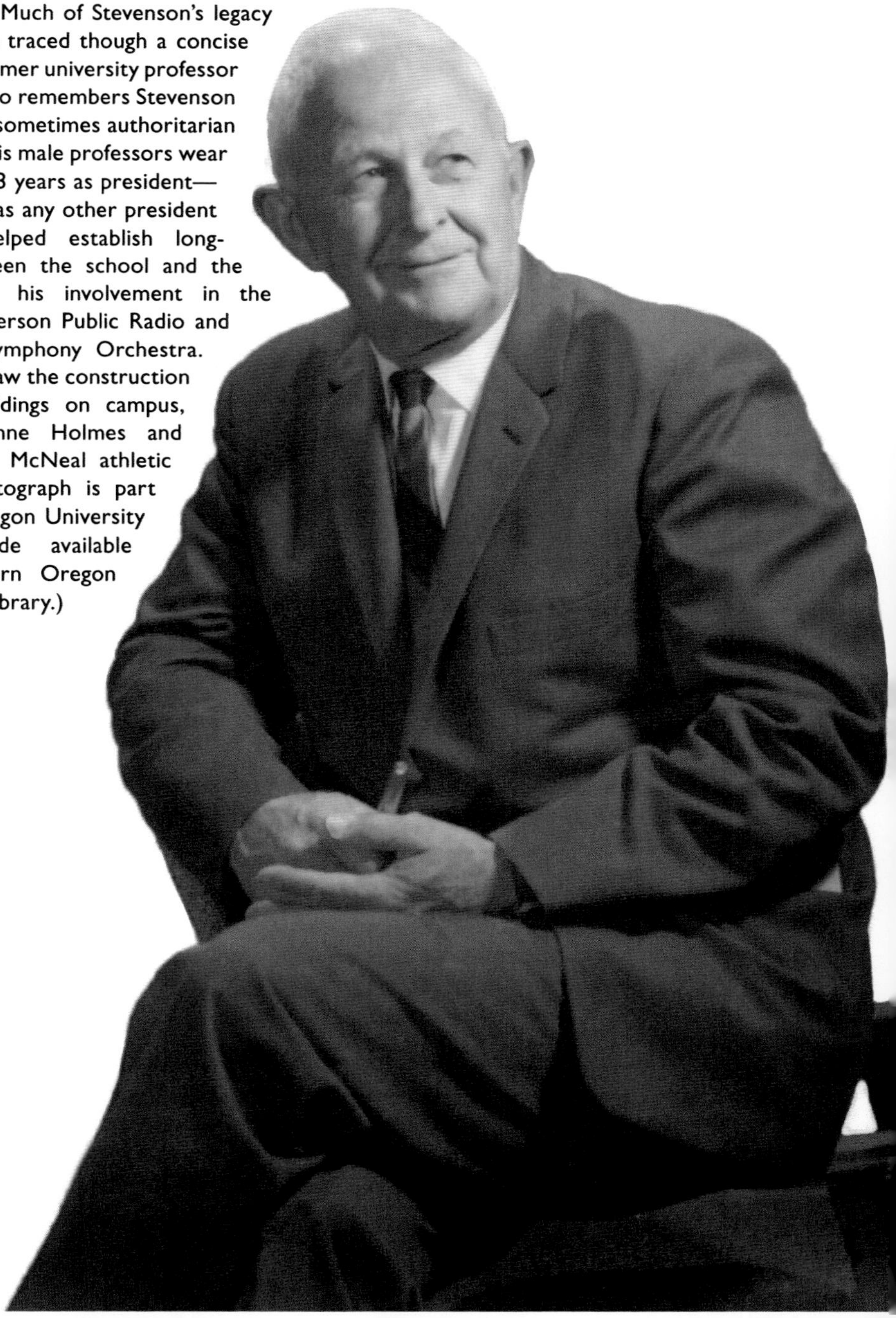

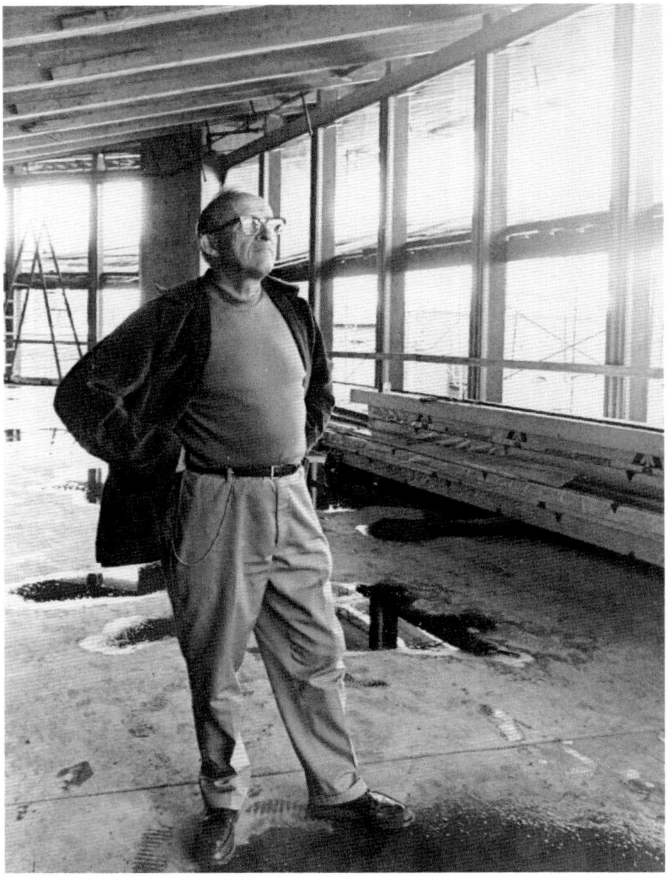

Angus Bowmer (ABOVE AND OPPOSITE PAGE)
Arguably the most prolific individual in the history of Ashland, Angus Bowmer founded the Oregon Shakespeare Festival in 1935 and restarted it following its lapse during World War II, in which he enlisted. Bowmer moved to Ashland in 1931 to teach English composition and public speaking at Southern Oregon Normal School. It was during preparations for Ashland's 1935 Fourth of July celebration that Bowmer convinced the city to support a three-day festival production of Shakespearian plays. The plays were staged inside the concrete skeleton of Ashland's former Chautauqua building, which today houses the festival's Allen Elizabethan Theater. Outside his involvement with the festival and college, Bowmer made significant contributions toward the advancement of theater arts in Ashland. In the early 1950s, Bowmer began to refurbish the decrepit Lithia Theater. He restored the theater's original name, the Vining Theater, and used it to house plays put on by a small company of actors he organized to perform during the Shakespeare festival's off season. Unfortunately, the theater was consumed by a fire during 1952, ending its use as a playhouse. Serving as artistic director from the festival's inception through 1971, Bowmer performed 32 roles in 43 separate stagings and produced all of William Shakespeare's 37 plays. He carried on an intimate involvement with the festival until his death in 1979. In 1970, the OSF opened the 600-seat Angus Bowmer Theater, named after the festival's beloved founder. Two years prior to his death, Bowmer received the first Governor's Award for Significant Contributions to the Advancement of the Arts in Oregon. Bowmer is pictured above in the incomplete lobby of the Angus Bowmer Theater; opposite getting his costume prepped by his first wife, Lois Bowmer; and opposite pointing with his pen at a model of the Elizabethan Theater while posing with Allan Harris above the actual theater. (All courtesy of the Oregon Shakespeare Festival.)

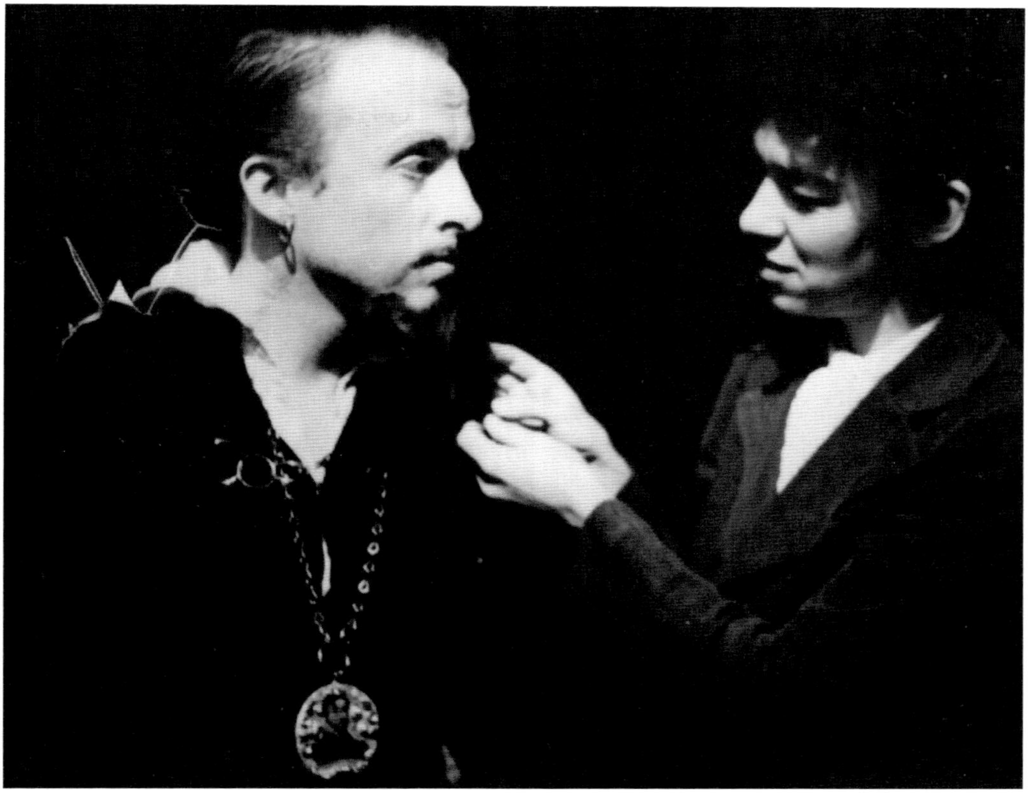

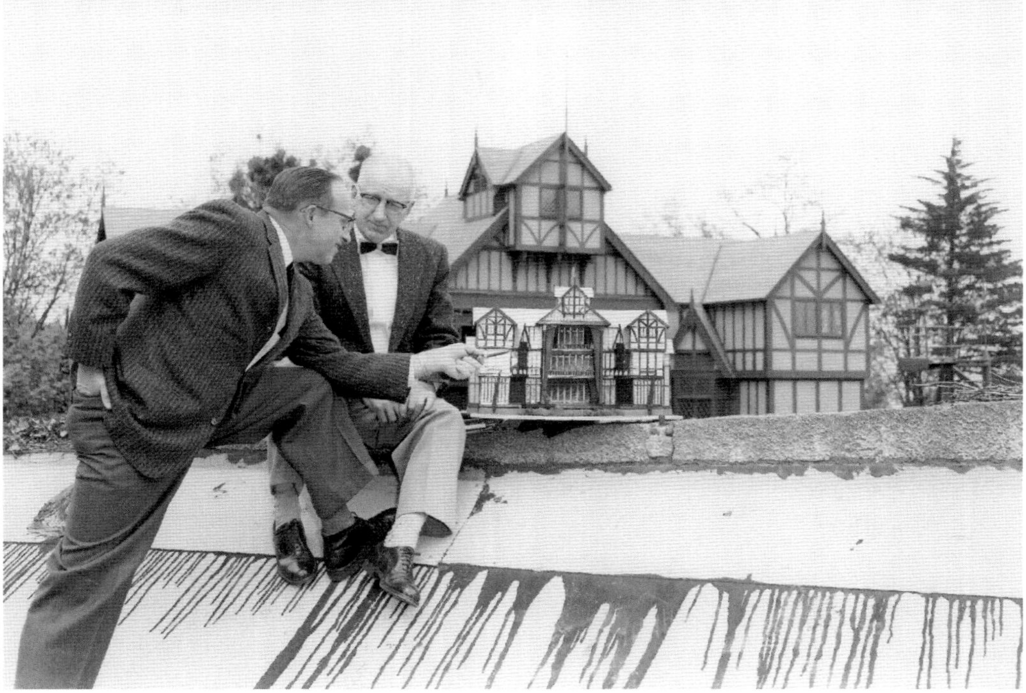

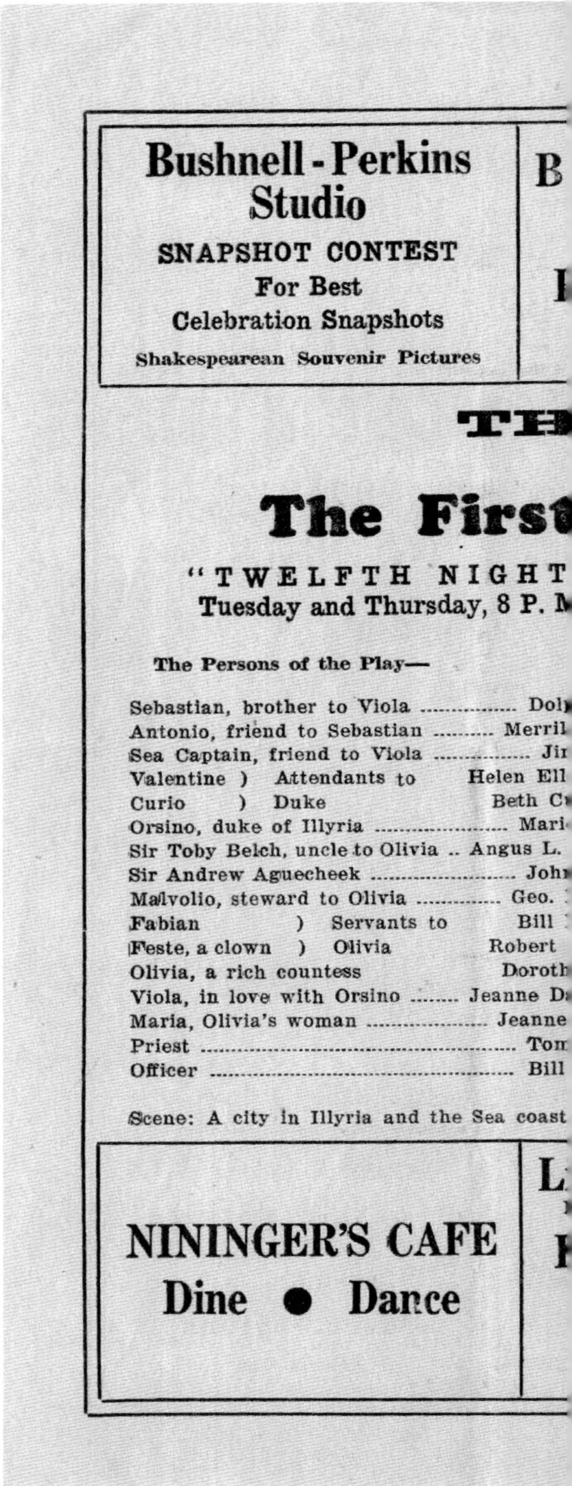
Bushnell - Perkins Studio

SNAPSHOT CONTEST
For Best
Celebration Snapshots
Shakespearean Souvenir Pictures

The First

"TWELFTH NIGHT
Tuesday and Thursday, 8 P.

The Persons of the Play—

Sebastian, brother to Viola .... Dol
Antonio, friend to Sebastian .... Merril
Sea Captain, friend to Viola .... Ji
Valentine) Attendants to Helen Ell
Curio) Duke Beth C
Orsino, duke of Illyria .... Mari
Sir Toby Belch, uncle to Olivia .. Angus L.
Sir Andrew Aguecheek .... Joh
Malvolio, steward to Olivia .... Geo.
Fabian) Servants to Bill
Feste, a clown) Olivia Robert
Olivia, a rich countess Doroth
Viola, in love with Orsino .... Jeanne D
Maria, Olivia's woman .... Jeanne
Priest .... Tom
Officer .... Bill

Scene: A city in Illyria and the Sea coast

NININGER'S CAFE
Dine ● Dance

Oregon Shakespeare Festival Original Playbill
The first Oregon Shakespeare Festival was held in conjunction with the Ashland Fourth of July celebration in 1935. In addition to theater performances, there were boxing matches held on the stage inside the remnants of the town's old Chautauqua building. The fights were scheduled to help the production break even financially, but it was actually the plays that attracted the most patrons and money. (Courtesy of the Oregon Shakespeare Festival.)

Draught
and
LUNCHES
Pool Hall
Park Entrance

McNAIR BROS.
The Rexall Store
Vacation Needs

Ashland
GROCETERIA
—ASHLAND'S—
SUPER
FOOD MARKET

ITY OF ASHLAND

—PRESENTS—

nual Shakespearean Festival

Under the Direction of
ANGUS L. BOWMER

PRODUCTION STAFF

stumes designed by .... Lois M. Bowmer
nstruction Manager .... R. Berry
ardrobe Mistresses ....
.... Maxine Gearhart, Billie Brandes
operties .... Jeanne Fabrick
ectrician .... Tom Palmer
ok Holder .... Noma Weaver
ke-up .... Marion Ady, Angus Bowmer
blicity .... Gordon MacCracken

sic orchestrated and directed by Lawrence Hubert

ORCHESTRA PERSONNEL

Violins
Mary Roberson, Frances Aikens
Alicia Coggins, Ruth Hardy
Florence Hubert, Laverne Roberson
Leslie Kincaid, Jean Billings

Viola
Andrew Johnson

Cello
Phyllis Sparr

Flute
Lorraine Sparr

Piano
Flossie Thompson

Reeds
Rosa Franko

"MERCHANT OF VENICE"
Wednesday at 8 P. M.

The Persons of the Play—
Duke of Venice .... Marion Frost
Prince of Morocco) Suitors to .... John Harr
Prince of Arragon) Portia .... Karl Moore
Antonio, a Merchant of Venice .... Ed. Butze
Bassanio, his friend .... Robert Stedman
Gratiano) Friends to .... Geo. F. Smith
Salanio) Antonio and .... Merrill Gunter
Salarino) Bassanio .... Tom Palmer
Lorenzo, in love with Jessica .... Jim Foster
Shylock, a rich Jew .... Angus L. Bowmer
Launcelot Gobbo .... John Chipley
A servant to Shylock
Old Gobbo, father to Launcelot .... Bill Cottrell
Leonardo, servant to Bassanio .. Helen Ellenberger
Stephano, servant to Portia .... Beth Cummings
Tubal, friend to Shylock .... Bill Cottrell
Portia, a rich heiress .... Helen Edmiston
Nerissa, her waiting maid .... Beverly Young
Jessica, daughter to Shylock .... Wanada Aldrich
Curtain boys .... Audrey Lofland, Wilma Copple
Magnificoes and other attendants: Bob Root, Maxine Gearhart, Vernon Clark, Jack Sanderson, Don Darnielle.
Scene: Partly at Venice and partly at Belmont, the seat of Portia, on the continent.

atre THURS.
RES FRI.
RADDOCK
-15 Rounds
plus —
BAXTER in
PAMPAS MOON"

STEVE'S SERVICE
Steve Zarka, Proprietor
PHONE 68
Your Smiling Associated Dealer
Across Street From Lithia Hotel
ASHLAND, OREGON

FORTMILLER'S
THE QUALITY STORE
Departments for Men's and
Ladies' Clothing and
Furnishings
SHOES · DRY GOODS
C. W. Fortmiller J. P. Daugherty

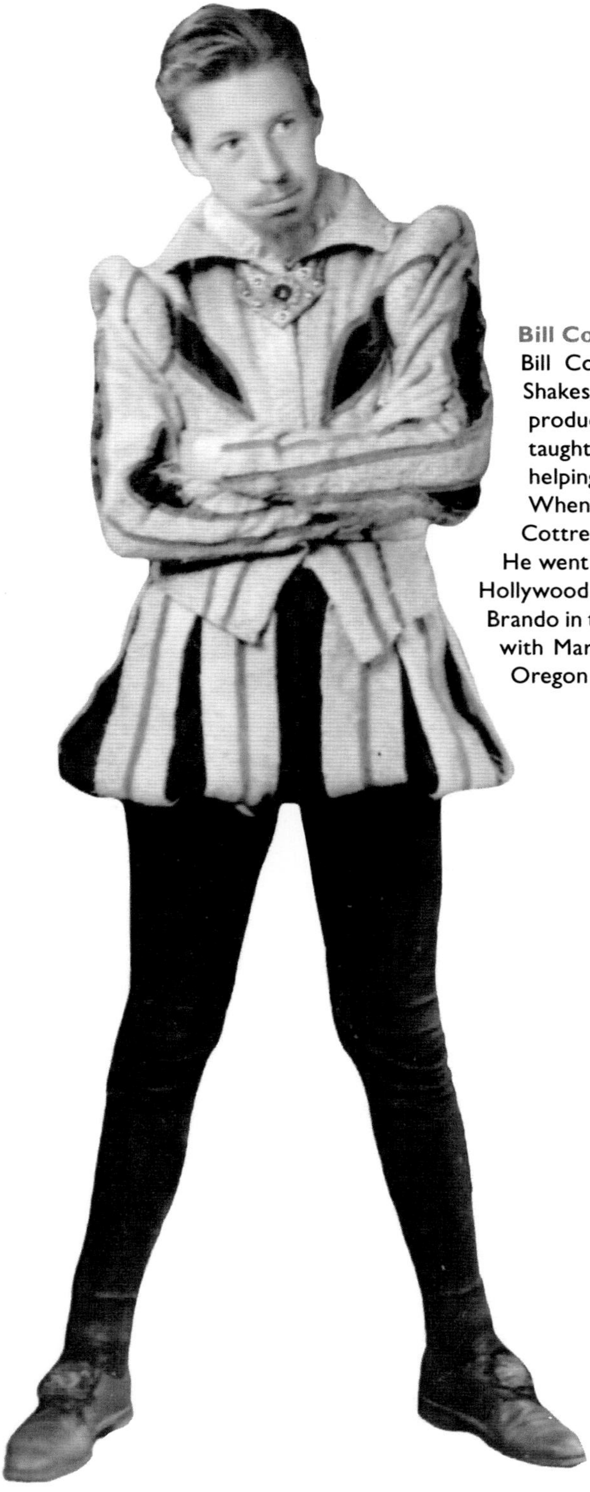

Bill Cottrell

Bill Cottrell was an original member of the Oregon Shakespeare Festival company, acting in the first productions in 1935. A Rogue Valley native, Cottrell taught at the Cornish School of the Arts in Seattle before helping founder Angus Bowmer get the festival started. When Bowmer spent a year away from OSF in 1940, Cottrell acted in and directed all four plays that season. He went on to act in theater and movies in New York and Hollywood, was a personal Shakespeare coach to Marlon Brando in the 1953 film *Julius Caesar*, and studied Shakespeare with Marilyn Monroe. He died in 2001. (Courtesy of the Oregon Shakespeare Festival.)

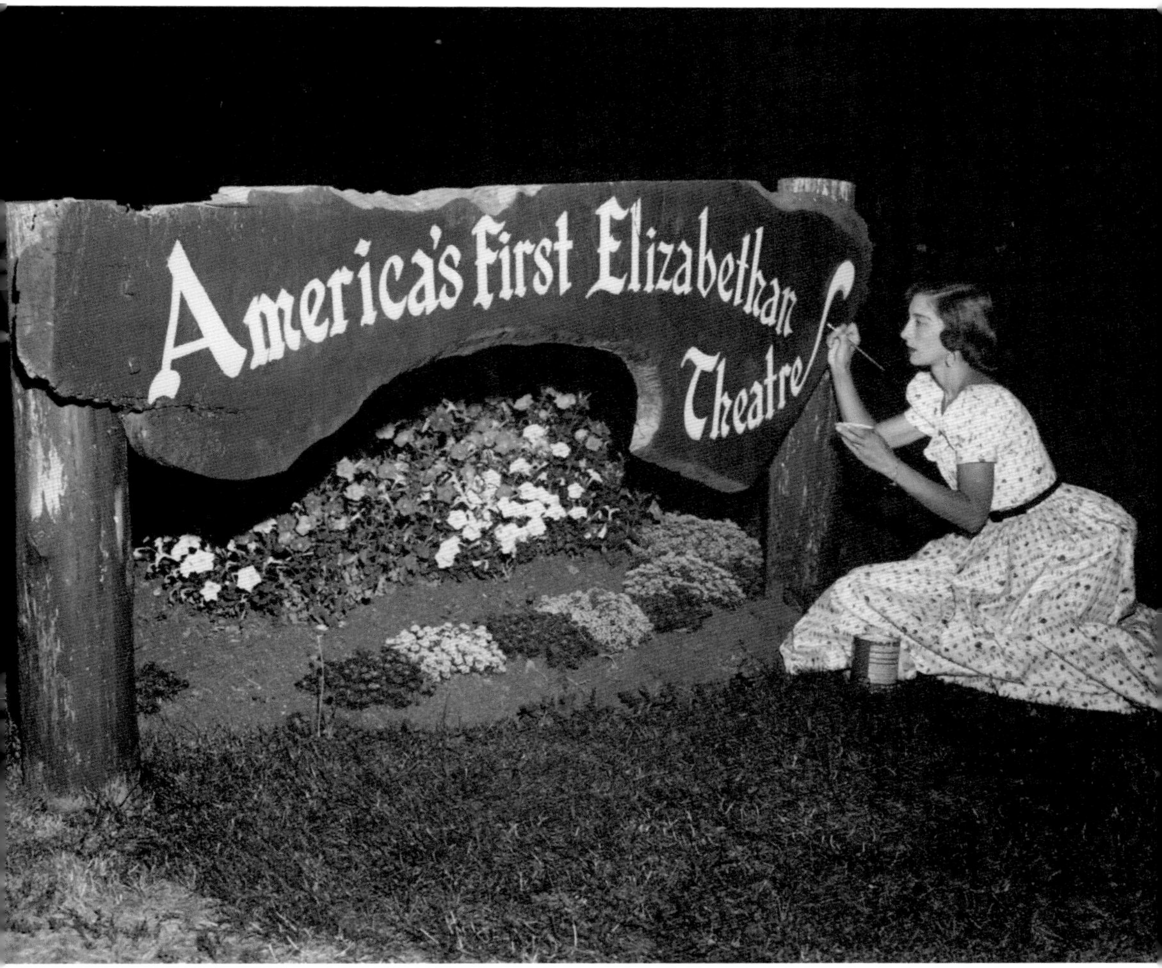

Martha Dawkins

Martha Dawkins was a Tudor Guild volunteer when a local lumberman donated a large slab of wood to the festival. She had the idea to turn the wood into a hand-painted sign for the Elizabethan Theater, reading, "America's First Elizabethan Theatre." Dawkins was president of the Tudor Guild—a volunteer organization that supports the Oregon Shakespeare Festival through financial contributions—in 1956, and her sign still stands on the festival campus today. (Courtesy of the Oregon Shakespeare Festival.)

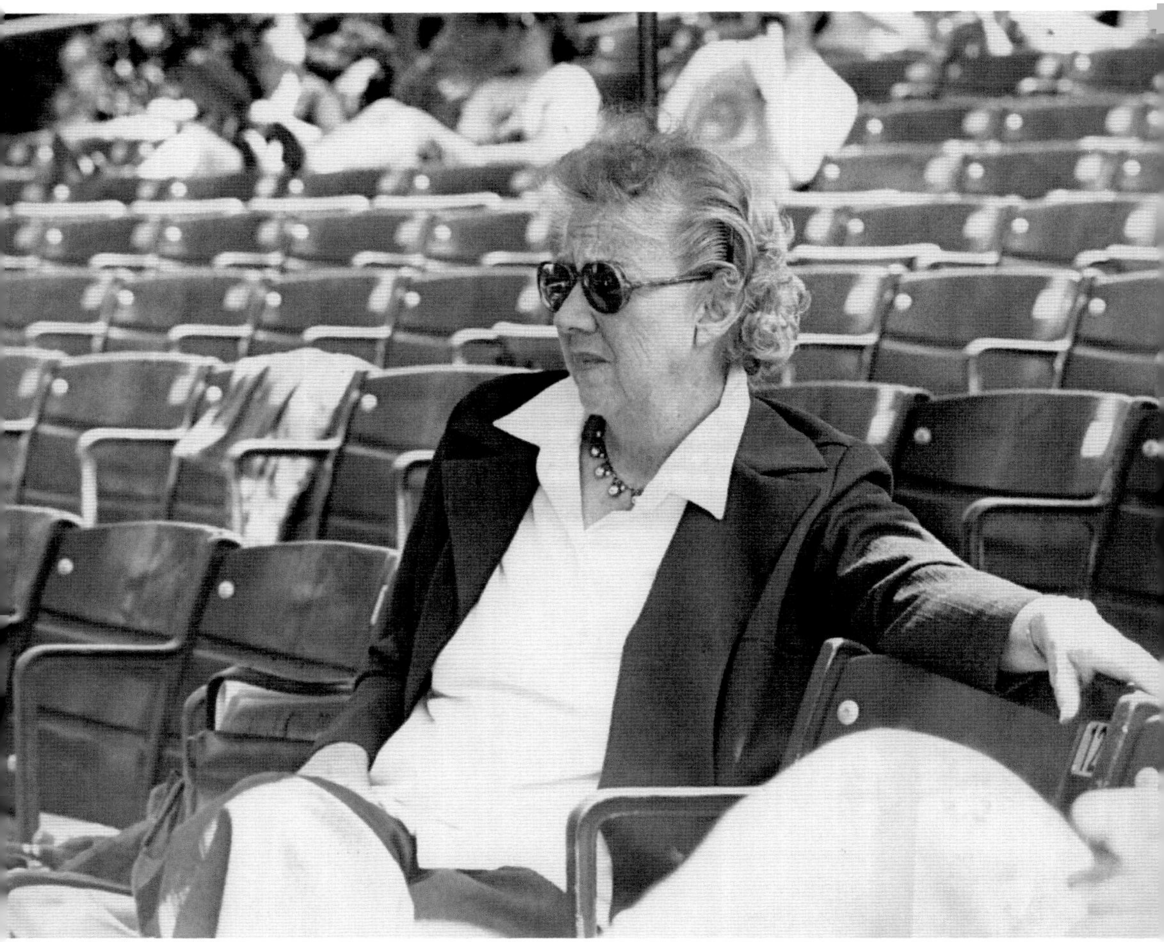

Gertrude Bowmer

Gertrude Bowmer was a volunteer ticket seller at the Oregon Shakespeare Festival when she met Angus Bowmer, the festival's founder. The two married in 1940, Angus Bowmer's second go at marriage. Once a high school French teacher and an employee of the Jackson County clerk's office, Bowmer went on to act as an assistant and secretary to her husband and was recognized by many for her wonderful memory. After his death in 1979, she continued on as a festival volunteer and was honorary chairwoman at the 50th anniversary of OSF in 1985. She died in 1994. (Courtesy of the Oregon Shakespeare Festival.)

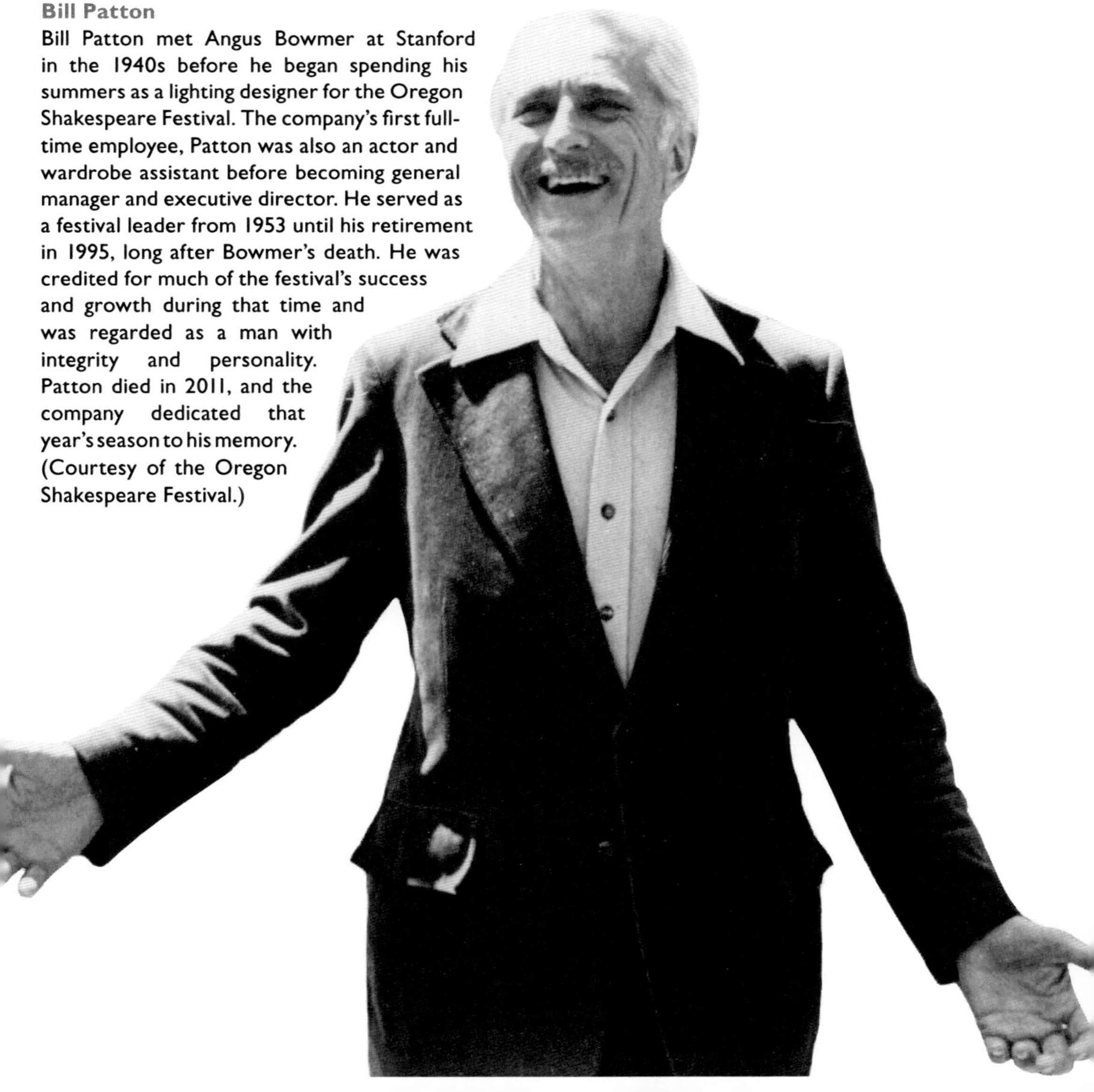

Bill Patton
Bill Patton met Angus Bowmer at Stanford in the 1940s before he began spending his summers as a lighting designer for the Oregon Shakespeare Festival. The company's first full-time employee, Patton was also an actor and wardrobe assistant before becoming general manager and executive director. He served as a festival leader from 1953 until his retirement in 1995, long after Bowmer's death. He was credited for much of the festival's success and growth during that time and was regarded as a man with integrity and personality. Patton died in 2011, and the company dedicated that year's season to his memory. (Courtesy of the Oregon Shakespeare Festival.)

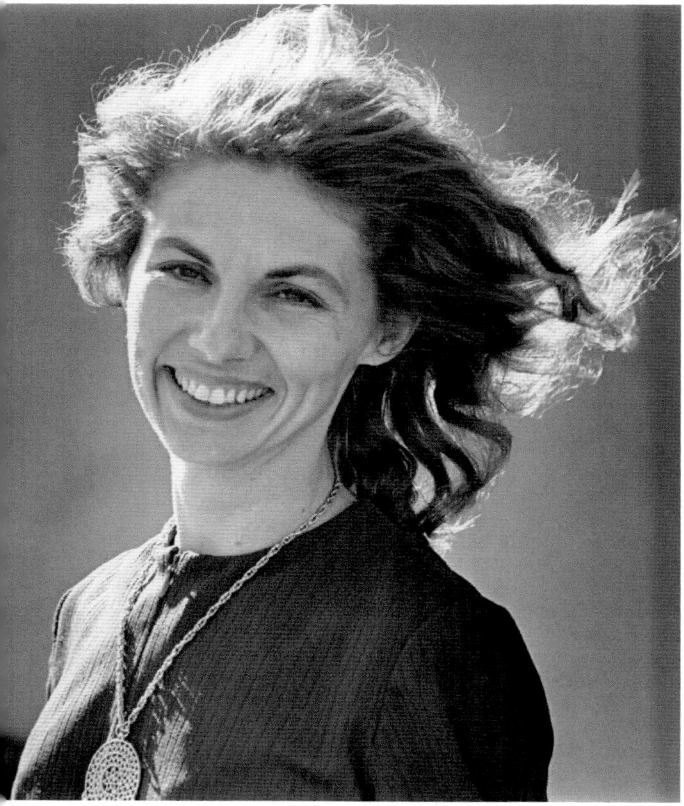

Shirley Patton
Shirley Patton called Angus Bowmer in 1958, hoping to act in the Oregon Shakespeare Festival. That season, she was given roles in *The Merchant of Venice* and *Troilus and Cressida*, and went on to spend 30 seasons with OSF. She married general manager and executive director Bill Patton. Still a familiar face in Ashland's theater community, after leaving OSF, she continued acting at other local theaters, including the Camelot Theater in Talent, Oregon. Her latest role there wrapped up in early 2014. (Both, courtesy of the Oregon Shakespeare Festival.)

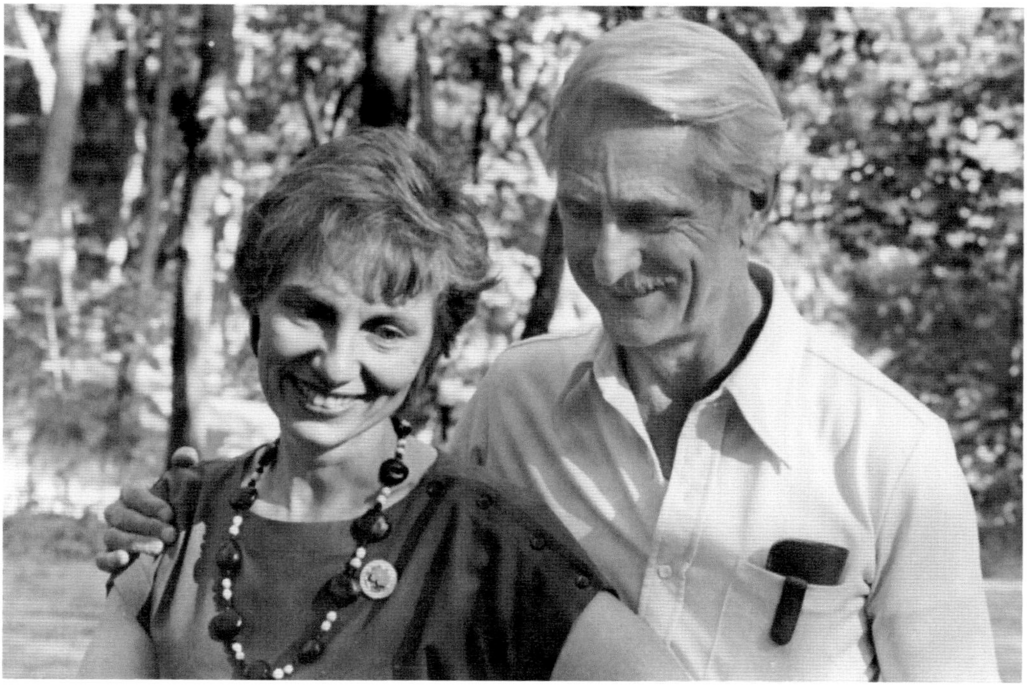

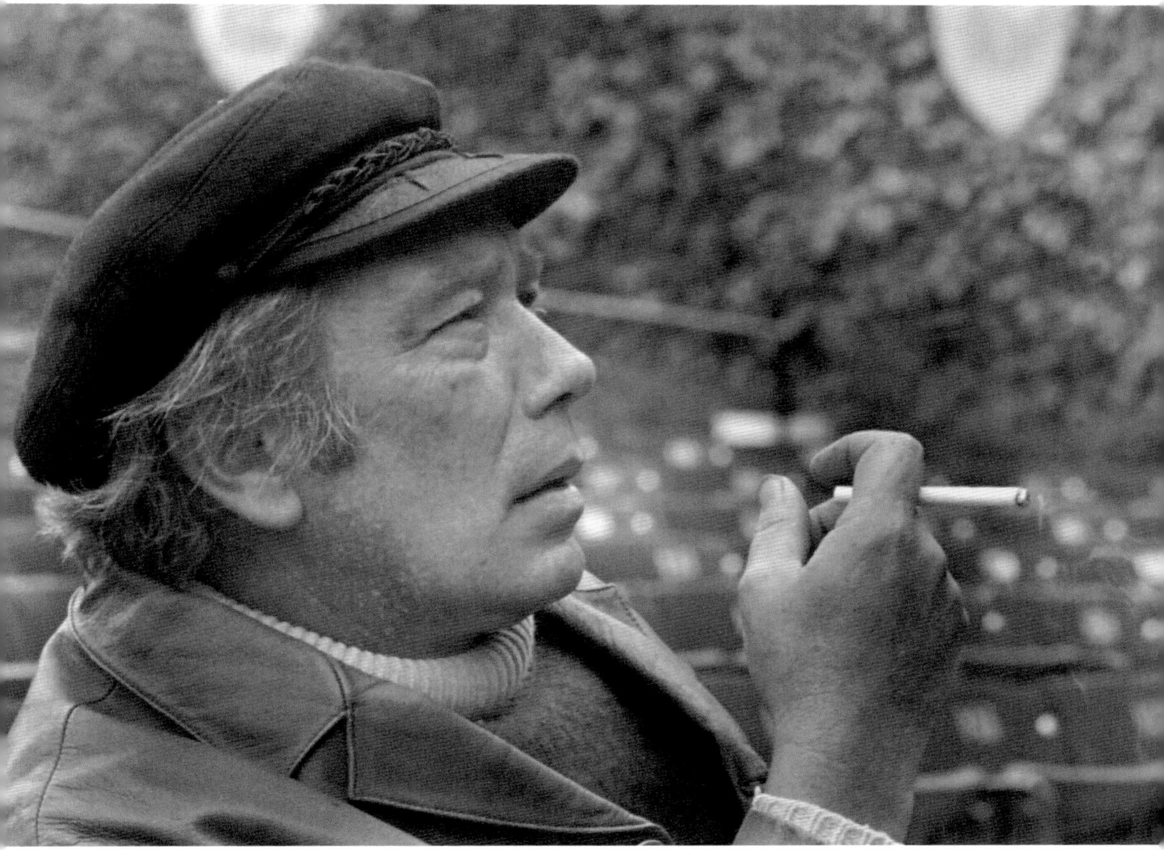

Jerry Turner
Jerry Turner served as the artistic director of the Oregon Shakespeare Festival from 1971 through 1991. During his tenure there, he helped lift the festival from a regionally renowned theater company to one of global notoriety. When Turner took on the role of artistic director, the Oregon Shakespeare Festival, with one theater—the Elizabethan—was attracting about 150,000 patrons a year. When he stepped down, the festival had added the Angus Bowmer Theater and the Black Swan and was serving over 400,000 annually. In 1983, the festival won a Tony Award for outstanding achievement in regional theater. Turner, who joined the festival as an actor in 1957 and held a doctorate in theater, was well known as a traditionalist and a risk-taker concerning his productions. He died of heart failure in September 2004 while living in Olympia, Washington. (Courtesy of the Oregon Shakespeare Festival.)

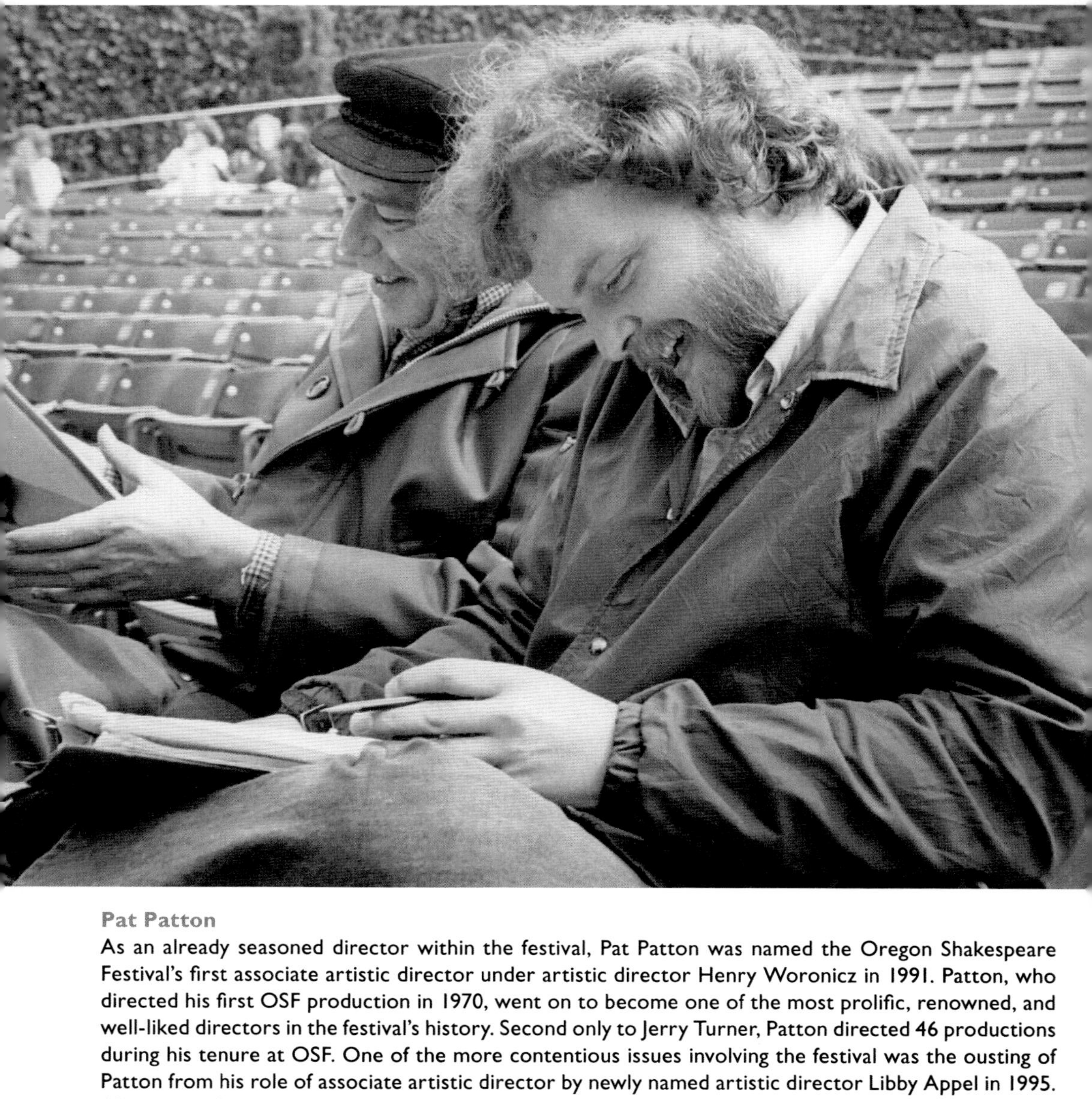

Pat Patton

As an already seasoned director within the festival, Pat Patton was named the Oregon Shakespeare Festival's first associate artistic director under artistic director Henry Woronicz in 1991. Patton, who directed his first OSF production in 1970, went on to become one of the most prolific, renowned, and well-liked directors in the festival's history. Second only to Jerry Turner, Patton directed 46 productions during his tenure at OSF. One of the more contentious issues involving the festival was the ousting of Patton from his role of associate artistic director by newly named artistic director Libby Appel in 1995. (Courtesy of the Oregon Shakespeare Festival.)

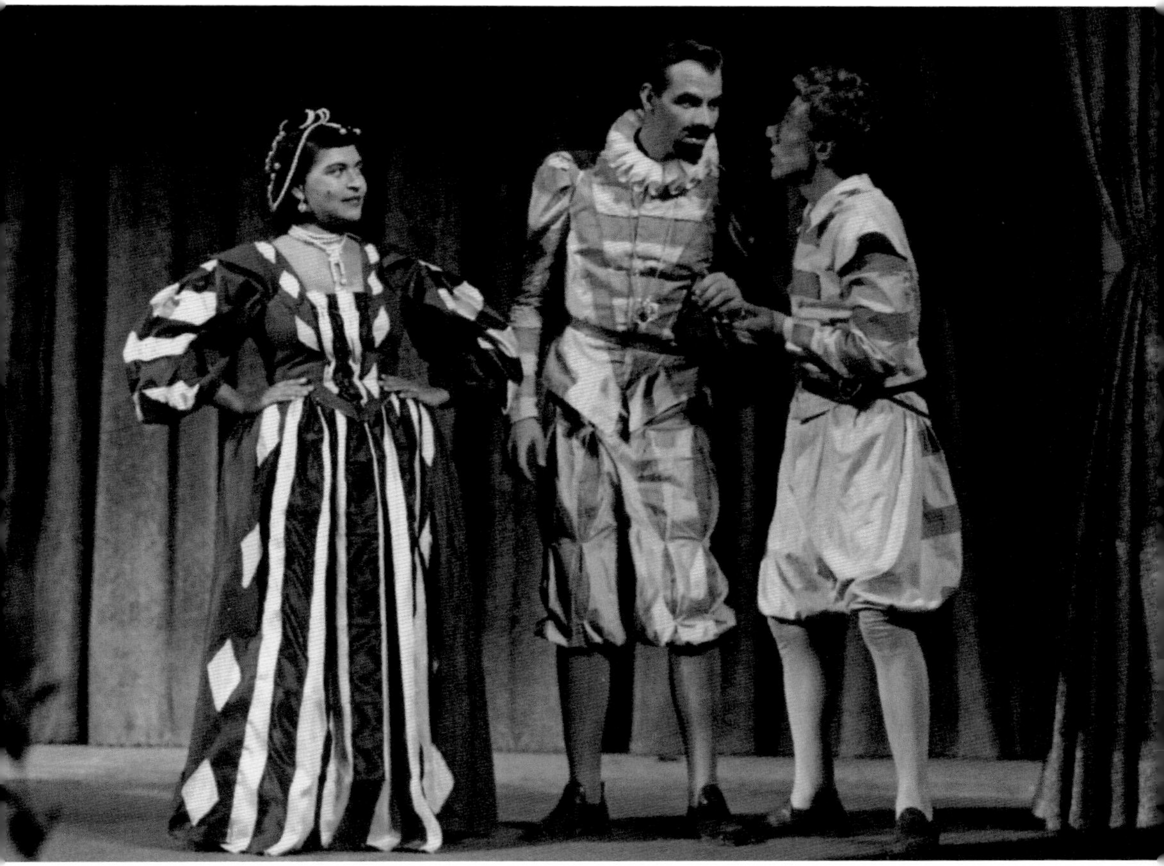

Patricia Norman

Patricia Norman, a talented actress, dancer, and singer, was the Oregon Shakespeare Festival's first African American company member. She played her first role, the courtesan in *The Comedy of Errors*, in 1950. In a county with an almost nonexistent African American population during the 1950s, Norman was the only African American actor at OSF in that decade. Former company member Carl Ritchie says he remembers Norman could not find anyone in Ashland to rent her a room, so she stayed in a dorm on the college campus. She was escorted to and from her dorm and around town by other company members because of the threat of violence stemming from widespread discrimination against African Americans in Ashland. (Courtesy of the Oregon Shakespeare Festival.)

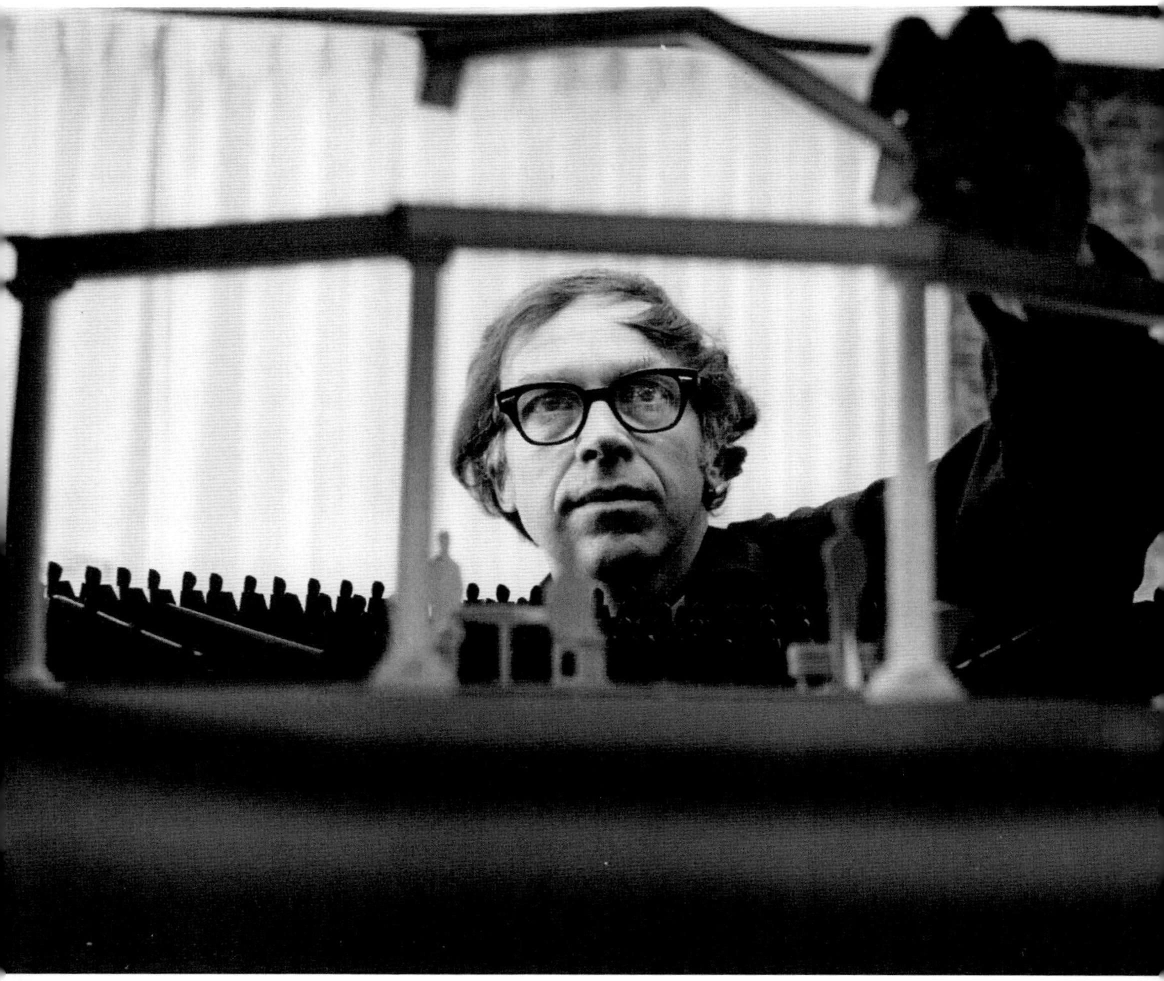

Richard L. Hay
Oregon Shakespeare Festival senior scenic theater designer Richard L. Hay was a Stanford theater student in the 1940s when he met Oregon Shakespeare Festival pillars Bill Patton and Angus Bowmer. He temporarily left behind his graduate studies in architecture to pursue set design for OSF during the summer of 1950. He continued as a seasonal designer and technical director through the 1950s and beyond, helping design the Elizabethan Theater, the Angus Bowmer Theatre, and the New Theater in 2002, which would eventually become the Thomas Theatre. He has created sets for more than 240 OSF productions and designed theaters and sets for numerous theaters outside Ashland. Hay has been a Fulbright Scholar in England and won an Oregon Governor's Award for the Arts. The 2014 season was Hay's 57th with the festival. (Courtesy of the Oregon Shakespeare Festival.)

Graciela "Señora Chela" Tapp-Knocks
Señora Chela Tapp-Knocks led the effort to foster ties between Ashland and its sister city, Guanajuato, Mexico. She began teaching foreign language and literature at Southern Oregon University in 1966 and acted as a virtual ambassador between the two cities. The sister city program has encouraged academic and cultural exchanges between citizens of the two cities, and has helped nurture a link between the two countries. An obelisk in Guanajuato and a bench in Ashland's Lithia Park both honor Señora Chela. (Courtesy of Graciela "Señora Chela" Tapp-Knocks.)

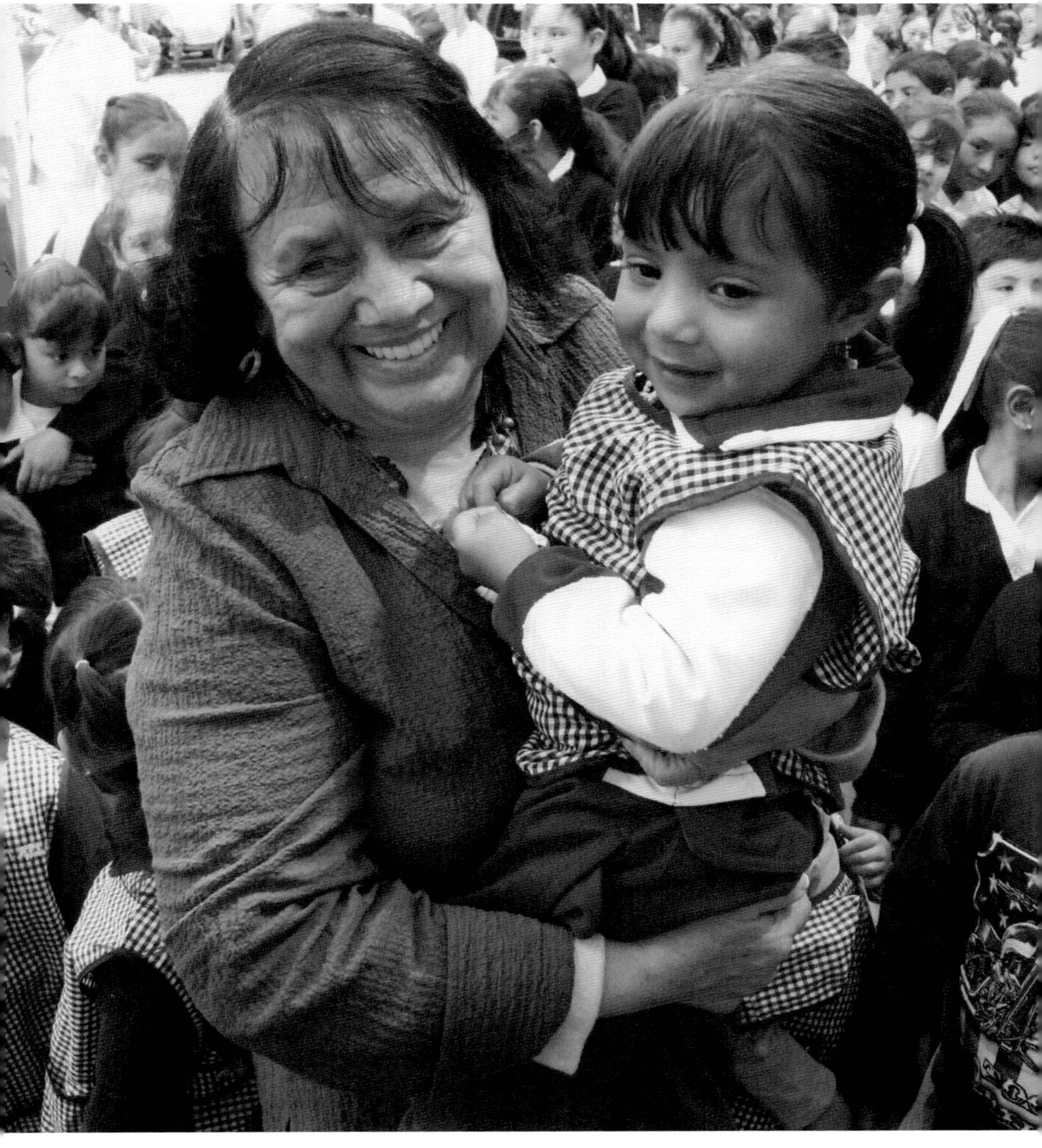

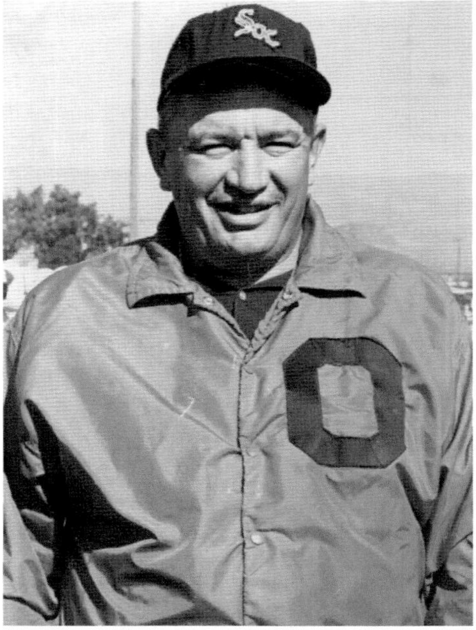

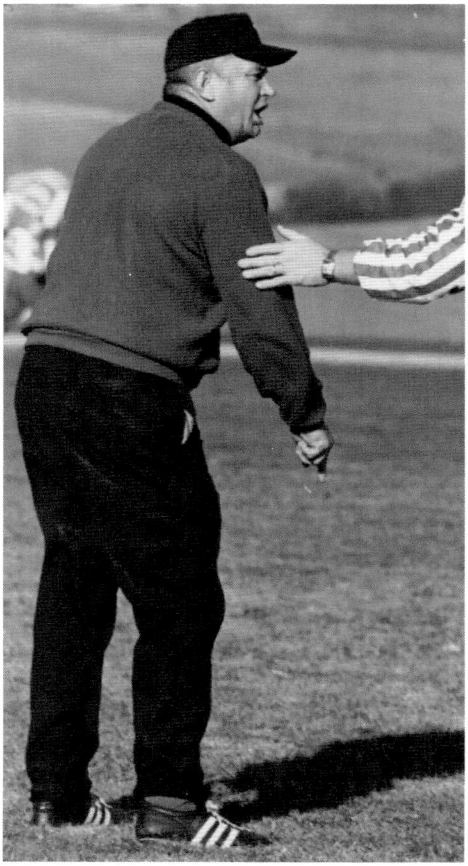

Al Akins

Southern Oregon University's head football coach of 15 years, from 1955 through 1969, Al Akins helped lead the Raiders to 71 wins and seven conference championships. He remains the Raiders' winningest coach. Following Akins's retirement, it took the Raiders nearly 20 years to reach the postseason again. Prior to leading SOU's football program, Akins played from 1946 through 1948 in the All-American Football Conference. During his professional tenure, he played halfback and defensive back for the Cleveland Browns, Brooklyn Dodgers, and Buffalo Bills. He was also an assistant coach for the football team at Lewis & Clark College from 1950 through 1954. (These photographs are part of the Southern Oregon University Archives and made available courtesy of Southern Oregon University Hannon Library.)

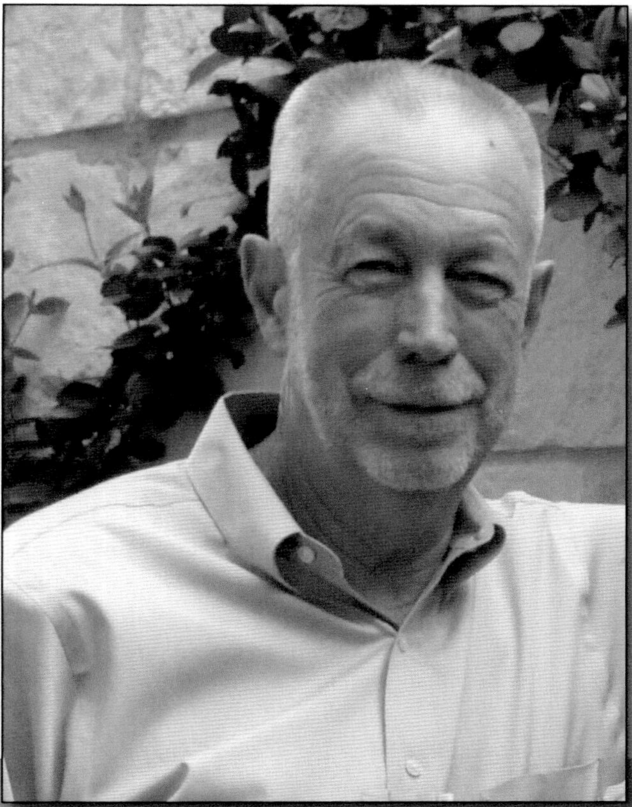

John Weisinger

John Weisinger started planting his east-facing hillside vineyard in 1978, after close friend Frank Wisnovsky, then owner of Valley View Vineyard, agreed to sell him enough cuts of Gewürztraminer grapevines for a 1.5-acre vineyard. Weisinger, originally from Texas, knew the Rogue Valley historically had been one of the oldest wine-producing regions west of the Rocky Mountains, and he had the courage to act on it. Before jumping head first into the wine industry, he enjoyed a career as a Presbyterian minister and youth counselor. Growing grapes and making wine outside Ashland mostly as a hobby led to his founding of Ashland Winery in 1988, known now as Weisinger Family Winery. (Both, courtesy of the Weisinger family.)

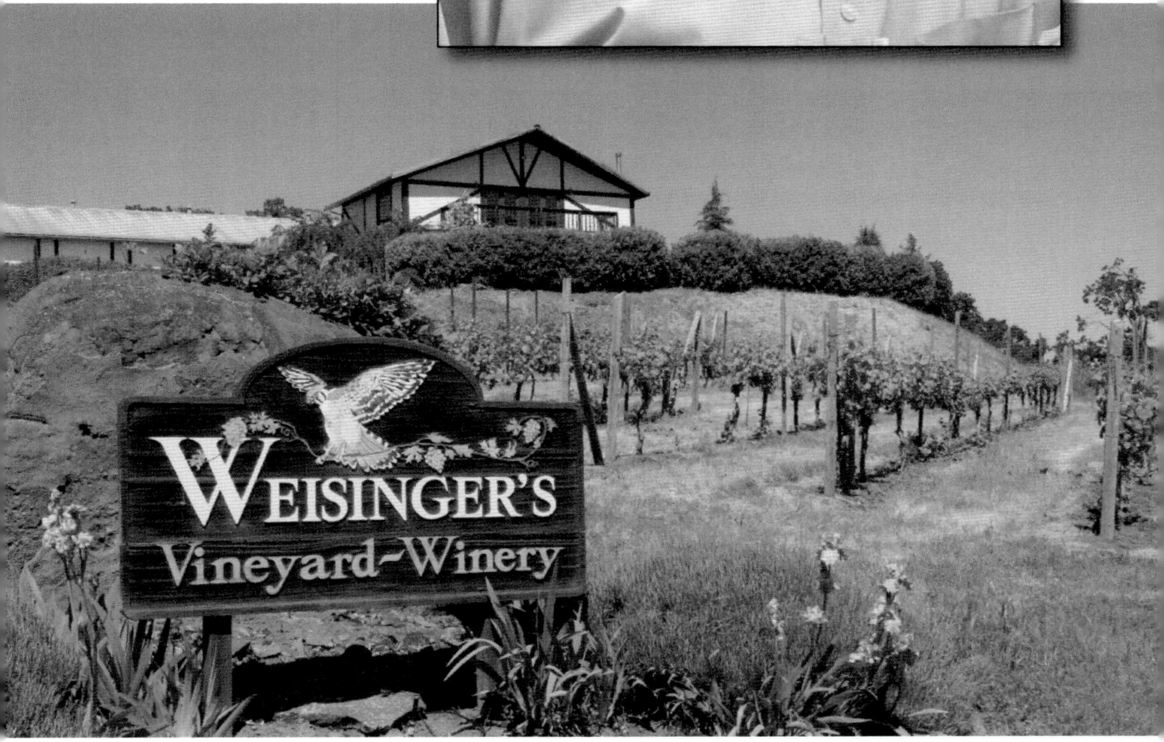

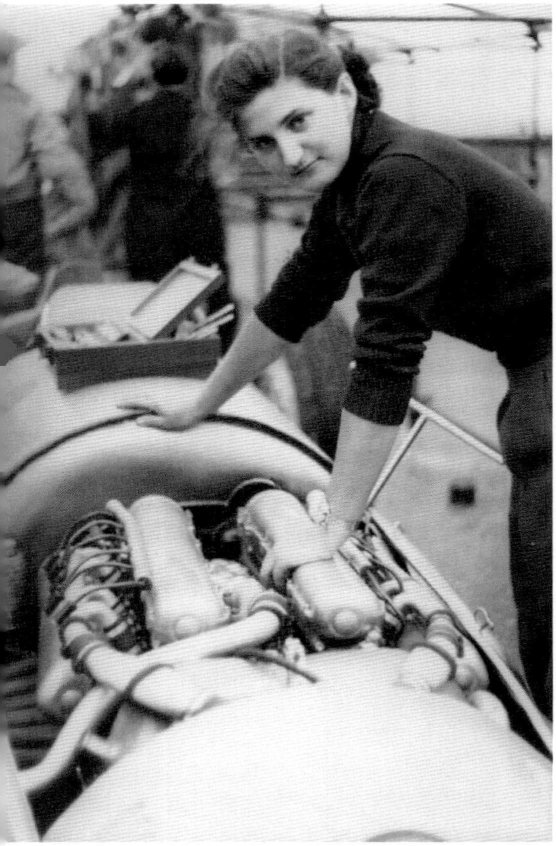

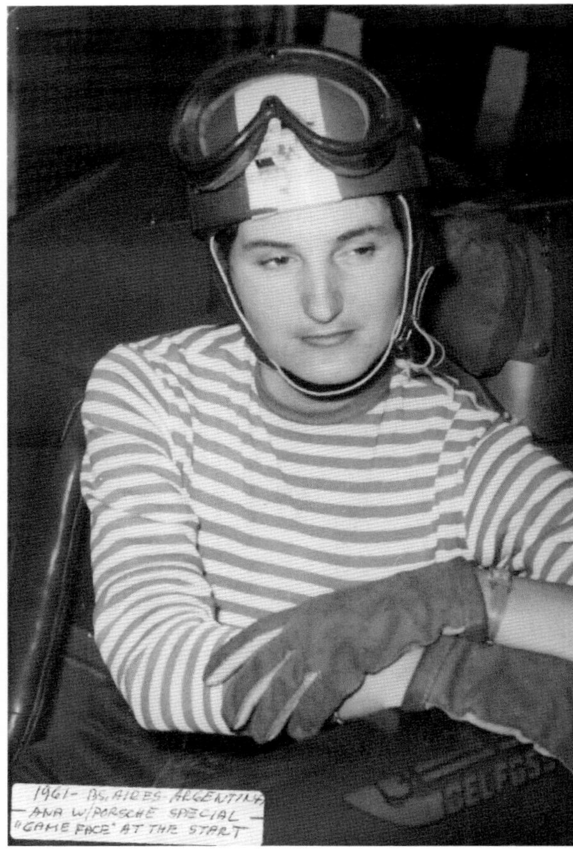

Ana Delfosse (ABOVE AND OPPOSITE PAGE)
Ashland residents remember Argentina-native Ana Delfosse as the longtime manager of the 76 gas station in south Ashland, but few may know that in the 1950s, she was a racecar driver and "the famous woman mechanic" for one of Grand Prix's greatest racers of all time—Juan "The Maestro" Fangio. At the age of 22, Delfosse was part of the five-time world championship Formula One team in 1953, when women were few and far between in the sport. Ana met her husband, Curt, a racecar designer and mechanic, while working in Fangio's garage in Buenos Aires, Argentina. The couple wed in 1955, later opening a small custom Porsche garage in Buenos Aires, and moved to San Diego in 1961, where Curt continued designing racecars. The couple established Delfosse Racing in San Diego and became the first domestic distributor to start importing German-made Bilstein car shocks, which are some of the most popular imported shocks in the United States today. In 1977, the Delfosses retired from racing and moved to the Applegate Valley. They garnered some fame in the late 1980s after moving to Ashland to open a service station and selling then-specialty German-made tire chains for motorists about to embark on the climb over Siskiyou Pass. Delfosse has not driven a proper racecar since the 1960s, but is satisfied these days with the calmness of her life outside Ashland and the occasional thrill of driving her friend's Porsche up Greensprings Highway. Delfosse is pictured opposite standing beside the Mercedes Benz of Juan Fangio with the 1955 Mercedes Benz Formula One team. She is also pictured above leaning over the engine bay of a Formula One racecar and in the cockpit of a Delfosse Racing–prepared Porsche before a race in Argentina in 1961. (All courtesy of Ana Delfosse.)

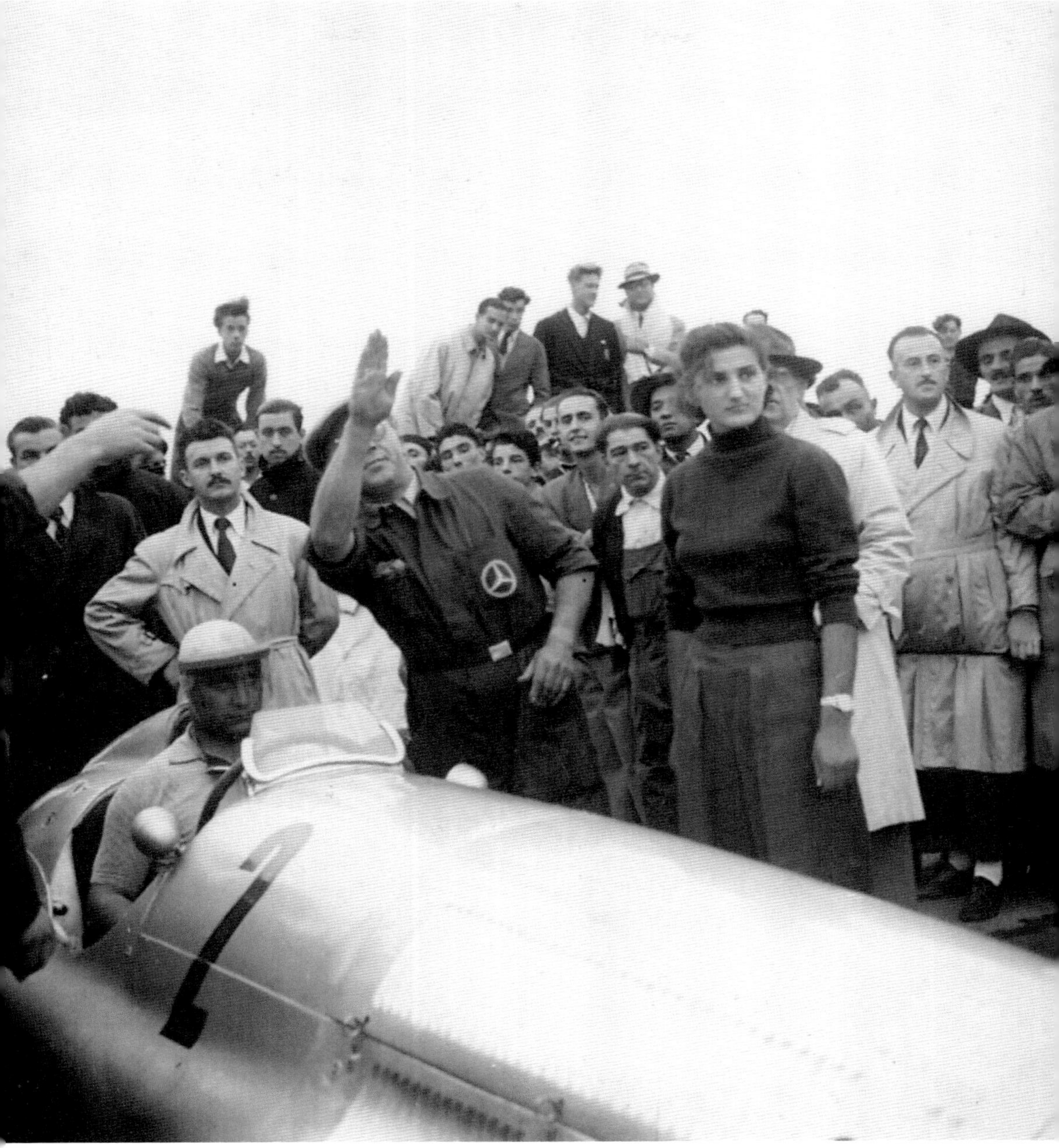

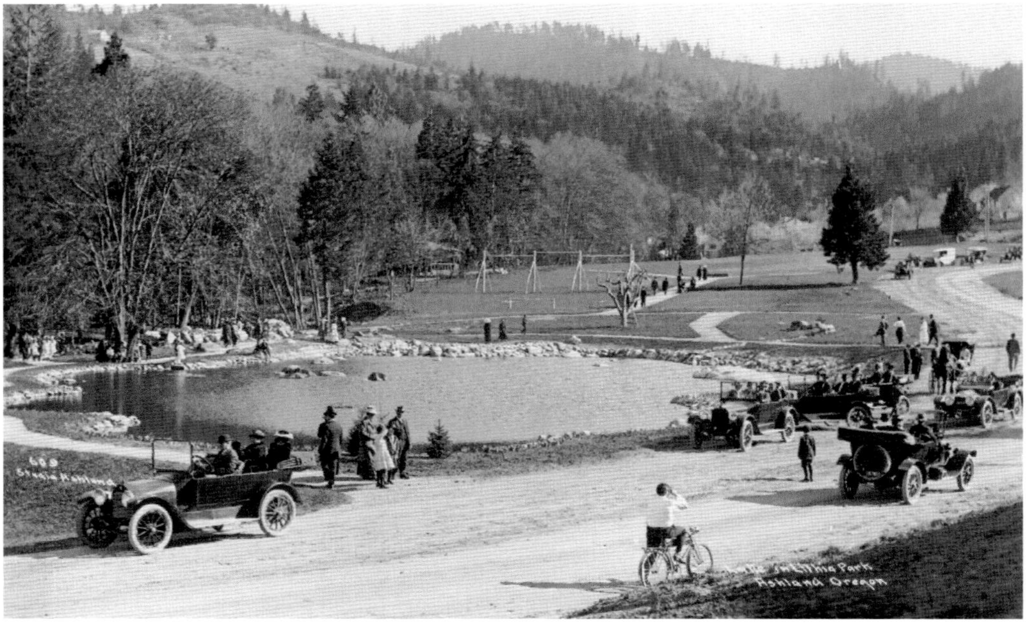

Lithia Park

John McLaren was commissioned by the town of Ashland in 1914 to design the landscape of the original Lithia Park, which has continued to grow following its original parcel, adjacent to Ashland's downtown plaza. McLaren's landscape for the first 18 acres of Lithia followed Ashland Creek and included native and introduced plants and ornamental varieties chosen for hardiness and color. In 1982, Lithia Park was designated a National Historic Place. McLaren was an active landscape architect in the San Francisco Bay Area—he also designed Golden Gate Park—and was credited with planting two million trees during his life. He died in 1943. (Both, courtesy of Terry Skibby and author.)

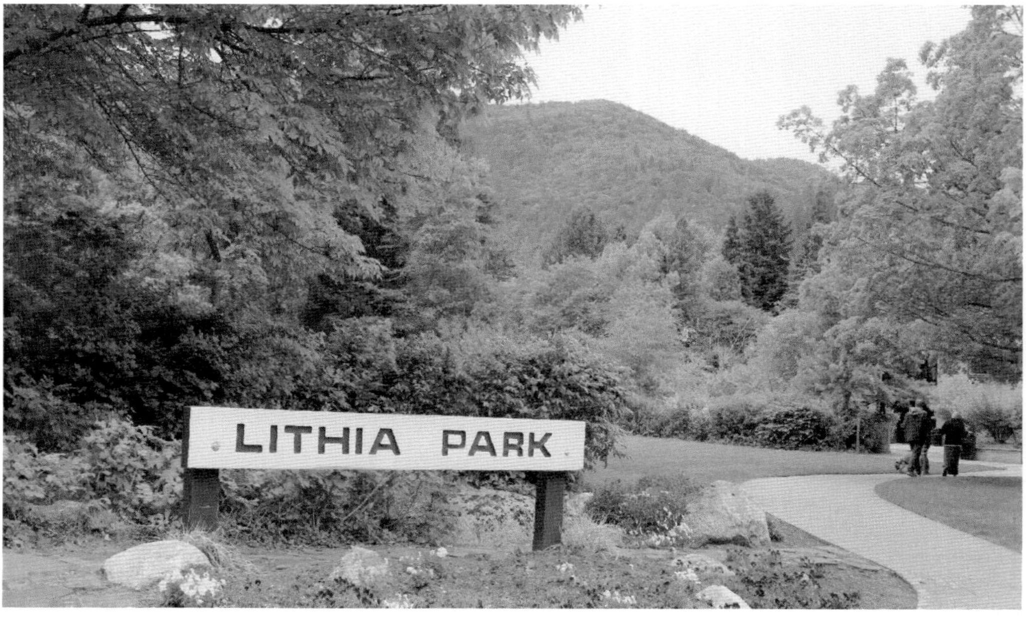

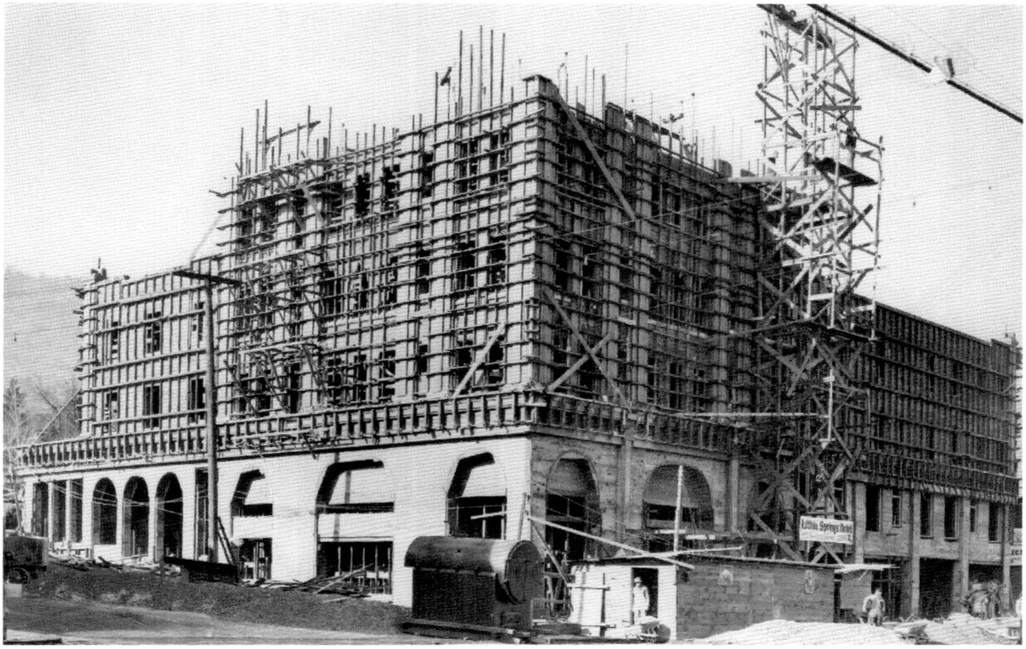

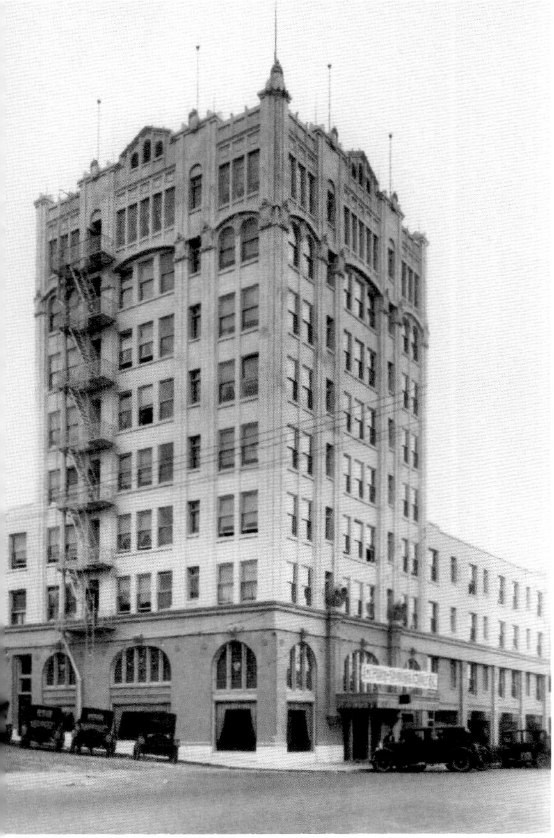

Ashland Springs Hotel

The 100-room, nine-story Lithia Springs Hotel was opened to guests along Ashland's main street on July 1, 1925. The lavish hotel was renamed the Mark Antony in 1960. Following a basement-to-roof remodel of the hotel initiated under new ownership in 1998, "The Mark" was renamed the Ashland Springs Hotel and featured 70 rooms. For some time, it was the tallest building between Portland and San Francisco and remains Ashland's most prominent building as the Ashland Springs Hotel. The original hotel, designed by Boise, Idaho–based architects John E. Tourtellotte and Charles F. Hummel, was listed in the National Register of Historic places in 1978. (Both, courtesy of Terry Skibby.)

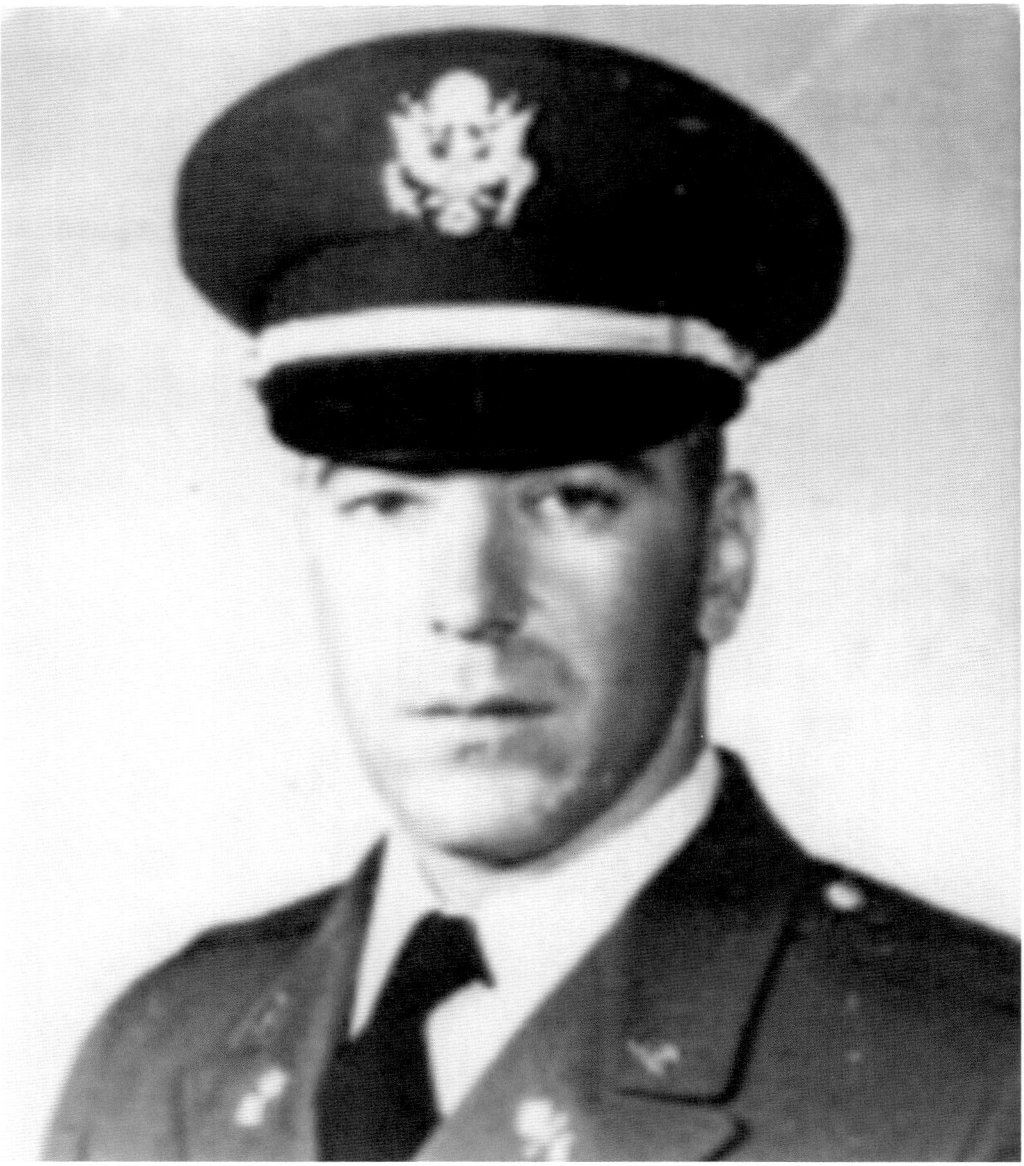

Steve Mason

Steve Mason was a decorated Vietnam veteran and a poet, considered the poet laureate of the Vietnam Veterans of America. He published three books of poetry, often writing on an old typewriter and without revising the poems, which he said had been in his head for many years before. He lived off and on in Ashland and late in his life became a proponent of Oregon's Death with Dignity Act. He testified before state committees in California in support of creating a law similar to Oregon's. Suffering from lung cancer, Mason died naturally in 2005 surrounded by his family in Ashland. (Courtesy of US Army.)

CHAPTER FOUR

Ashlandia

1981–2014

Ashland's population stood at about 15,000 going into the 1980s, and the formerly timber-dependent town was about to find itself in severe need of an economic makeover. Progressiveness was becoming a celebrated ideal in Ashland, and the town's citizens voted to become a nuclear-free zone in 1982 in response mostly to Pres. Ronald Reagan's national defense policy. The same year, Southern Oregon State College opened a theater arts building on its campus, and Al and Margaret Meyer donated $100,000 toward a fundraising effort for building a public swimming pool in Ashland. In 1984, it was estimated that the Oregon Shakespearean Festival and Southern Oregon State College contributed nearly $100 million annually to Ashland's economy, and property values in the town were higher than anywhere in the Rogue Valley. A year later, the Oregon Shakespearean Festival celebrated its 50th year with annual attendance topping 300,000. In 1988, the festival's name was changed to the Oregon Shakespeare Festival. Friends of Ashland, a group of community members dedicated to citizen involvement concerning urban development and land use planning, was formed in 1988, and Ashland became known for its critical, thorough, and citizen-involved city planning process. That year, citizens voiced opposition to a massive natural history museum as a tourist attraction for the town and multimillion-dollar destination resort. Both projects were blocked. The museum would eventually be built on a much smaller scale but went under and now houses ScienceWorks Hands-On Museum. In 1986, the Oregon Cabaret Theater opened in Ashland, further establishing the town as a theater lover's paradise.

Entering the 1990s, city leaders proposed a $1 million renovation of downtown. The town's reputation hinged on tourism and with it came a sharp influx of people centered on the Oregon Shakespeare Festival and downtown area. Eventually, the plan, which included a redesign of the Ashland Plaza, was accepted but not without extensive public discussion and debate. In 1993, Ashland's well-known food and beverage tax was approved by voters. Initially it was a 1 percent levy, but was increased to 5 percent by the city council just two months after its inception. The same year, in December 1992, Ashland held its first Festival of Light celebration, which attracts thousands of revelers from across the valley to watch over a million holiday lights flicker on at the culmination of a crowd countdown led by Santa Claus. It was in the 1990s that Ashland became known as a mecca for the home free, homeless, and vagabonds of all style who found the town's liberal zeitgeist and temperate climate appealing. There was also no shortage of heavy-pocketed, change-dropping tourists streaming along Ashland's sidewalks, which promoted panhandling. Many local businesses, including the Oregon Shakespeare Festival and chamber of commerce, voiced concern over the aggressiveness, consistency, and number of people panhandling for money in Ashland. In 1995, partly to address the issue, Ashland enacted a street camping ban—an issue that is still contested by opponents.

Ashland's infamous flood of 1997 plowed through downtown and drowned the ground level of buildings in others areas of town on New Year's Day. The result was devastating: nearly $4 million in damage and political upheaval among city officials. Despite the disastrous winter and contentious spring following the flood, 1997 was not an all-negative year in Ashland. The town's population had reached 18,560, Southern Oregon State College became Southern Oregon University—with about

4,500 students enrolled at the school—and Ashland High School's speech and debate team won its seventh state title in eight years. In the year before the new millennium, Ashland's Railroad District was listed in the National Register of Historic Places, and the Shakespeare Festival announced plans to replace its Black Swan Theater with another intimate but equally versatile theater. The New Theater was opened in 2002 and was renamed the Thomas Theater in 2013. In 2001, the Ashland Independent Film festival was founded, which attracts about 20,000 patrons annually.

For the last decade and a half, Ashland, a quaint, mountain foothills town of about 20,200—mocked by some and celebrated by others as the "People's Republic of Ashland," "Ashlandia," or "Ashlantis,"—has continued to build on its reputation as one of Oregon's most liberal and progressive cities. In actuality, its people now are not as liberal as they are idealistic and determined. Ideal to Ashlanders is a state of perpetually progressing and promoting acceptance, sustainability, and livability and instilling those same responsibilities in future generations. The city, as any city does, continues to suffer from hardships and celebrate triumphs of varying magnitude. Whether it be the Oak Knoll fire in 2010, which torched 11 homes and damaged several others in south Ashland's Oak Knoll neighborhood; a tourist season–threatening cracked main beam inside the Bowmer Theater of the Oregon Shakespeare Festival during the summer of 2011; or the tragic and unsolved 2011 murder of beloved 23-year-old Ashland resident David Michael Grubbs on the Central Ashland Bike Path, the people of Ashland have always found a way to pull together and rise from each of those hardships as a stronger and more refined community—and nothing could be more legendary.

Sen. Lenn Hannon

Serving nearly 30 years in the Oregon state senate between 1974 and 2001, Ashlander Lenn Hannon stands as Oregon's second-longest-serving state senator. Hannon, a graduate of Ashland High School and former student at Southern Oregon State College, switched from the Democratic to the Republican Party in 1980 and was well known and admired for his bipartisanship as an elected official. As a senior leader in the senate, Hannon helped secure $20 million in state funds for the construction of a library at Southern Oregon University. In 2004, the school named the library the Lenn and Dixie Hannon Library after the former senator and his wife. It is known now as the Hannon Library. (This photograph is part of the Southern Oregon University Archives and made available courtesy of Southern Oregon University Hannon Library.)

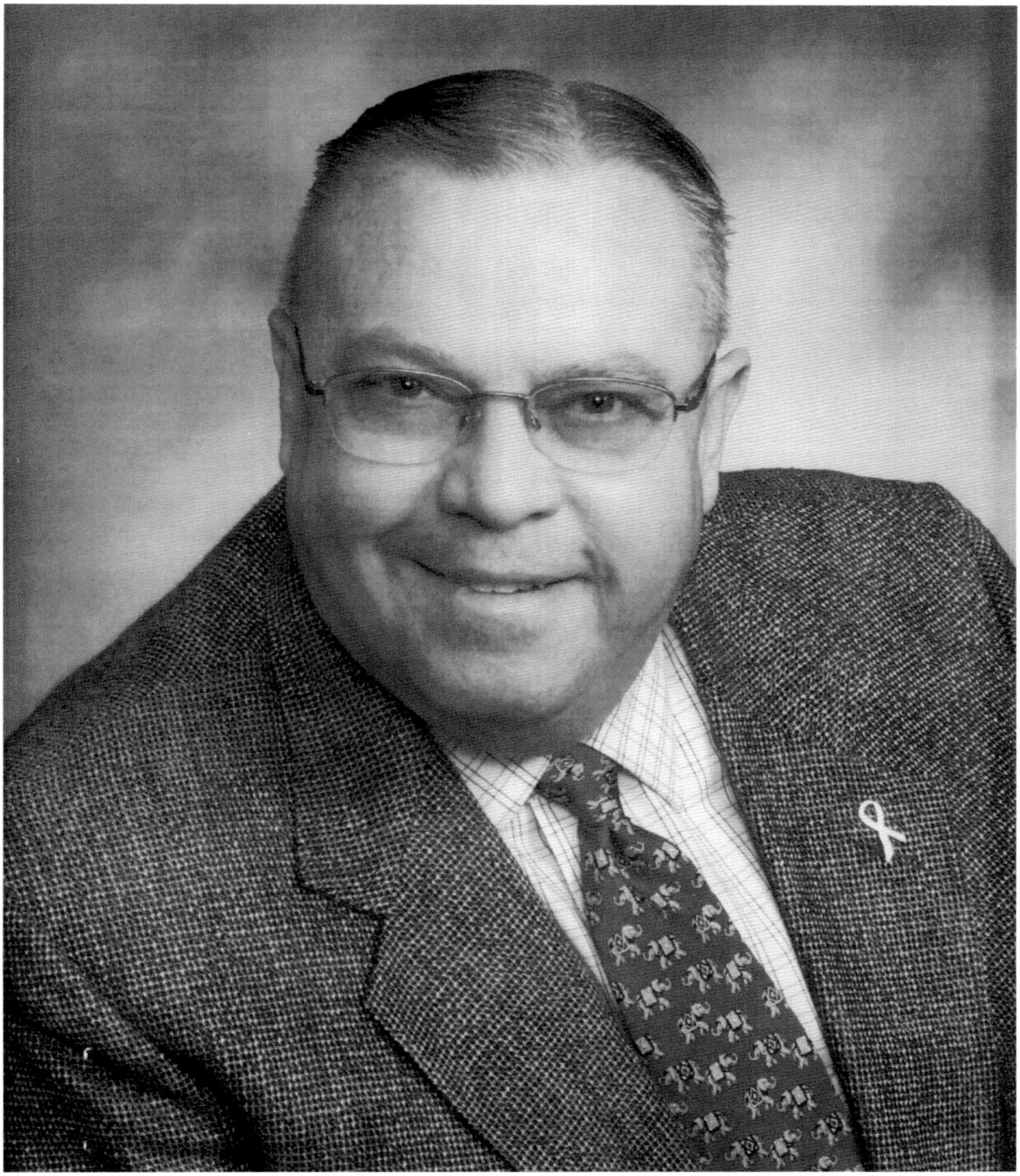

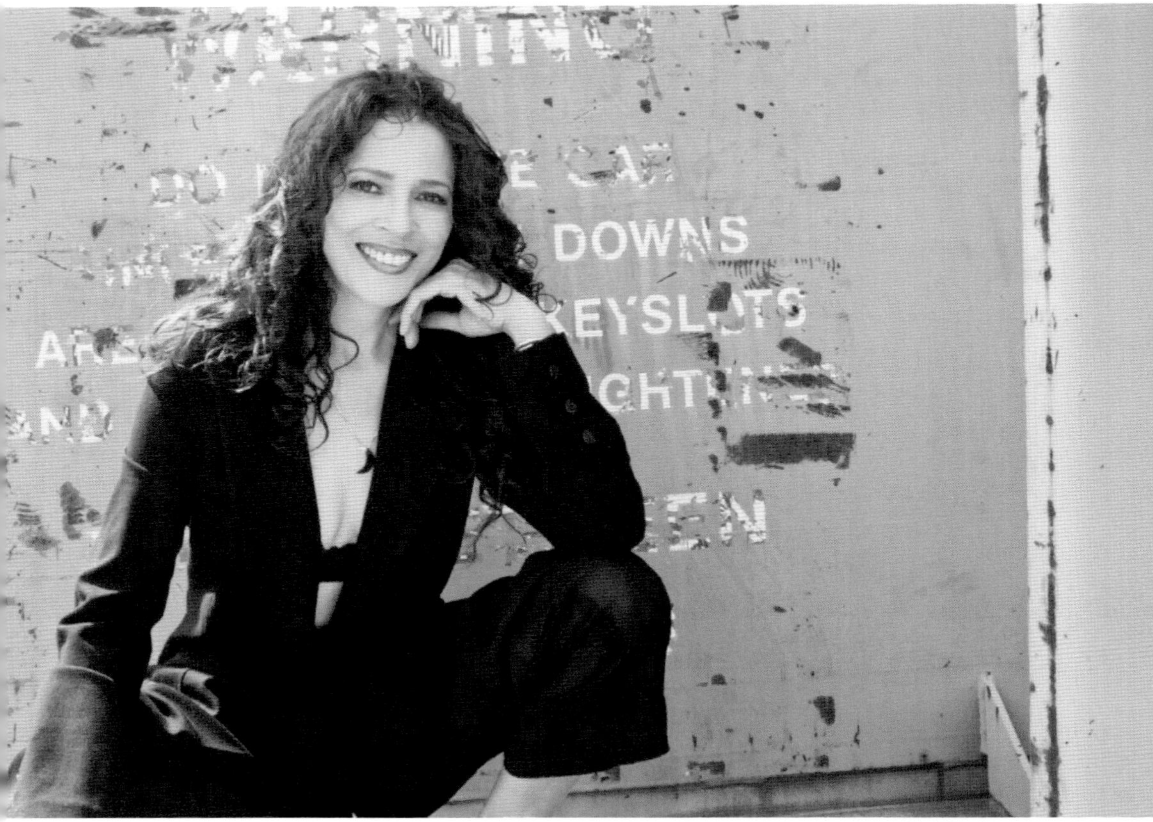

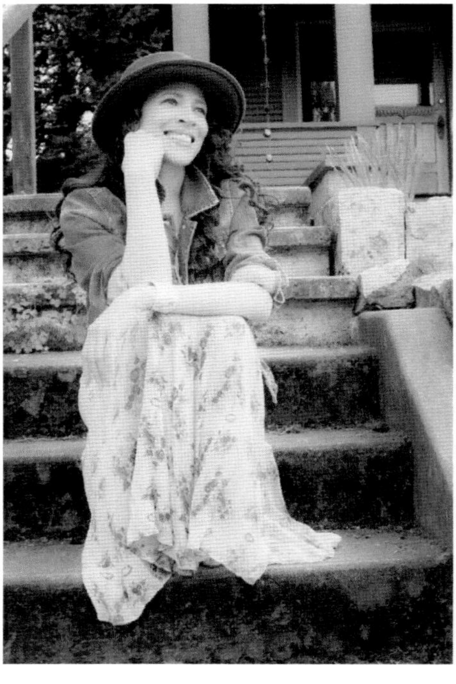

Tai Babilonia

Tai Babilonia is an accomplished Olympic pairs figure skater who competed for 43 years before retiring from the sport and moving to Ashland. With her longtime skating partner, Randy Gardner, Babilonia was the 1979 world champion and a five-time US national champion. The pair qualified for the 1976 and 1980 winter Olympics. She was inducted into the US Figure Skating Hall of Fame in 1991. Immediately after arriving in Ashland in 2008, she began helping with fundraisers to improve the Ashland ice rink. She also designs a female skaters' clothing line called Tai. (Both, courtesy of Pam Danielle.)

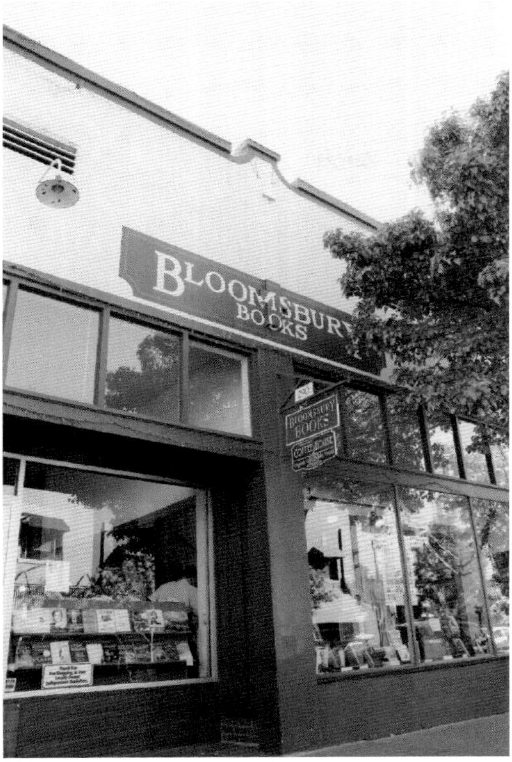

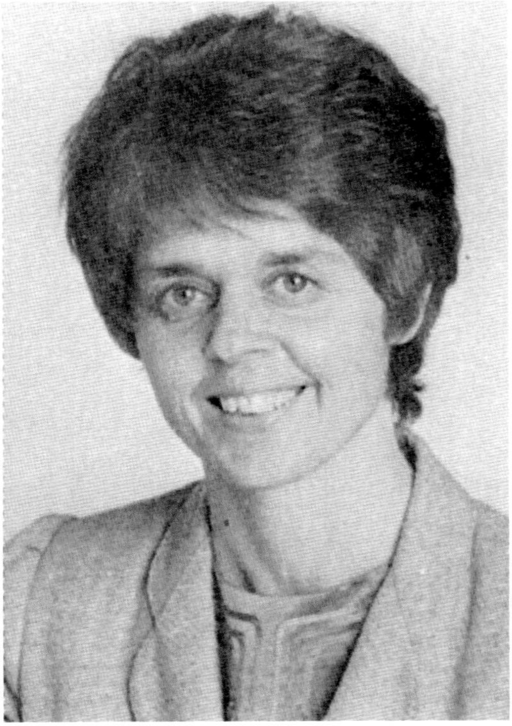

Nancy Peterson
Nancy Peterson was an Ashland City Council member and a state representative in the Oregon House of Representatives in the 1980s representing eastern Jackson County, District 52. Peterson, elected to her first of four terms in 1984, was a Democrat known for her work advocating for education, health, and human services, as well as the environment. She helped persuade legislators to require private health insurance companies to cover gynecological exams and advocated for the Oregon Health Plan. She was also a partner in Bloomsbury Books, which opened in 1980. She died in Ashland in 1997 from cancer. (Top, author photograph; bottom, courtesy of Oregon legislature.)

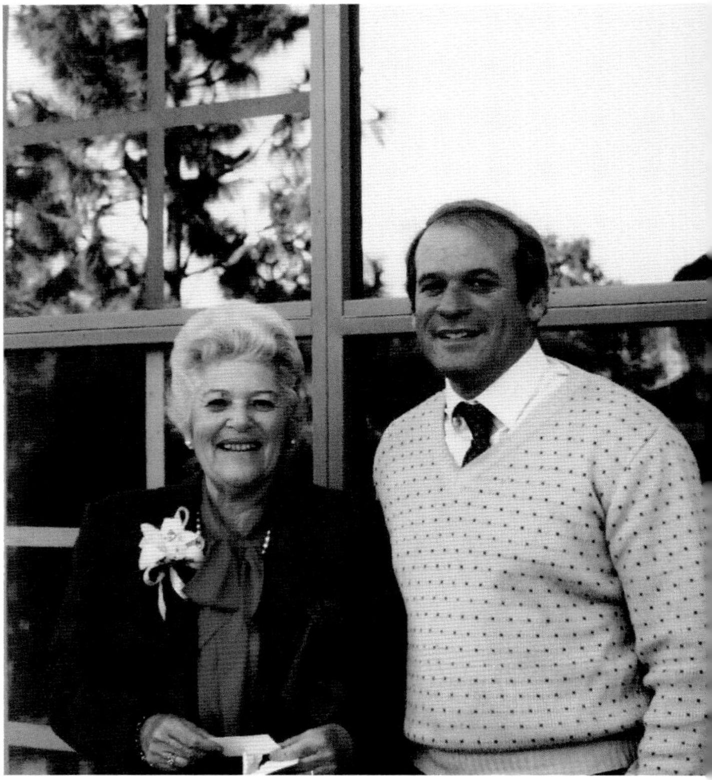

William and Florence Schneider
Following a five-year community fundraising effort and a generous donation from William and Florence Schneider, the Schneider Museum of Art on the campus of Southern Oregon University opened in the fall of 1986. The museum was designed to embrace the surrounding landscape and architecture of SOU by Portland architect Will Martin. The museum is named after Bill's parents Samuel and May Schneider. (Right, courtesy of Burton Schneider; below, author photograph.)

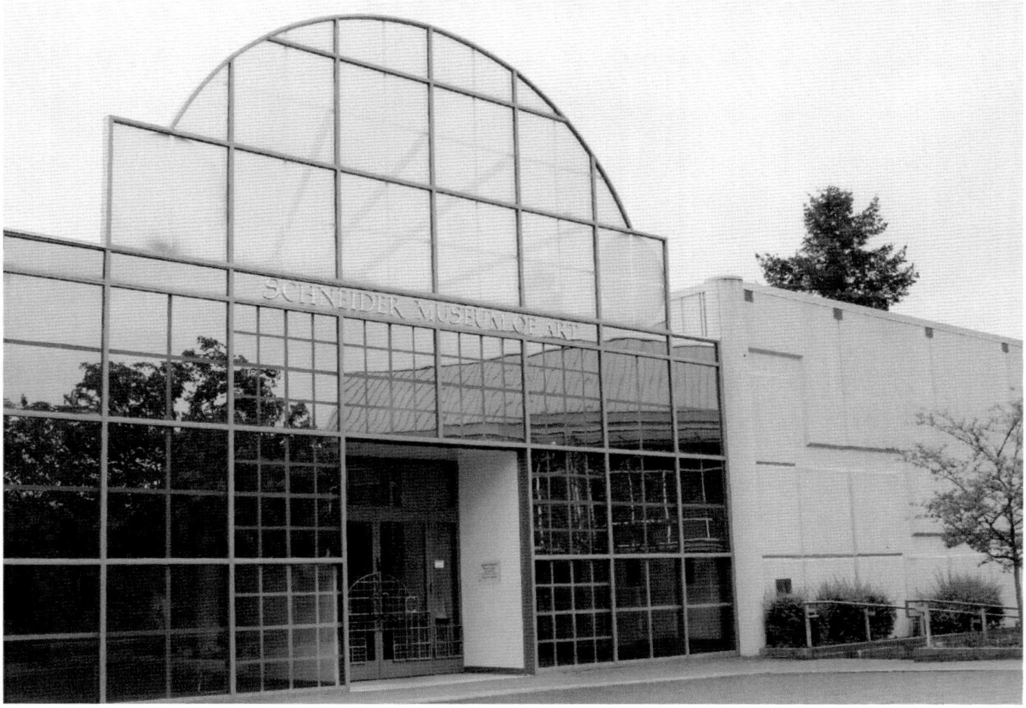

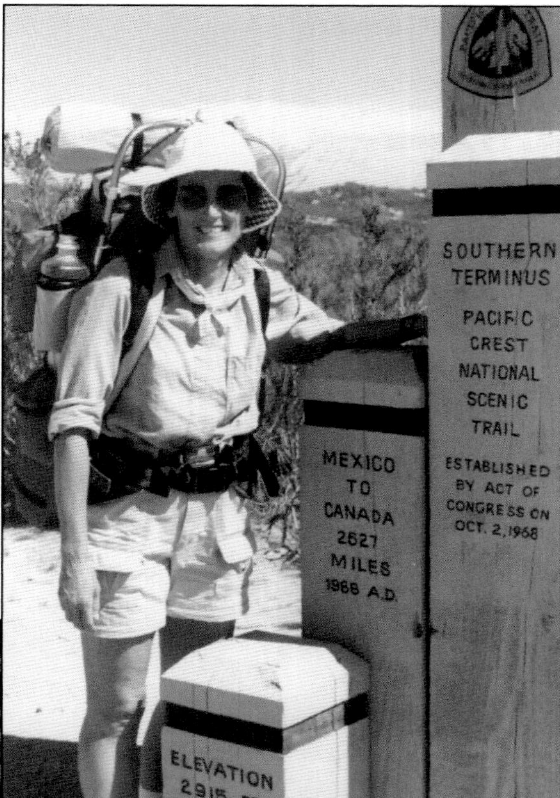

Lolly Skillman

Lolly Skillman first hiked across the Oregon section of the Pacific Crest Trail in 1985. She then completed the California section five years later and, lastly, the Washington section in 1992. She joined the Pacific Crest Trail board of directors and personally adopted a section of the trail from Crater Lake to the California border. Once a realtor, she and husband Don Skillman together have written *25 Hikes along the Pacific Crest Trail* and *Pedaling Across America*, which is about their cycling journey from Oregon to Virginia Beach. An Ashlander for many years, she now lives in Apache Junction, Arizona. (Both, courtesy of Lolly Skillman.)

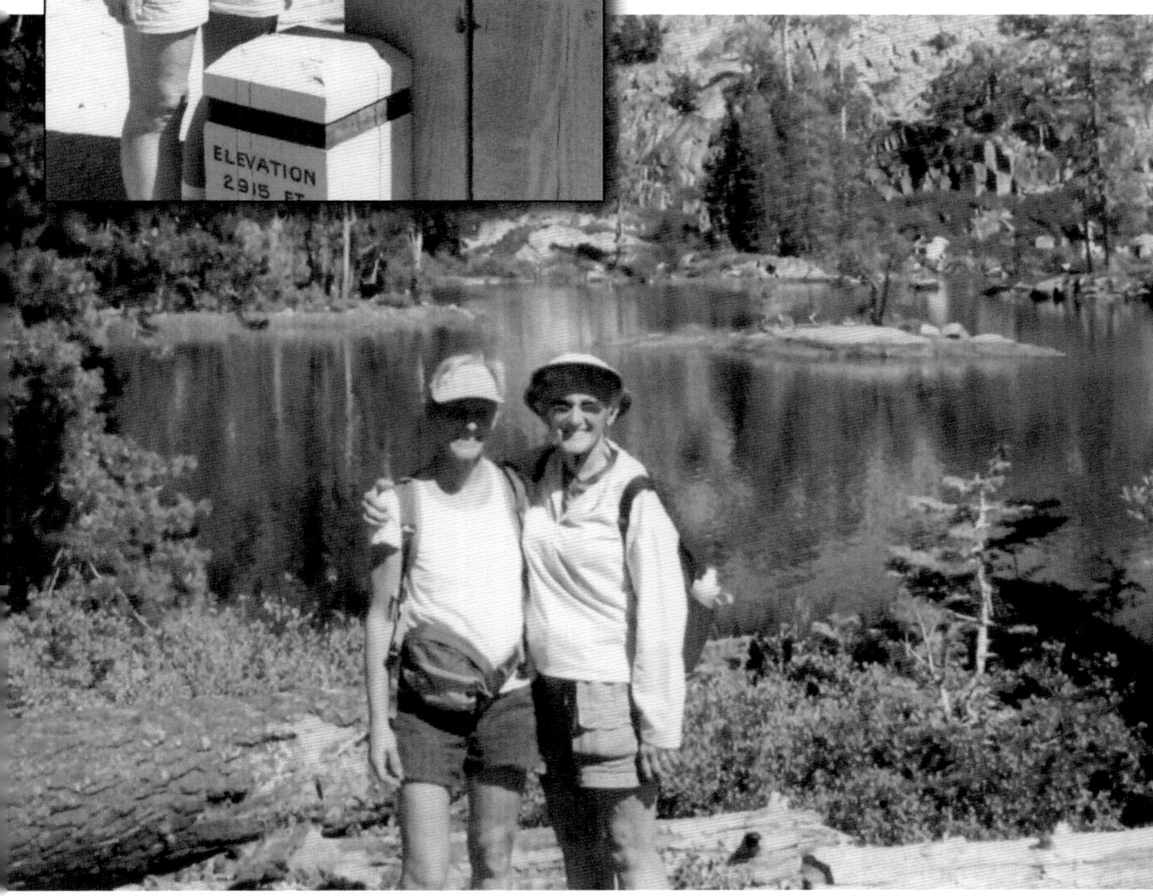

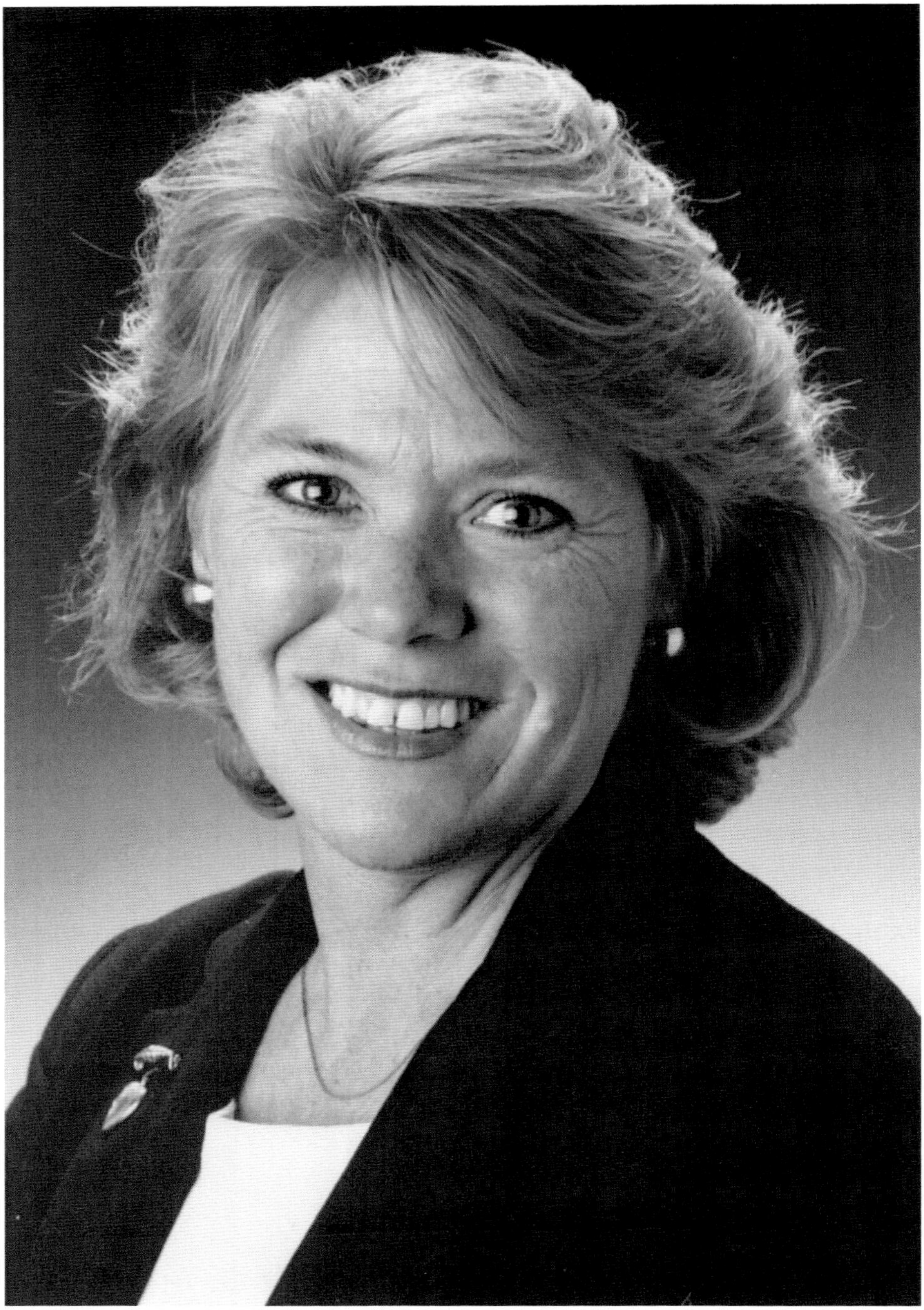

Mayor Cathy Golden
At the age of 34, not only was Cathy Golden the youngest mayor ever elected in Ashland, she was also the city's first female mayor. Golden put strong emphasis on balancing Ashland's quality of life with its growth, an attitude that has continued to drive planning policy in the city. Golden went on to be reelected in 1992. (Courtesy of the City of Ashland.)

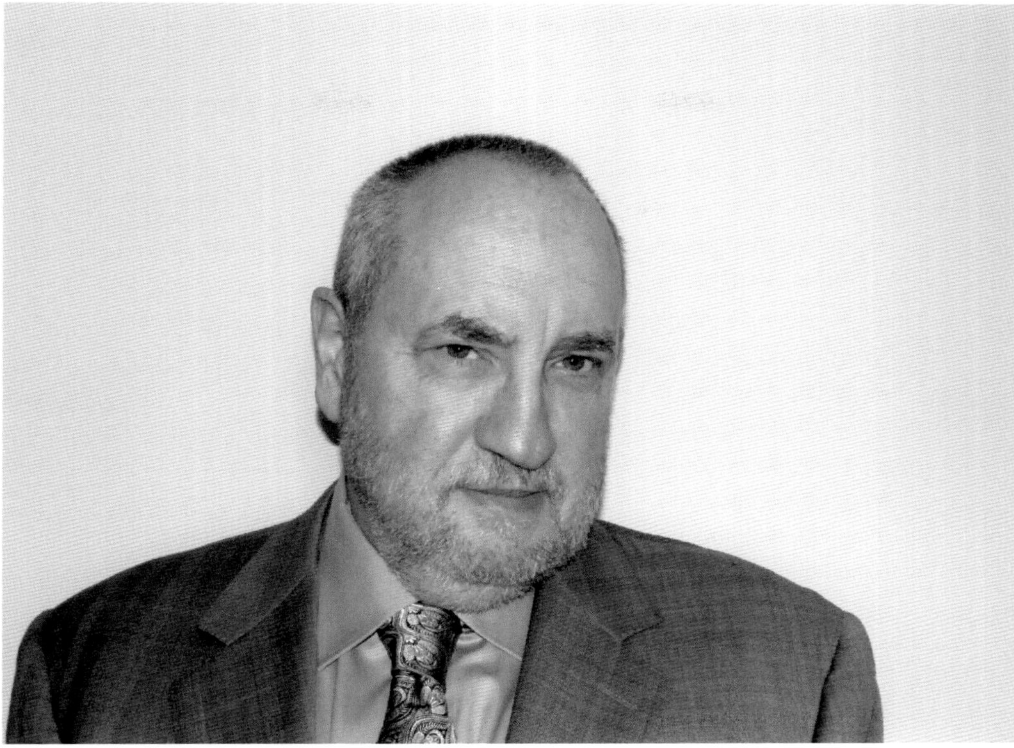

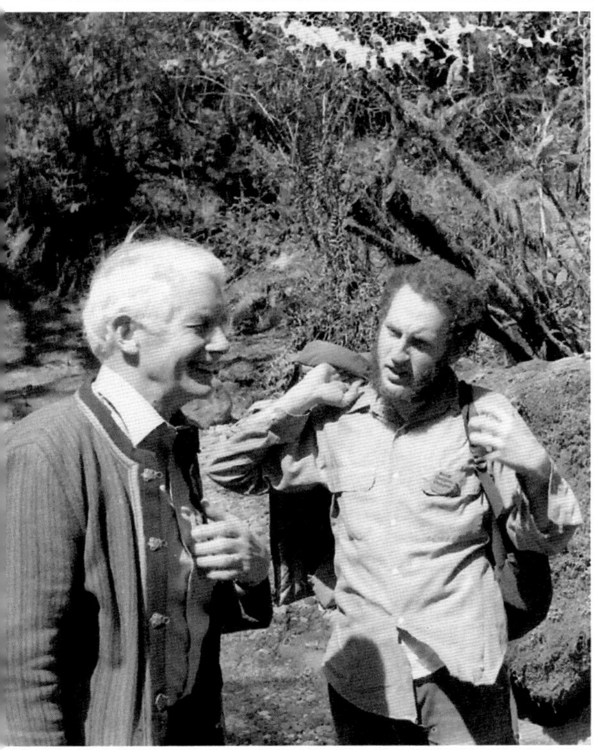

Andy Kerr
Conservationist Andy Kerr is an environmental activist and the former executive director of the Oregon Natural Resources Council—now Oregon Wild. Kerr was an active participant in the timber wars of the 1980s, fighting to save the Pacific Northwest's old-growth forests. An Oregon State University dropout, Kerr has been involved in the enactment of nearly 30 pieces of state and federal public lands conservation legislation and has lectured at universities across the nation. He has published several scholarly articles and two books, *Oregon Desert Guide: 70 Hikes* and *Oregon Wild: Endangered Forest Wilderness.* He splits his time between Ashland and Washington, DC, and still lobbies for wildlife, wilderness, and wild waters. A young Kerr is pictured at left in 1980 with legendary conservationist David Brower in what is now the Drift Creek Wilderness in Oregon's Coastal Range. (Above, courtesy of Andy Kerr; left, courtesy of Larch Archives.)

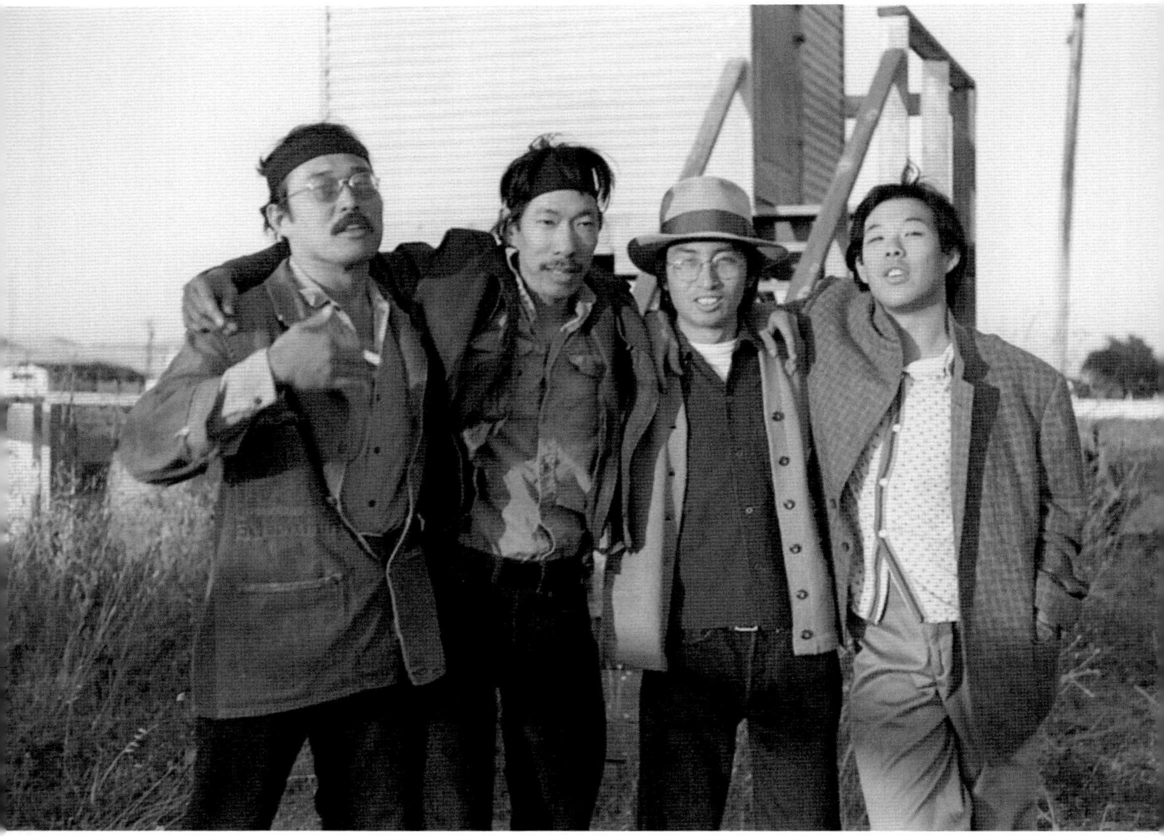

Lawson Inada

Lawson Inada is an emeritus professor of English at Southern Oregon University and was Oregon's fifth poet laureate, serving from 2007 to 2010. Appointed by Oregon governor Ted Kulongoski, Inada was the first person to fill the post since 1979. He began teaching at SOU in 1966, and has written five books and edited or appeared in several others. Lawson's 1971 book, *Before the War: Poems as They Happened*, detailed Inada's time spent with his family in internment camps during World War II and was the first book of poetry by a Japanese American published by a major publisher. He was a Guggenheim Fellow in 2004 and now lives in Medford, Oregon. Standing on the far left, he is pictured above with American playwright Frank Chin, novelist Shawn Wong, and actor Michael Chan. (Courtesy of Lawson Inada, photograph by Nancy Wong.)

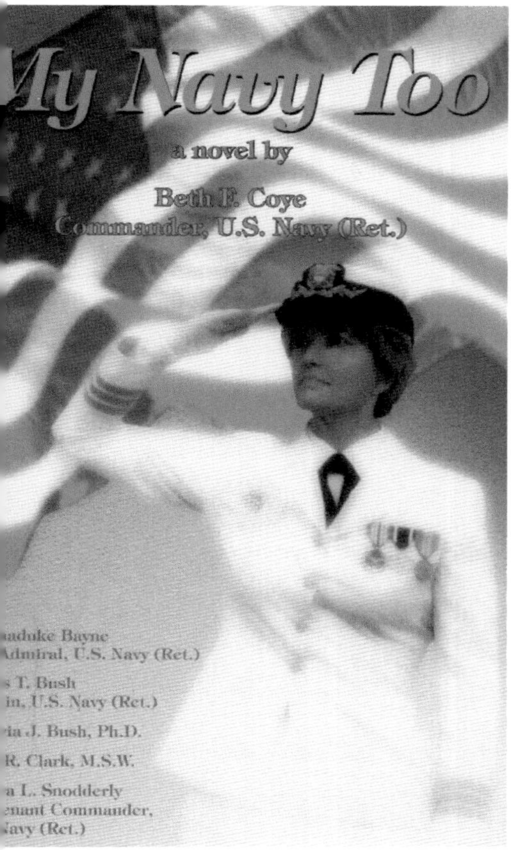

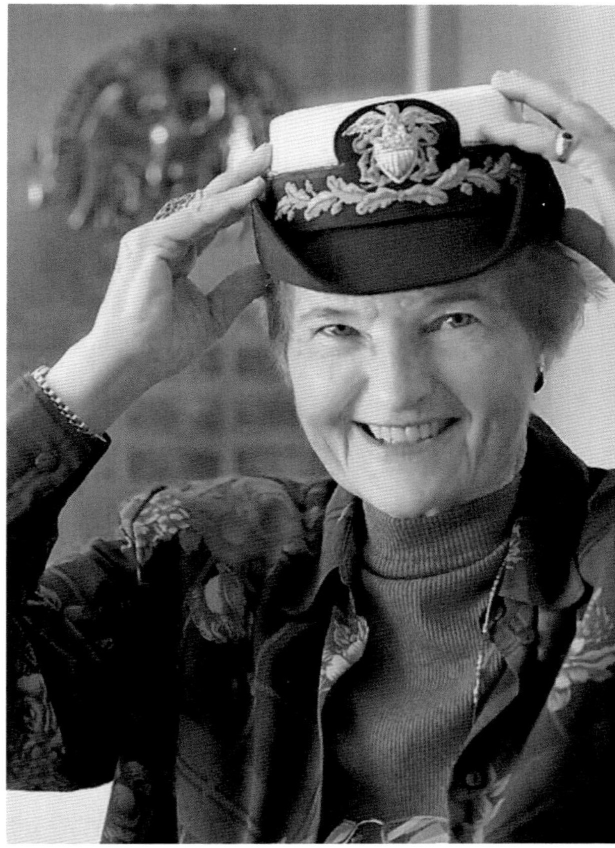

Beth Coy

Ashlander Beth Coye never served for the US Navy under the "Don't Ask, Don't Tell" (DADT) policy, but she fought as hard as anyone to tear it down. She climbed the Navy chain of command over the course of a 21-year career, mostly as a closeted lesbian. Joining in 1960, Coye came out with her sexual orientation to her mother in 1979, and less than a year later, resigned from the service. At the time, she was the commanding officer of a personnel support activity, a Navy administrative unit in San Diego, and one of the first female commanding officers in the Navy.

In April 2010, less than a year before Congress passed an act repealing the provision, she took a collection of letters from the Military Outreach Committee titled, "We Are Family, Too," to Capitol Hill so senators could read about the personal experiences of gays serving in the military under DADT. (Both, courtesy of Beth Coy.)

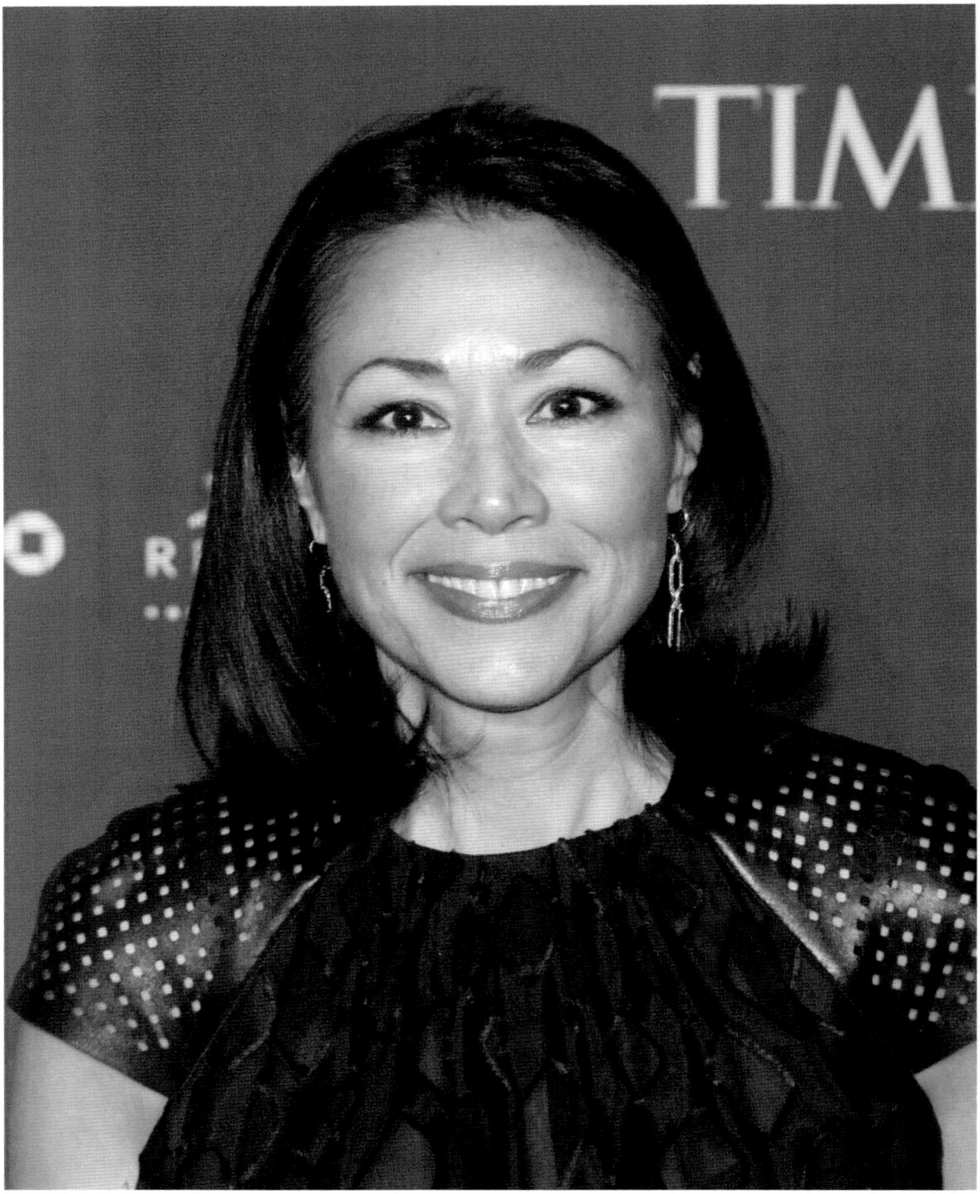

Ann Curry (ABOVE AND OPPOSITE PAGE)
Ann Curry graduated from Ashland High School and attended the University of Oregon before starting a long career in the news industry, most notably for NBC News as a host of *Dateline NBC* and *The Today Show*. She began her television career at KTVL news in Medford and soon become the station's first female reporter before moving to other stations. Curry has won three Emmy Awards for news reporting and has been an international reporting correspondent in Iraq and Afghanistan. Curry's father attended Southern Oregon University, and she was invited in 2010 to give the school's graduation commencement speech and receive an honorary doctorate in communication. (Above, courtesy of David Shankbone; opposite top, courtesy of Chad J. McNeeley of the US Department of Defense; opposite bottom, courtesy of US Department of State.)

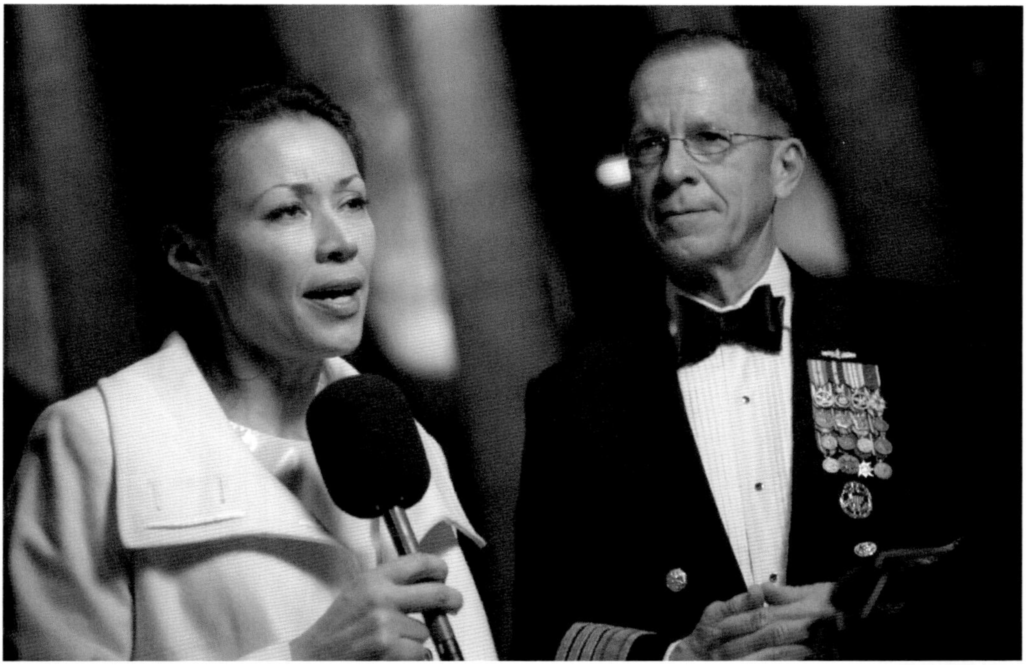

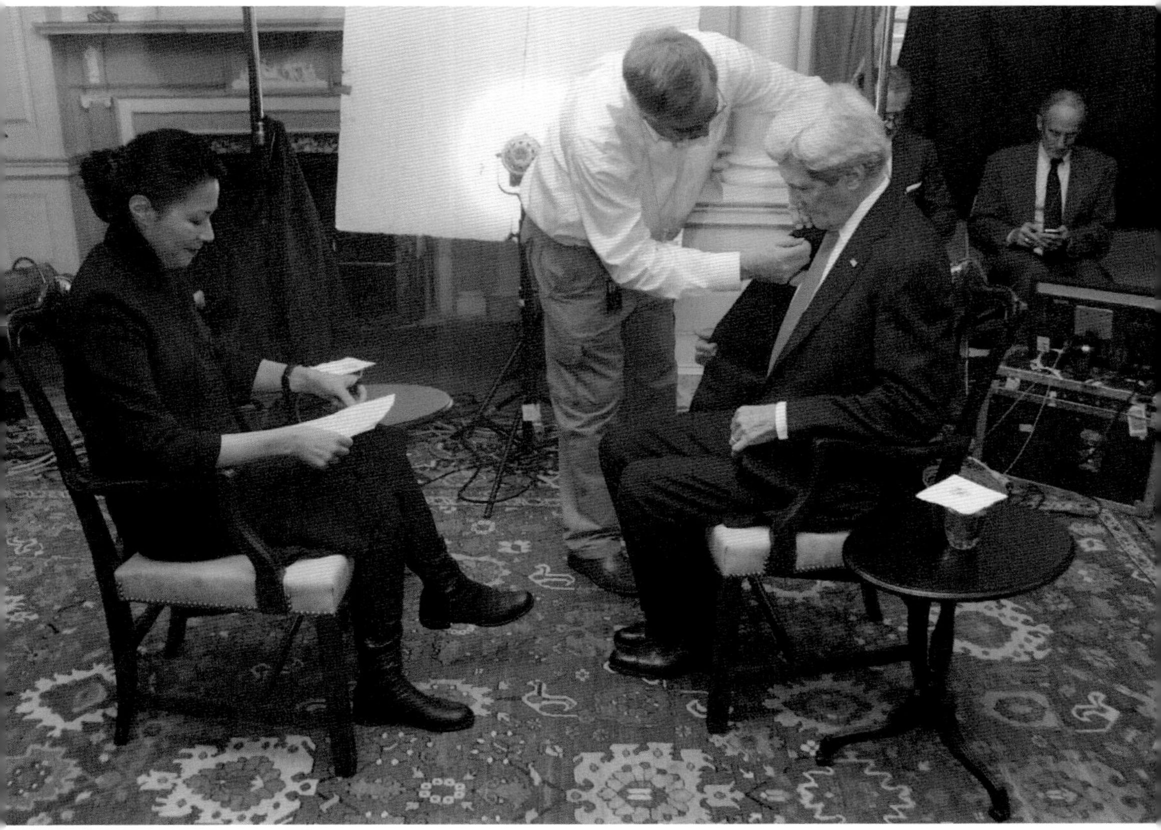

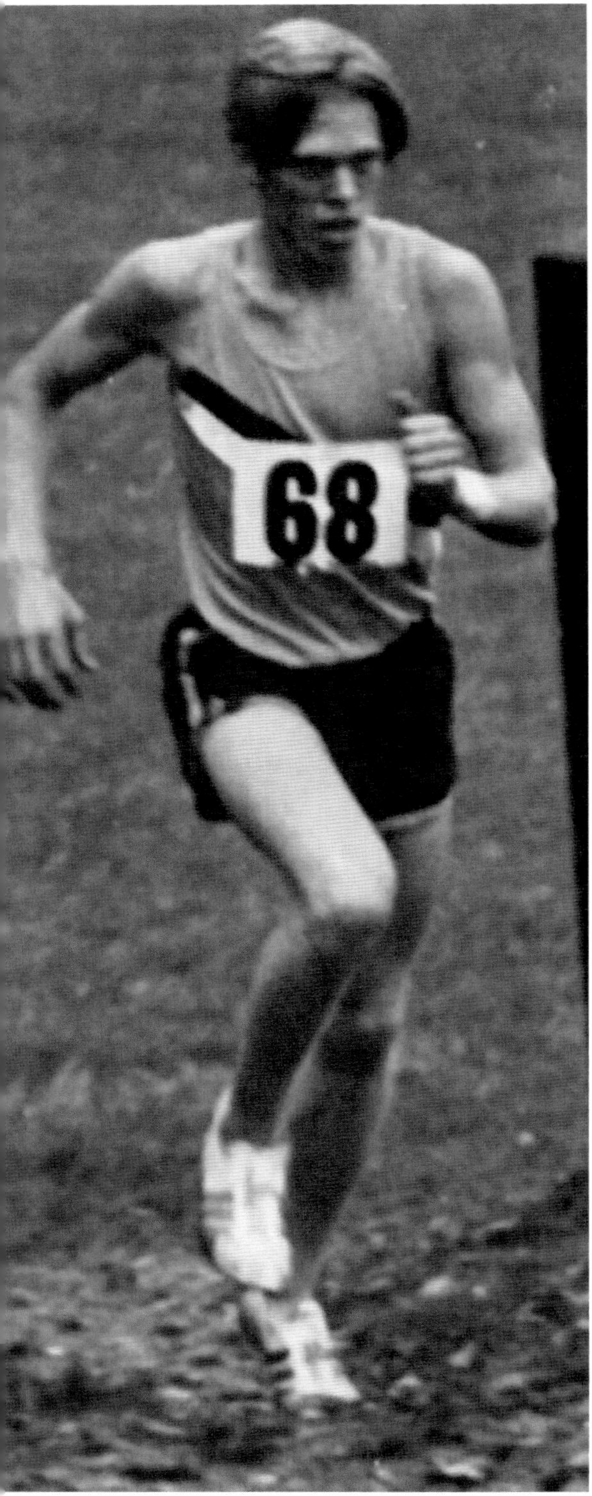

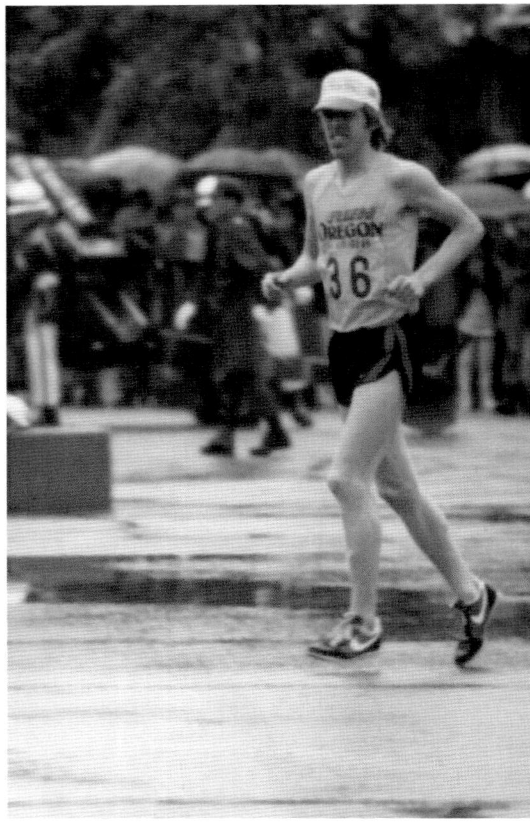

Ric Sayre (LEFT AND ABOVE)
Ric Sayre was a marathon runner who won the first Los Angeles Marathon in 1986 and a total of 12 of the 50 marathons he ran throughout his life. An Ashlander since 1981, Sayre was the winner of Medford's annual Pear Blossom Run in 1982 and excelled in other local races, including the Ashland Hill Climb between Lithia Park to the top of Mount Ashland. He was one of only four American men to qualify for the Olympic marathon trial five times and was the US national marathon champion in 1987. Sayre was also a 14-year employee of the Ashland Food Co-op. Sadly, he died unexpectedly in 2011. (Both, courtesy of Sayre family and Archbishop Hoban High School.)

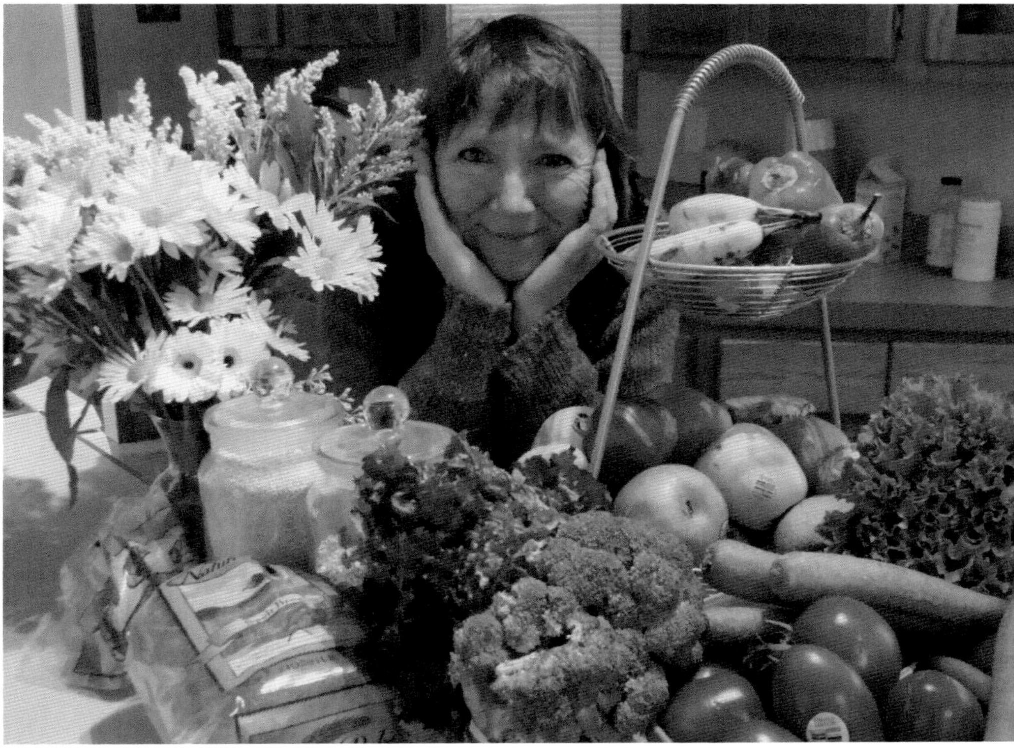

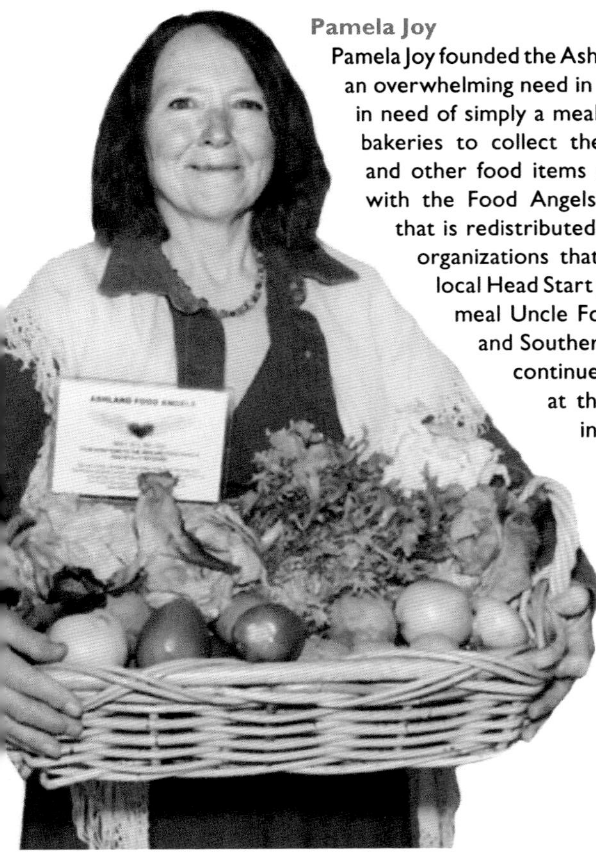

Pamela Joy

Pamela Joy founded the Ashland Food Angels in 1996. That year, recognizing an overwhelming need in the community for compassion toward people in need of simply a meal, Joy made agreements with local grocers and bakeries to collect the hundreds of pounds of still-good produce and other food items destined for the trash. Dozens of volunteers with the Food Angels drive around Ashland daily, collecting food that is redistributed through partnerships with a long line of local organizations that include the Ashland Emergency Food Bank, local Head Start program, the Peace House's weekly community meal Uncle Food's Diner, Jackson County Fuel Committee, and Southern Oregon University Family Housing. Joy, who continues to provide guidance through a leadership role at the nonprofit, has seen the Food Angels grow into one of Ashland's most prolific examples of community service and local sustainability. (Both, courtesy of Pamela Joy.)

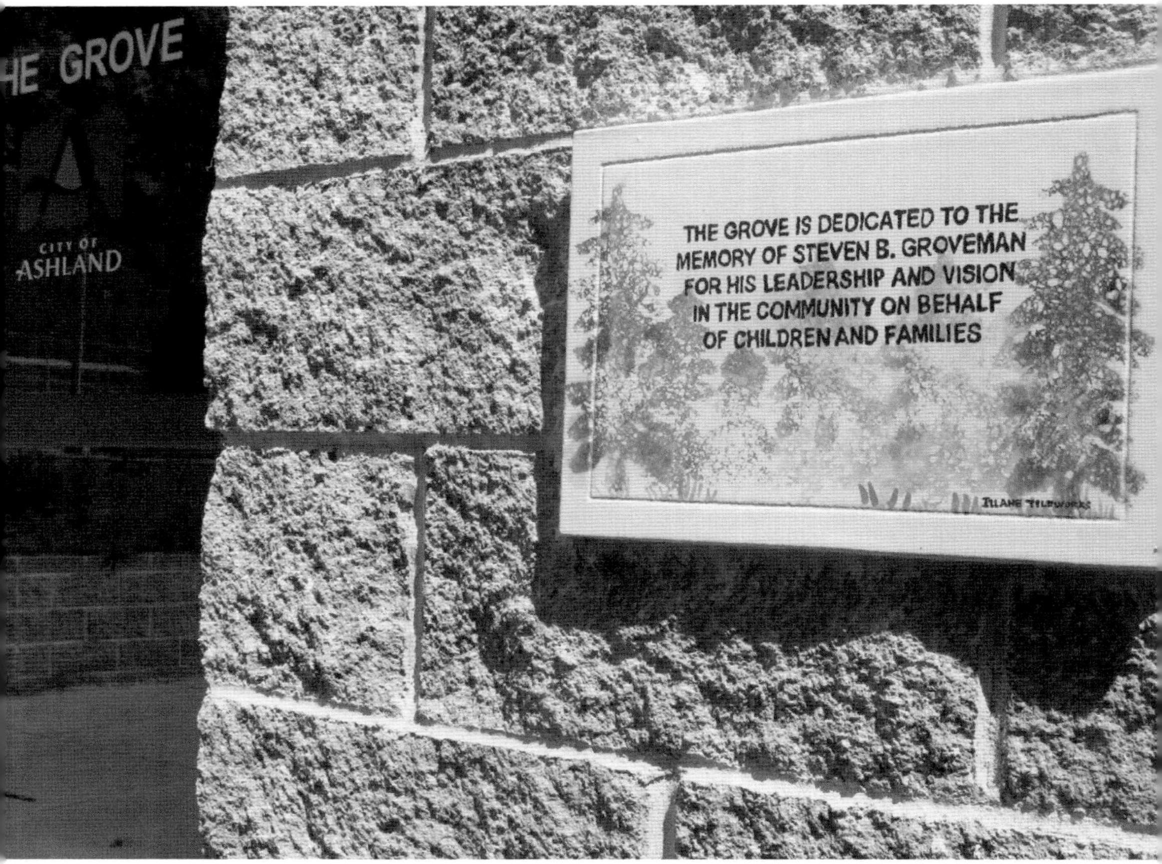

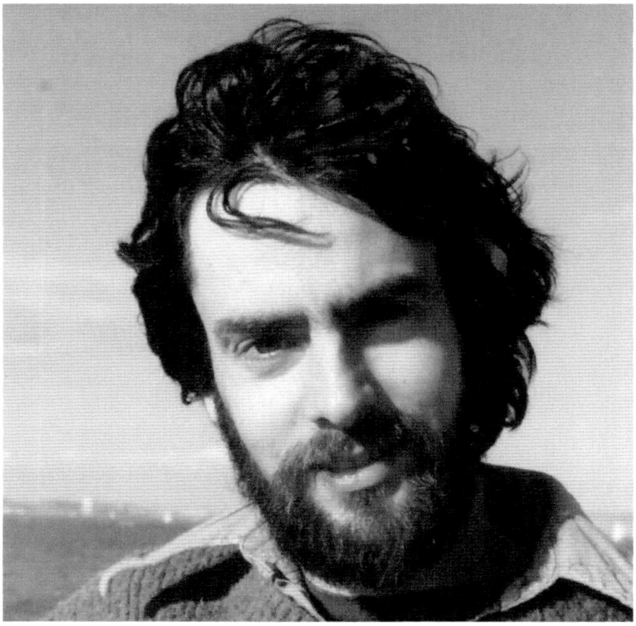

Steve Groveman

A tireless community activist, Steve Groveman is the namesake for the City of Ashland's Grove community center building. Originally, the building was dedicated to serving youth and families. Groveman was well known and respected for his work with at-risk teens. In 2000, Groveman, who had passed away following a battle with colon cancer in November 1999, was the first person to be named grand marshal of Ashland's Fourth of July Parade posthumously. He was also a talented musician and conceived the idea, which proved popular among local youth musicians, of housing a recording studio in the Grove building. (Both, courtesy of Groveman family.)

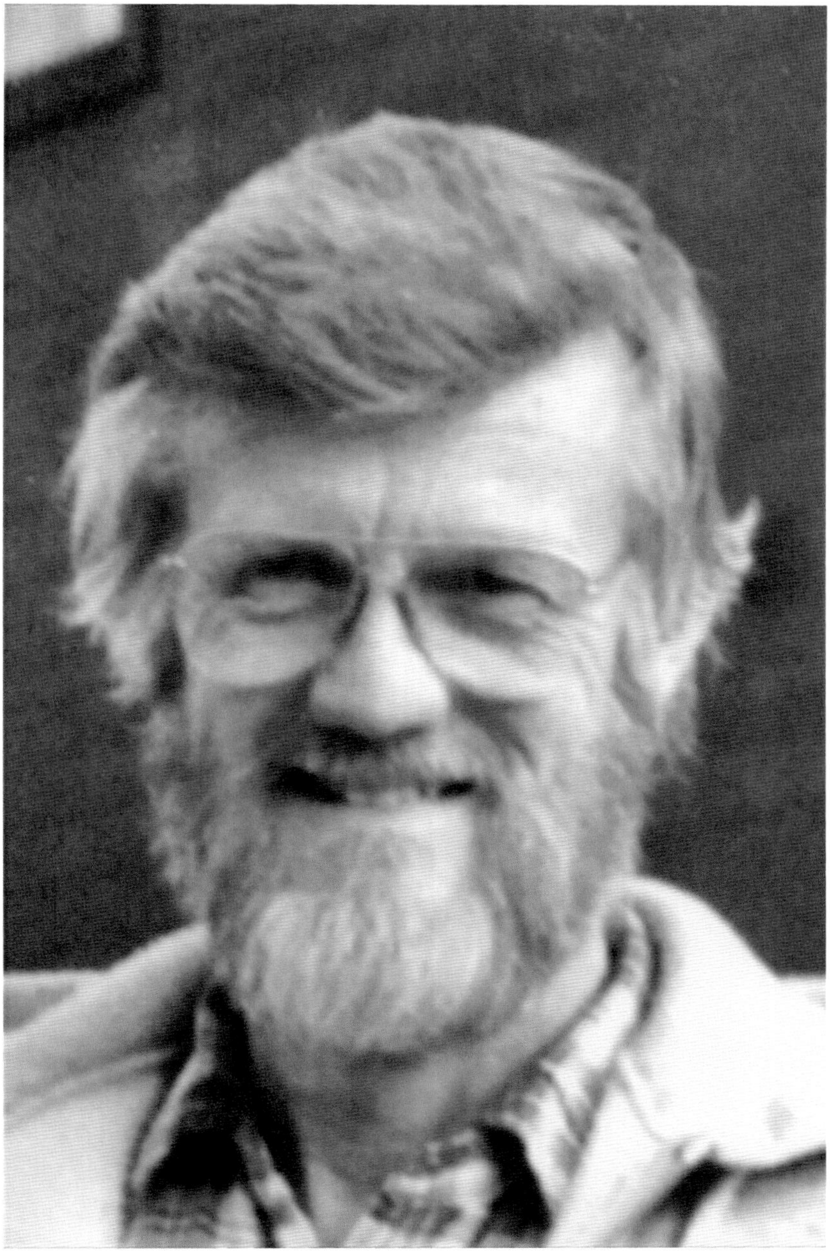

Robert J. Staal

Robert J. Staal was a US Department of Justice attorney who led the government's anti-monopoly suit against IBM from 1969 to 1982. A highly disputed case stemming from the market dominance of IBM during the 1960s, the case was ultimately dropped due to lack of merit. Staal was also an environmental activist who dedicated countless hours to protect land in Marin County, California, and southern Oregon. He advocated for the removal of the Savage Rapids Dam and protested the expansion of the Mount Ashland Ski Area. He lived in Ashland from retirement until his death in 2013. (Courtesy of Staal family.)

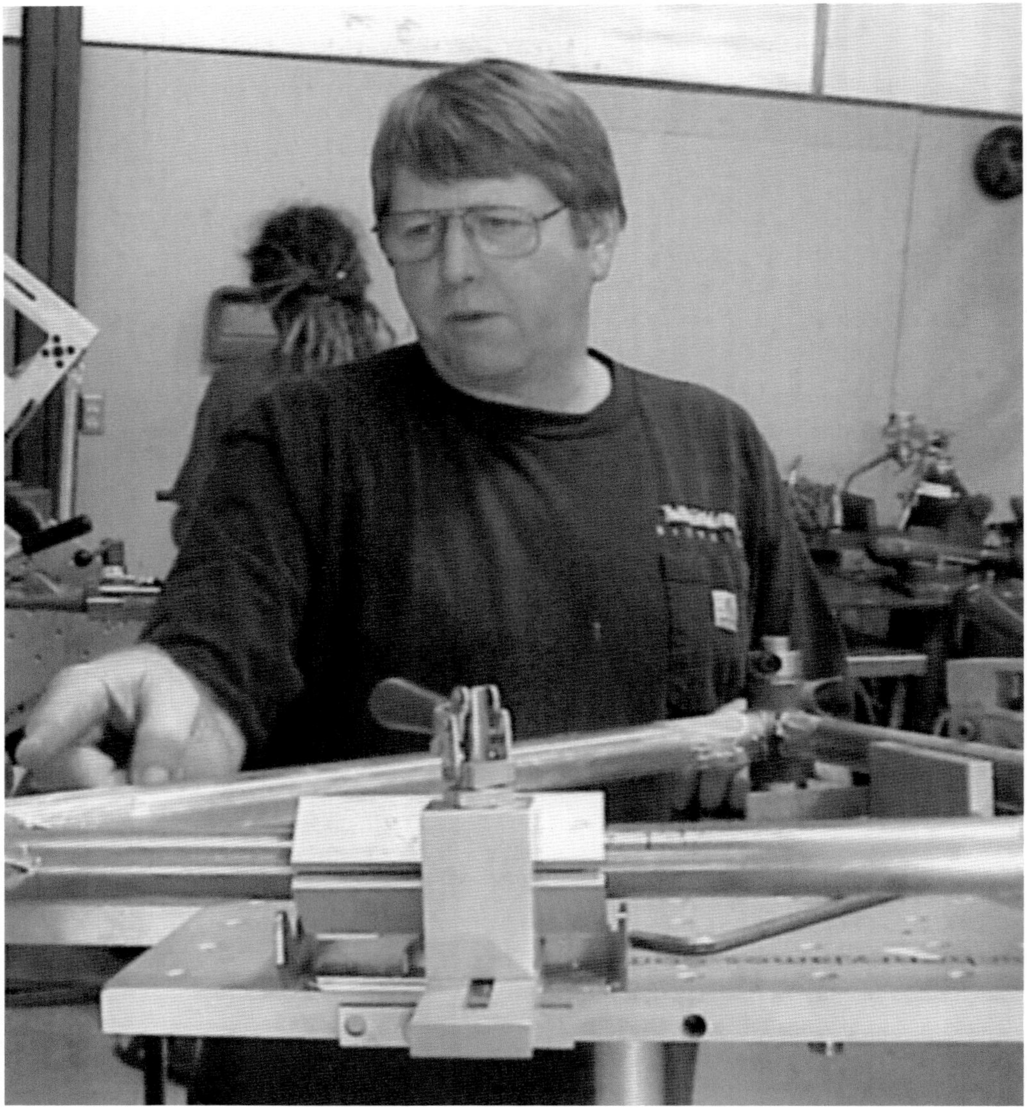

Ron Sutphin

Ron Sutphin is the president and owner of United Bicycle Institute in Ashland and has been an instructor there since it was founded in 1981. He was previously a retail bike shop manager and is a master mechanic and master frame builder. He purchased the company in 1986 from its founder and has grown it exponentially since. UBI is one of only two bike schools in the country and welcomes hundreds of students to classes each year. (Courtesy of Ron Sutphin.)

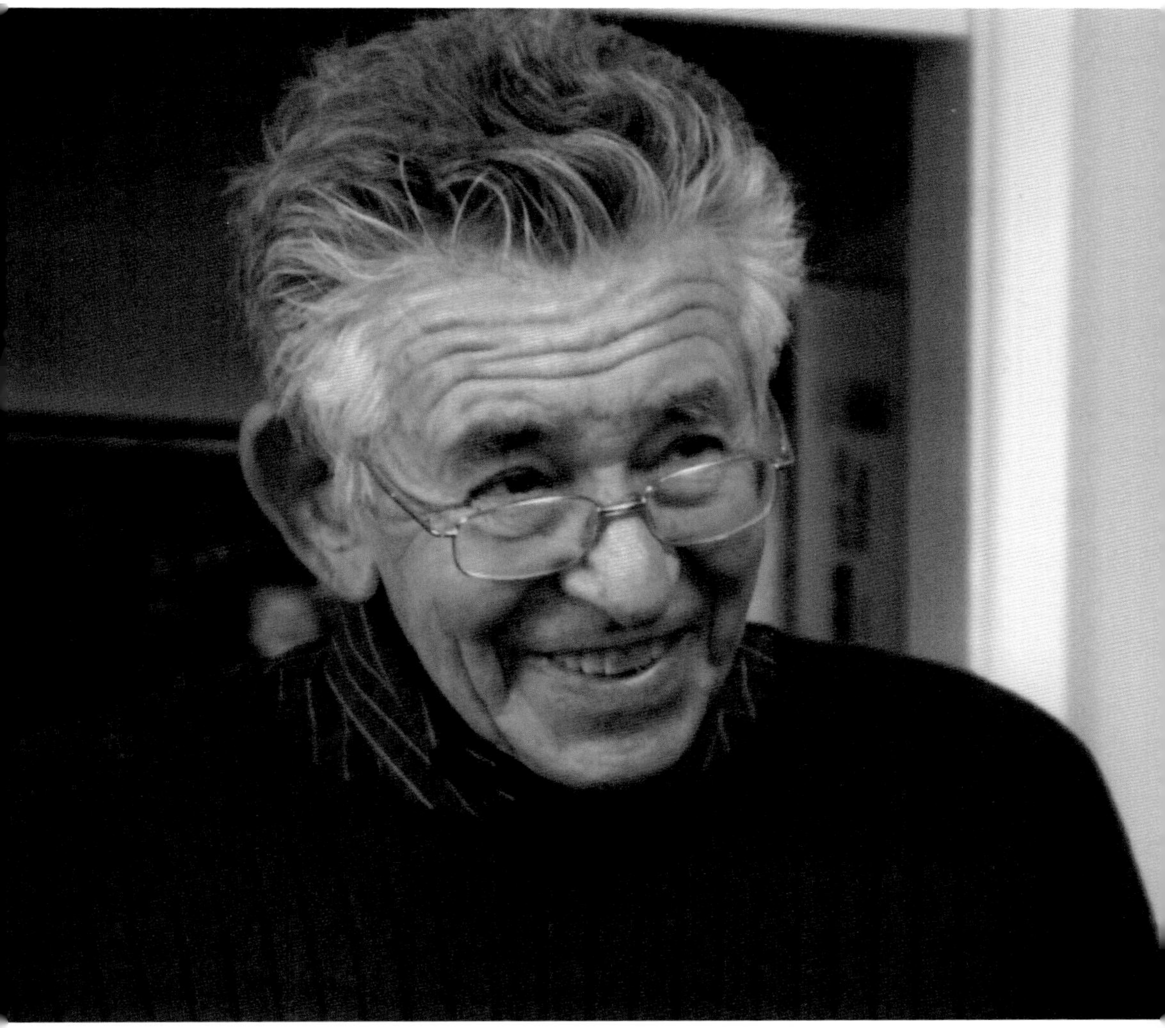

Ralph Temple

Ralph Temple was a tireless advocate for civil liberties, working as the legal director for the Washington, DC, branch of the American Civil Liberties Union for 14 years, including one year as executive director. He was active during the civil rights movement and was often at odds with the DC police for their role during public demonstrations. He retired in Ashland, where he continued to advocate for civil liberties in local cases involving homelessness, panhandling, and public nudity. Temple also worked for the right to demonstrate in Medford parks, opposing restrictive ordinances once in place by the city. He died in Ashland in 2011. (Courtesy of Dean Spillane Walker.)

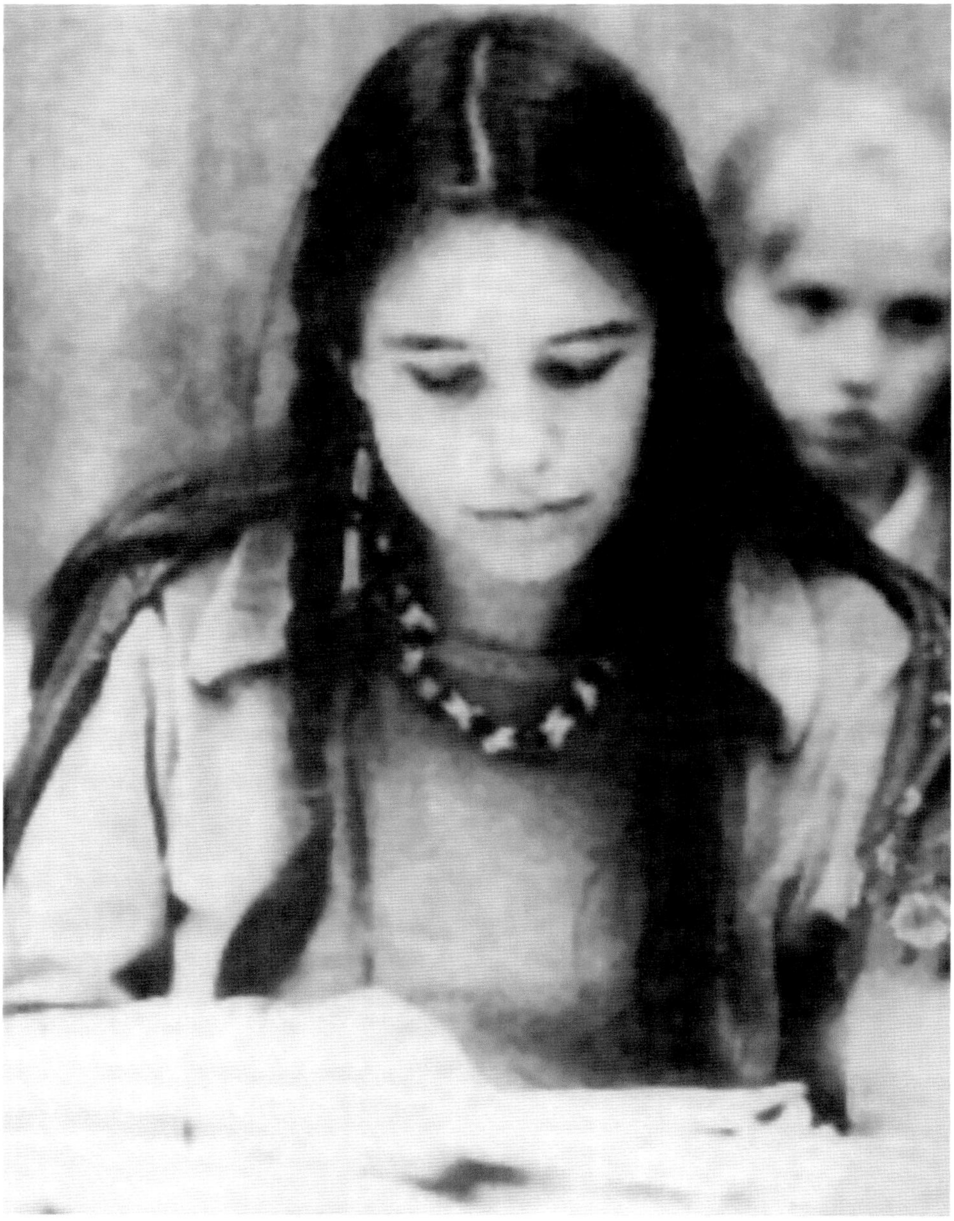

Winona LaDuke

Winona LaDuke is an Anishinaabekwe (Ojibwe) enrolled member of the Mississippi Band Anishinaabeg. She was raised mostly in Ashland and went on to attend Harvard University. After graduation, she moved to the White Earth Indian Reservation in Minnesota, where her father had once lived, and worked as an Indian activist and politician. Twice—in 1996 and 2000—she ran on the Green Party's presidential ticket as a vice president for Ralph Nader. She helped found the Indigenous Women's Network and in 2007 was inducted into the National Women's Hall of Fame to honor women who have helped with the development of the country. LaDuke is also a published author of three books. (Courtesy of Ökologix.)

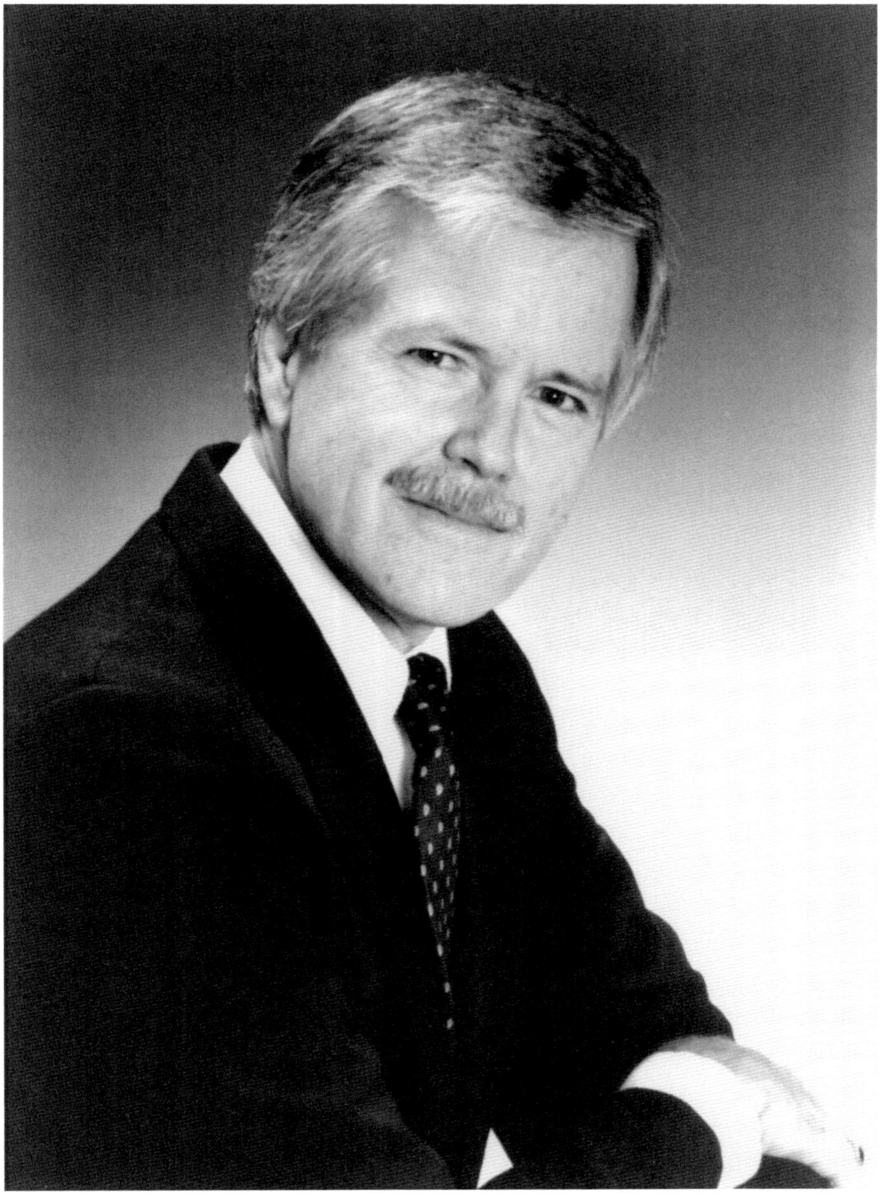

Brian Almquist
Leaving a big pair of shoes to fill, Brian Almquist retired from the role of city administrator of Ashland in 1998 after holding the position for 28 years. When the Seattle-based corporation Harbor Properties announced its plan to close Mount Ashland Ski Area in 1992, it was Almquist who called the first meeting that would eventually—after a million-dollar local fundraising effort—lead to the City of Ashland's owning the ski area. Almquist, among his many other accomplishments as city administrator, is foremost a savior of the ski area. In 2010, Almquist received the Ashland Community Hospital Foundation's Distinguished Service Award. He has served on the foundation's board since 1999, taking a short break before rejoining in 2001. He has also been a member of Ashland Rotary Club since 1977. (Courtesy of the City of Ashland.)

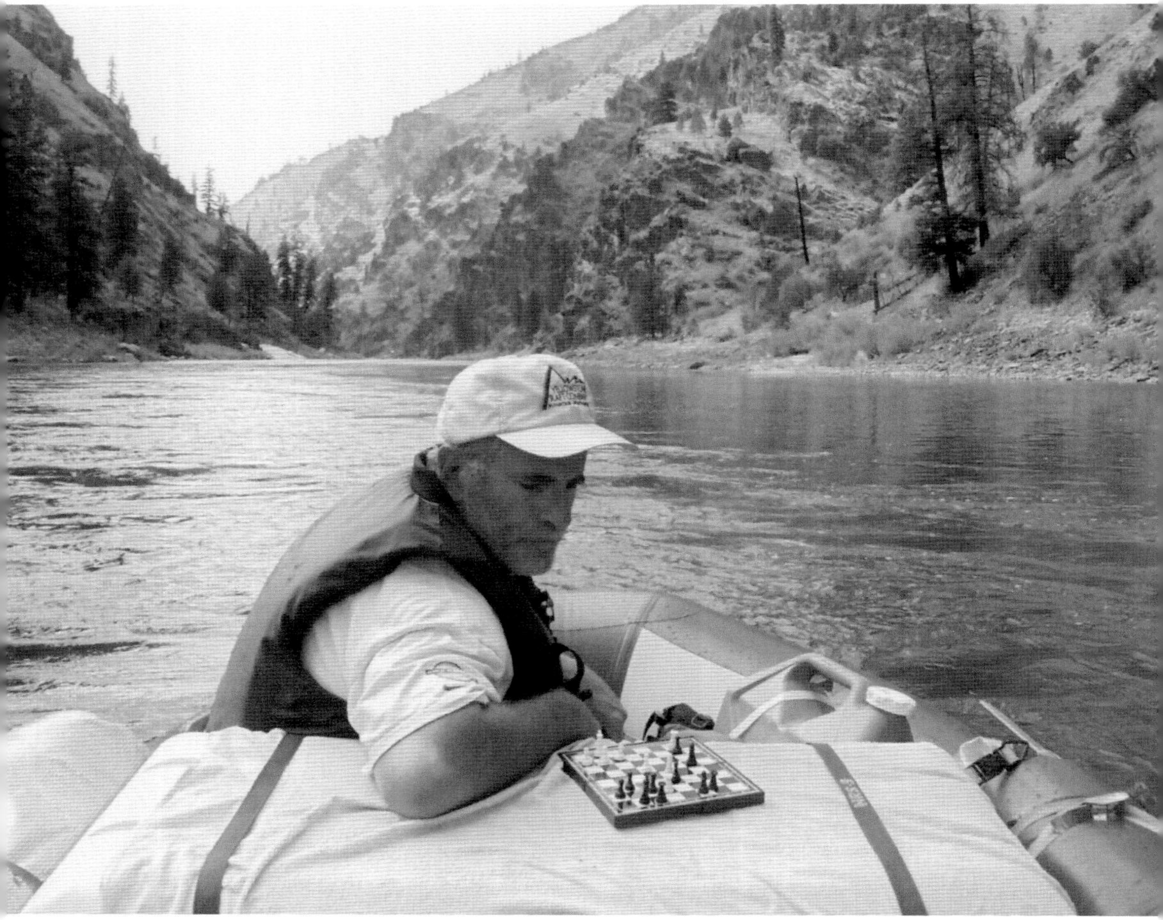

Jeff Golden (ABOVE AND OPPOSITE PAGE)
Born in Los Angeles and graduating from high school in Beverly Hills, Jeff Golden chronicled his journey of dropping out of Harvard University and moving to southern Oregon to live off the grid in his first book, *Watermelon Summer*. Active in broadcasting and editorial journalism, Golden also has a rich political career, serving as a Jackson County commissioner and chief of staff to the Oregon Senate president. He was a host of *The Jefferson Exchange* on National Public Radio for 10 years and now hosts *Immense Possibilities*, a weekly public television and Internet broadcast about people building vibrant communities. He lives in Ashland and remains politically active. (All, courtesy of Jeff Golden.)

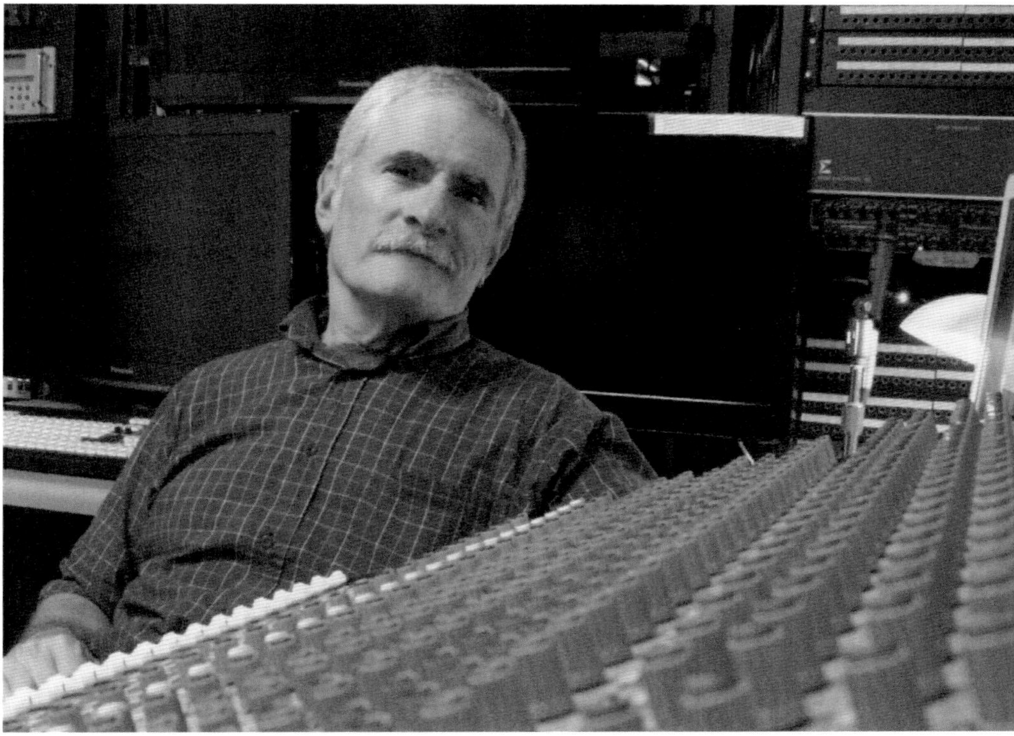

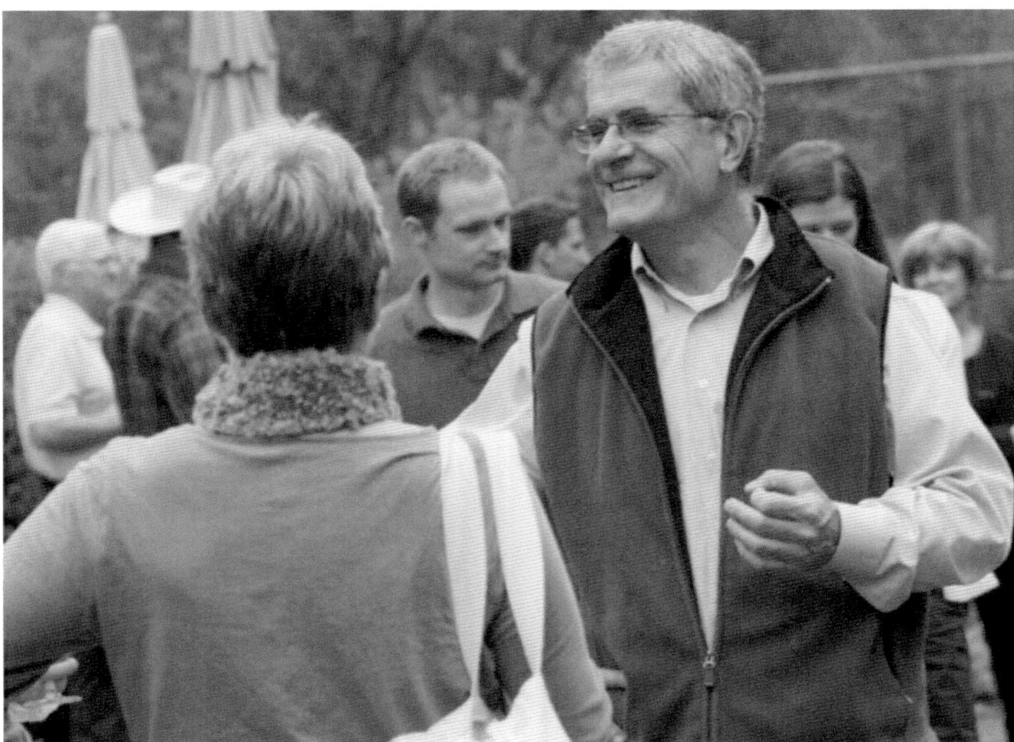

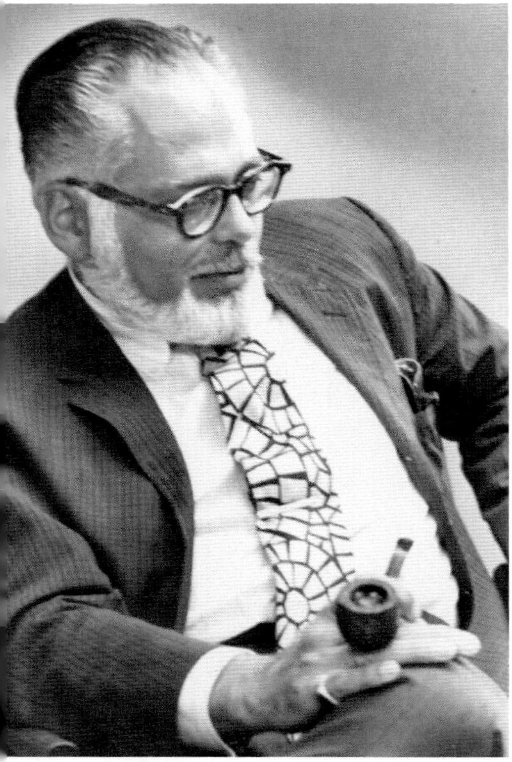

Leonard W. Levy
Pulitzer Prize of History–winner Leonard W. Levy was appointed a Distinguished Scholar in Residence while adjunct professor of history and political science at Southern Oregon State College in 1990. Author and contributor to dozens of highly regarded books, Levy was awarded the Pulitzer Prize in 1969 for his book *Origins of the Fifth Amendment*. Born in Toronto, Canada, Levy was educated at Columbia University and died in Ashland on August 24, 2006. Levy testified during the US Senate's Watergate hearings, and his distinguished work was cited several times in the Supreme Court. He is pictured below with former first lady of the United States Anna Eleanor Roosevelt. (Both, courtesy of Leslie Levy.)

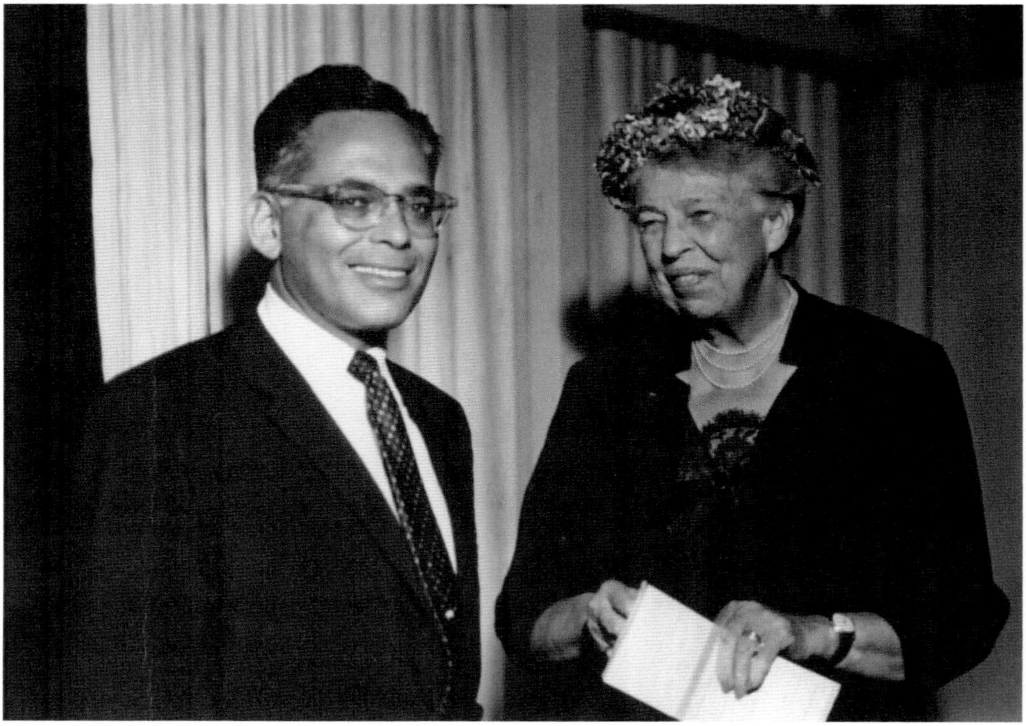

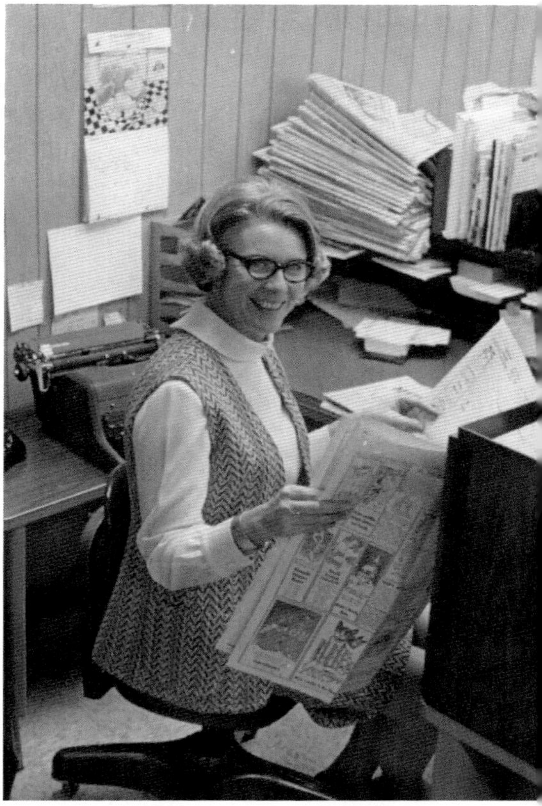

Marjorie Lutz O'Harra
Marjorie O'Harra is a lifelong Ashland resident and its foremost historian. Prior to her retirement, she worked as a reporter and feature writer for the *Ashland Daily Tidings* and as a writer and regional editor for the *Mail Tribune* in Medford. She also served as a Jackson County commissioner. Her books—*Ashland: The First 130 Years*, published in 1981 by the Southern Oregon Historical Society, and *Ashland in Transition: 1980s and 1990s*, published in 2000 by the *Ashland Daily Tidings*—portray the clearest and most concise history of Ashland. (Courtesy of Marjorie Lutz O'Harra.)

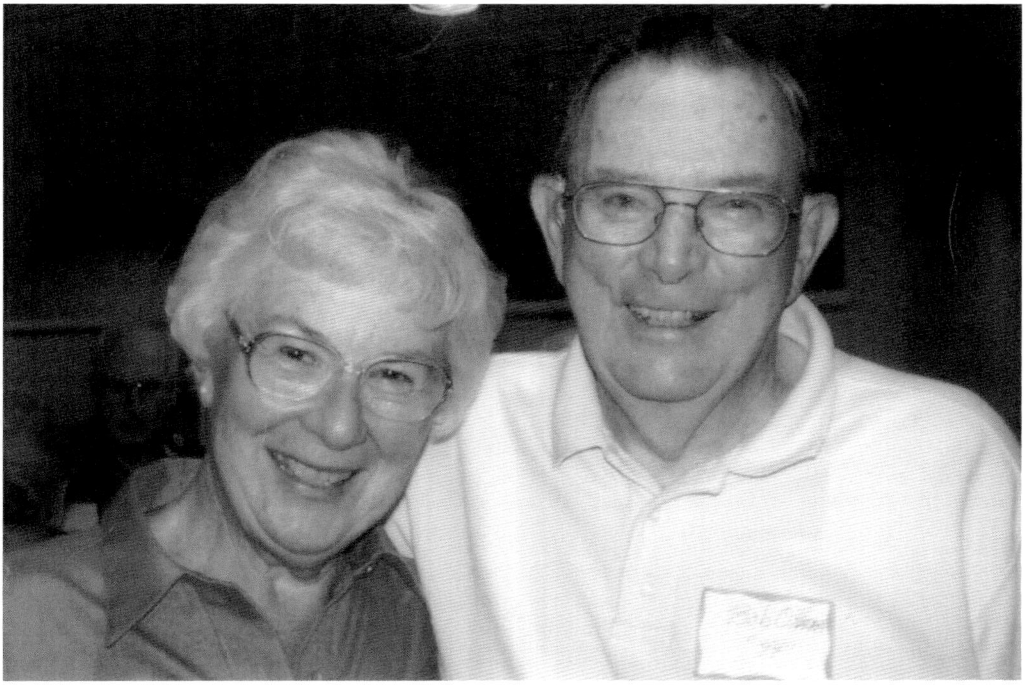

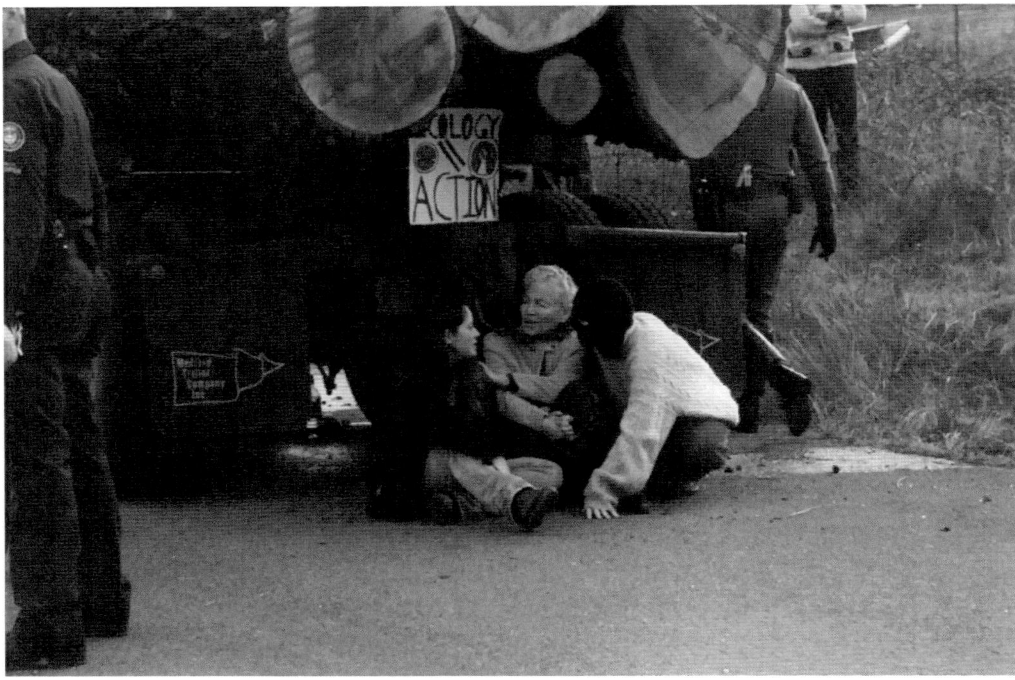

Dot Fisher-Smith

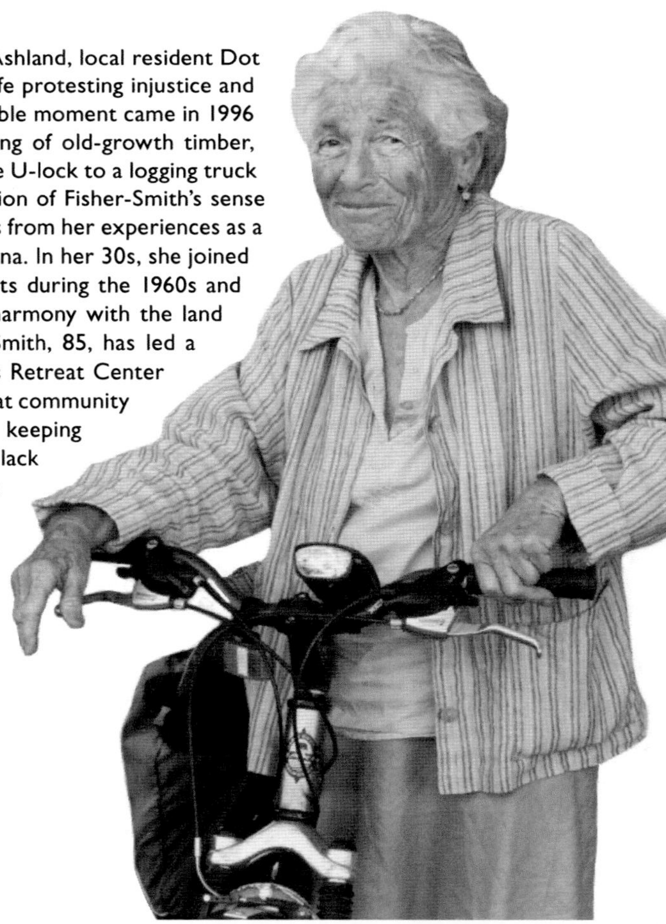

A co-founder of the Peace House in Ashland, local resident Dot Fisher-Smith has spent much of her life protesting injustice and social wrongs. Perhaps her most notable moment came in 1996 when she, while protesting the logging of old-growth timber, locked herself by the neck with bicycle U-lock to a logging truck near Croman Mill in Ashland. A portion of Fisher-Smith's sense of social responsibility no doubt stems from her experiences as a child growing up in segregated Louisiana. In her 30s, she joined the anti-war and anti-draft movements during the 1960s and moved to Oregon to live in closer harmony with the land in the 1970s. Most recently, Fisher-Smith, 85, has led a women's retreat at Buckhorn Springs Retreat Center outside Ashland, and can still be seen at community events, meetings, and gatherings keeping a pulse on the social progress or lack thereof in Ashland. (Courtesy of Dot Fisher-Smith and Jim Chamberlain.)

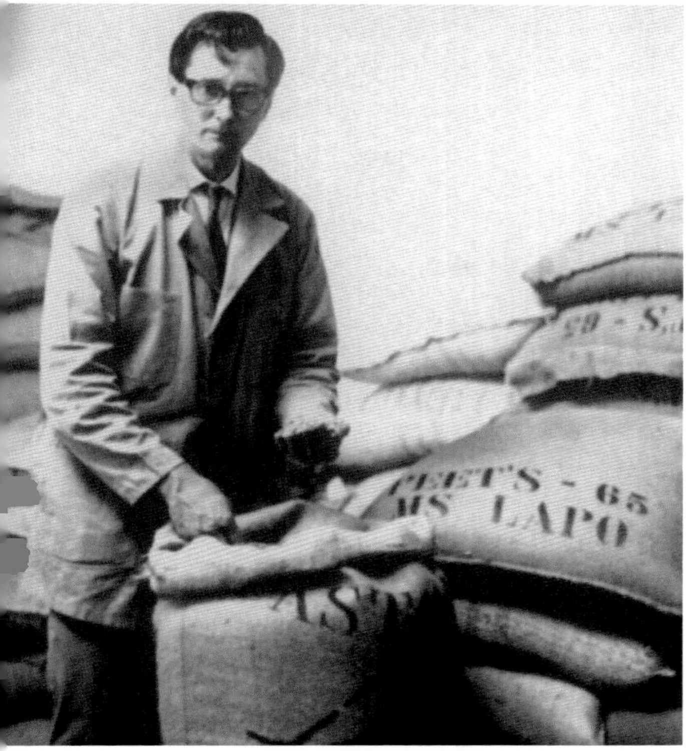

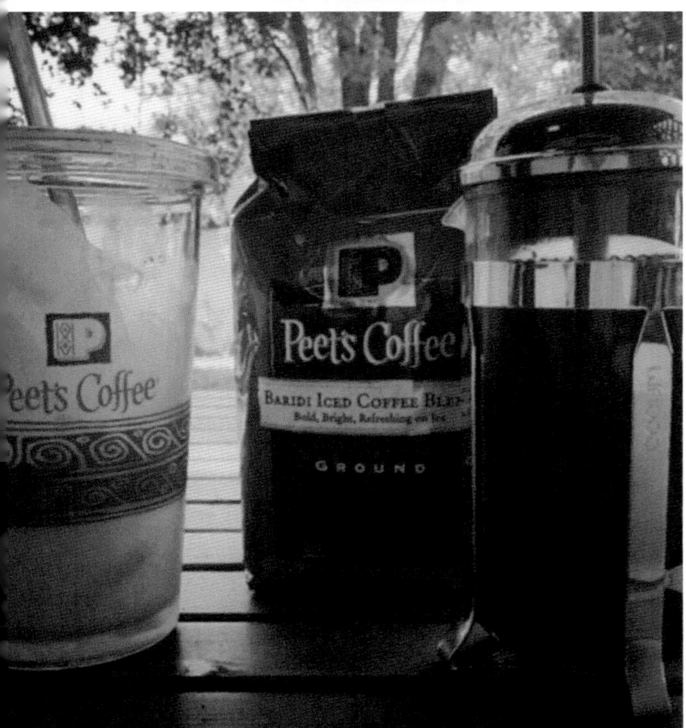

Alfred Peet
Alfred Peet founded Peet's Coffee & Tea in Berkeley, California, in 1966, the first to introduce custom coffee roasting to the United States. He is credited with teaching the coffee roasters who went on to create Starbucks in Seattle. In 2001, Peet moved to the Rogue Valley, first living at the Rogue Valley Manor and then at Mountain Meadows retirement community in Ashland. He died of bone cancer in 2007 at his home in Ashland. (Top, courtesy of Peet's Coffee & Tea; bottom, courtesy of Tony Webster.)

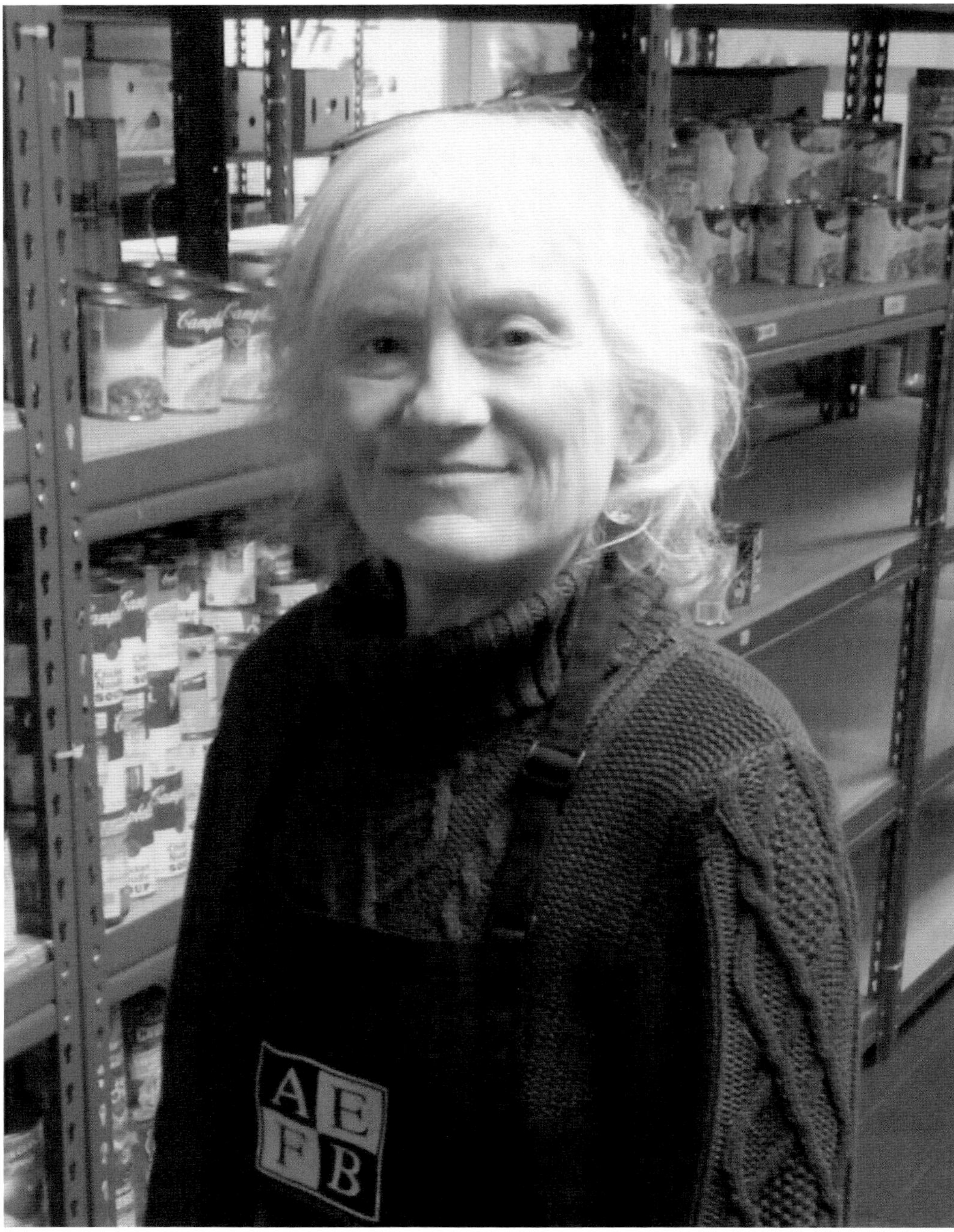
AEFB

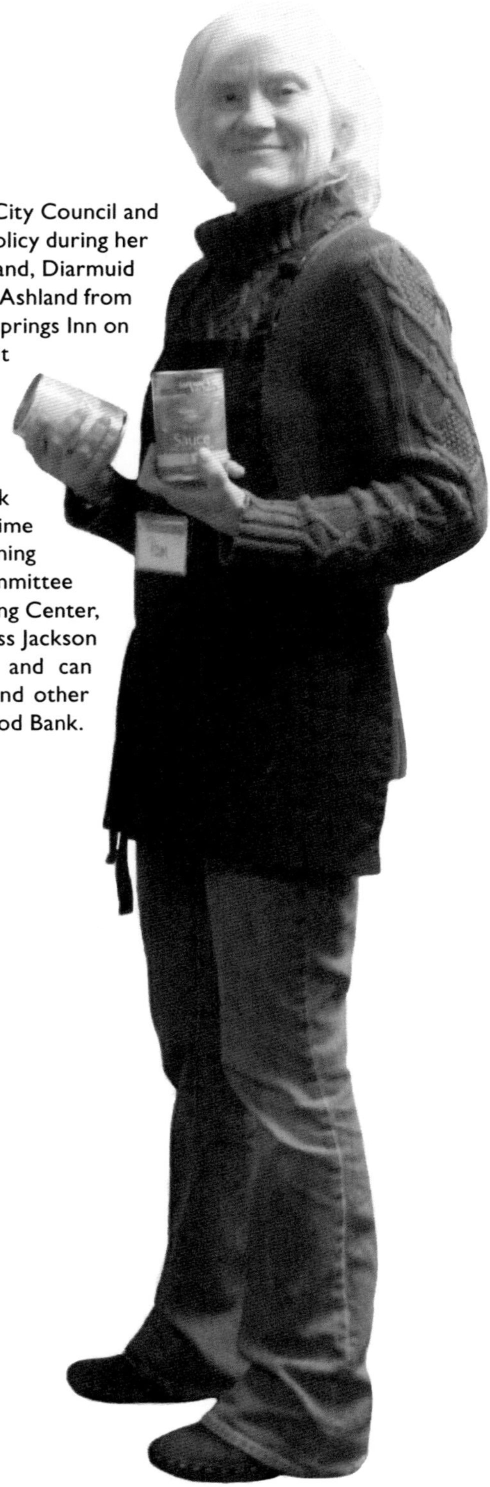

Pam Marsh (RIGHT AND OPPOSITE PAGE)
Ashlander Pam Marsh currently sits on the Ashland City Council and has been heavily involved in school district and city policy during her 20 years as an Ashland resident. Marsh and her husband, Diarmuid McGuire, moved their family to the mountains above Ashland from Palo Alto in 1994, taking up ownership of the Greensprings Inn on Highway 66. The family moved to Ashland in 2003, but continues to operate the stayover and restaurant. In 2013, Marsh, who is director of the Ashland Emergency Food Bank, helped the nonprofit secure ownership of its first permanent location in south Ashland. Last year, Marsh estimated the food bank served about 1,200 people each month. During her time in Ashland, Marsh has served on the Ashland Planning Commission and the Ashland Charter Review Committee and currently sits on the board of the Family Nurturing Center, whose aim is to prevent child abuse and neglect across Jackson County. Marsh is a tireless community advocate and can usually be found stacking or handing out produce and other food items at the always busy Ashland Emergency Food Bank. (Both, author photographs.)

Libby Appel

Libby Appel was the Oregon Shakespeare Festival's artistic director from 1995 to 2007, directing 32 plays at OSF during that time. She is credited with increasing the number of modern plays to grace the repertory theater's stages and diversifying the company by casting more women and minorities. The festival's first female artistic director, Appel worked to attract a younger, more diverse audience, while continuing to retain and attract OSF's traditional crowd. She also fostered and oversaw the creation of the festival's New Theater, now known as the Thomas Theater. After retiring, Appel moved to Santa Barbara, California, where she lives today. In 2012, Appel was awarded the Stephen and Christine Schwarzman Legacy Award for Lifetime Excellence and Achievement in Theater. (Courtesy of the Oregon Shakespeare Festival.)

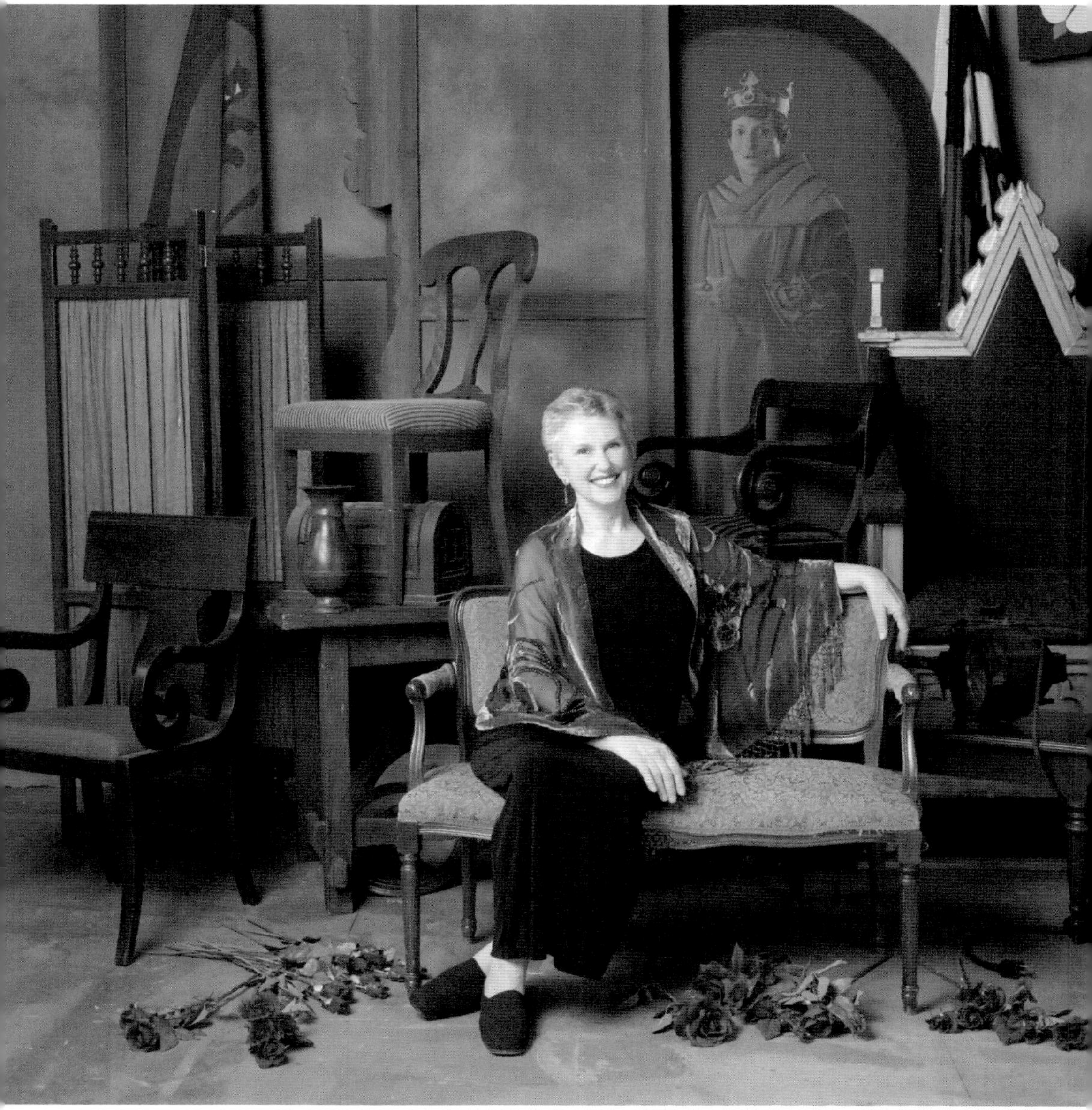

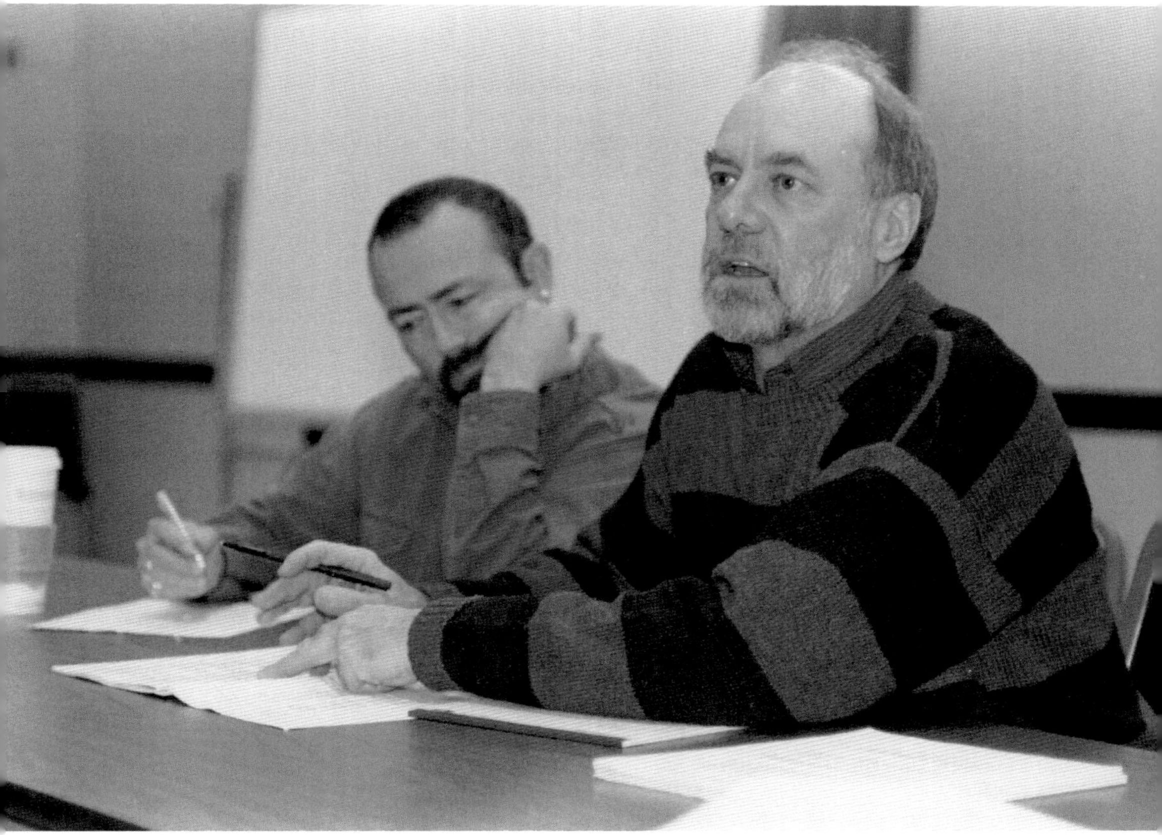

Paul Nicholson

New Zealand native Paul Nicholson was the general manager and then executive director of the Oregon Shakespeare Festival for 33 years, retiring in 2012. He helped the festival partner with the Actors Equality Association in 1984 to attract more experienced actors and oversaw OSF during a period when the festival nearly doubled its audience totals and increased its budget from $2.6 million to $30 million. Nicholson helped OSF move into the computer age and helped develop the repertory theater into a company that could attract professionals looking for careers. (Courtesy of the Oregon Shakespeare Festival.)

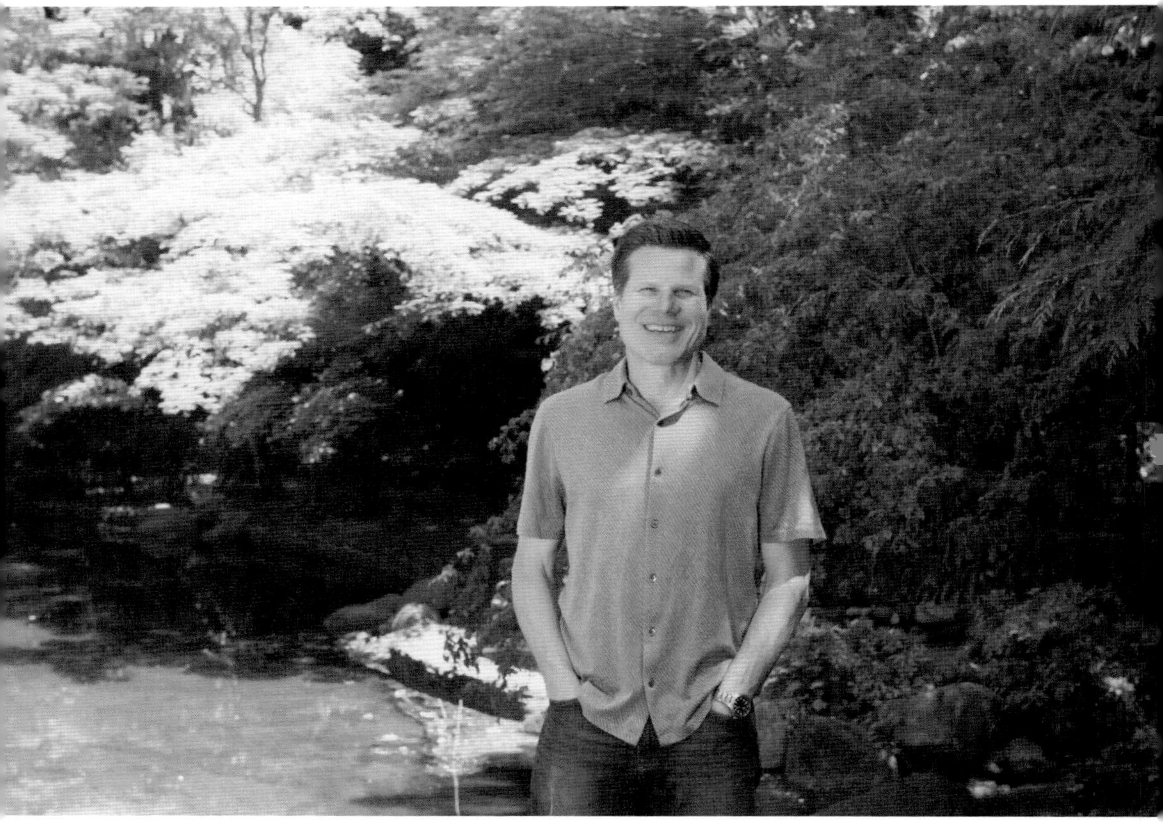

Bill Rauch

Bill Rauch became the fifth artistic director of the Oregon Shakespeare Festival in 2007, succeeding OSF founder Angus Bowmer and only three others since 1935. Rauch is a Harvard University graduate and enjoyed a long history in theater before coming to OSF as a guest director. In 12 seasons at OSF, he has directed 18 plays, including three world premieres. He has set a goal to commission up to 37 new plays at OSF through the American Revolutions: US History Cycle play series and helped initiate a community-based format for the festival's Green Show. Rauch also co-founded Cornerstone Theater Company, where he directed more than 40 plays with diverse rural and urban communities across the country between 1986 and 2006. In 2012, he received the Zelda Fichandler Award and has been honored numerous times in the past for his work as a director. (Courtesy of the Oregon Shakespeare Festival.)

Terry Skibby

Ashland resident Terry Skibby has dedicated most of his life toward photographing Ashland. His visual representations of Ashland's past play an integral part in the depiction of the town's history. His personal collection of original glass plates, negatives, and photographs acquired over the last 40 years numbers in the thousands. If it were not for 69-year-old Skibby's tireless devotion to the upkeep of his collection, much of Ashland's past would be an unsightly one. (Courtesy of Terry Skibby.)

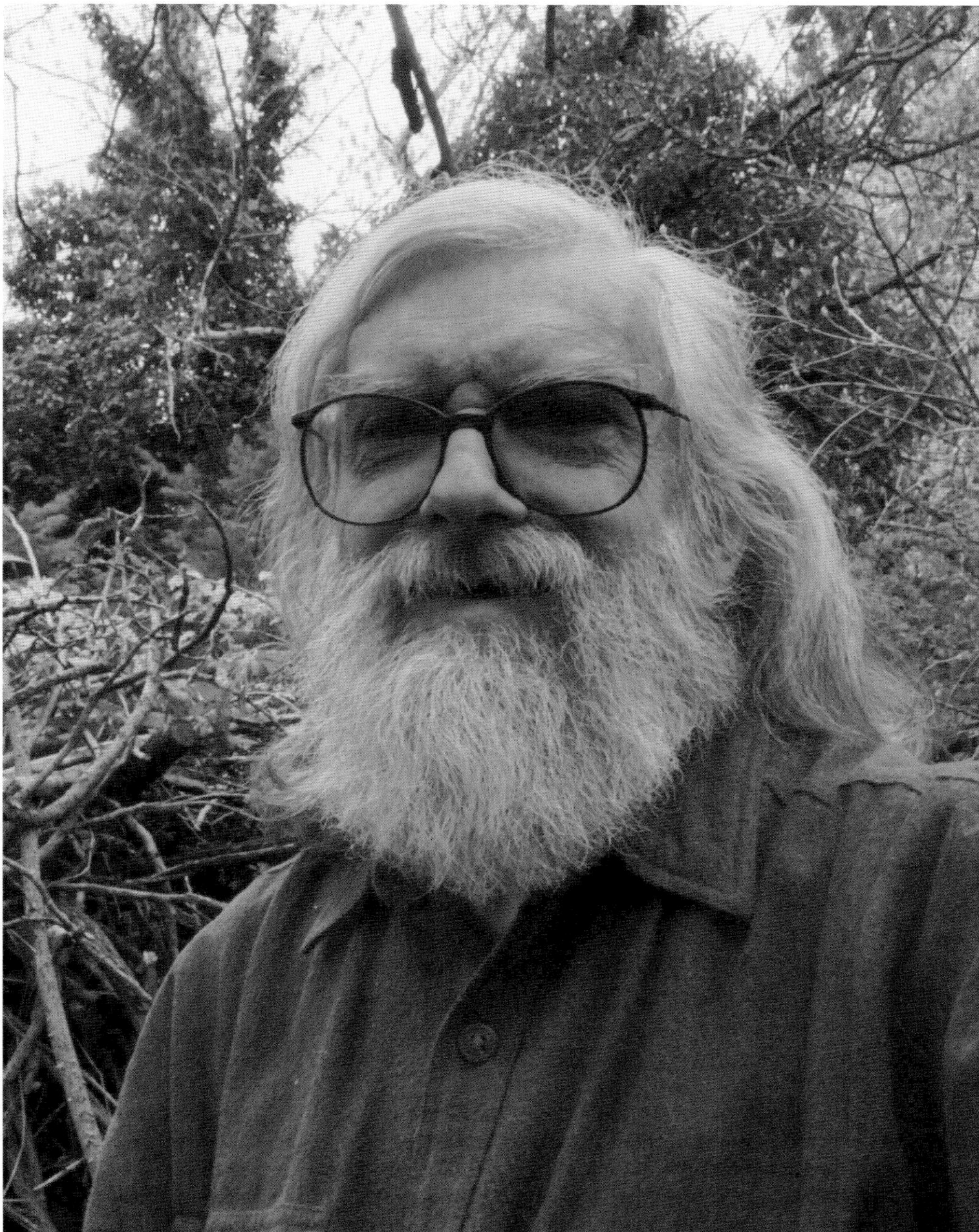

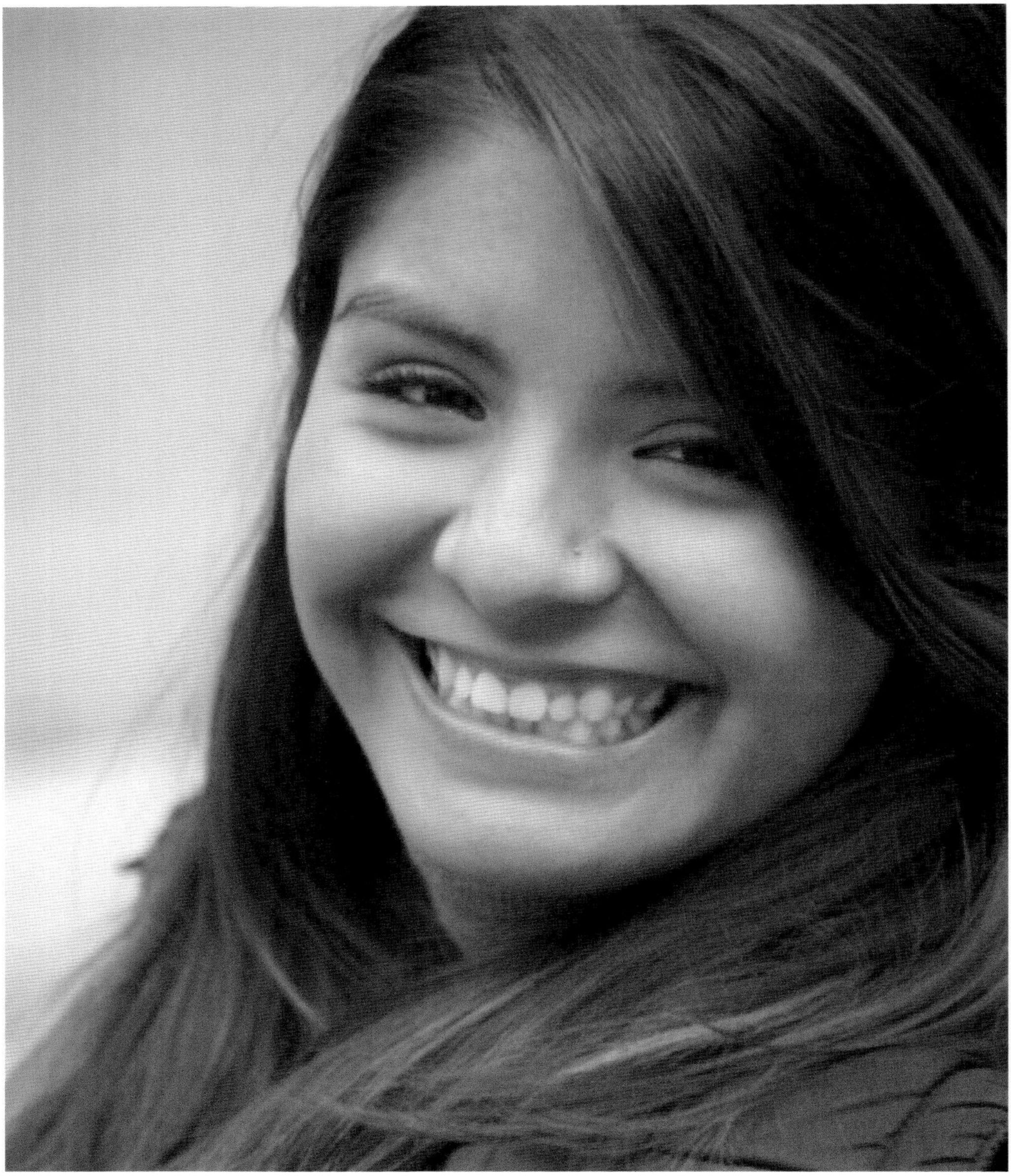

Diana Banda (ABOVE AND OPPOSITE PAGE)
Diana Banda did not begin to grasp the plight of her status as a US citizen until entering high school. Banda's family immigrated to southern Oregon from Mexico City when Banda was three, settling in Ashland because acquaintances and family lived nearby. Last year, when Banda, 22, made the decision to come out of the shadows as an undocumented illegal alien, it frightened her parents. Since publicly declaring her status as an undocumented youth, Banda has been arrested once, on May Day, by Portland police during an Undocumented and Unafraid march of about 1,500 people, organized by Northwest Immigrant Youth Alliance. Banda also helped form Oregon Dream Activists, which has chapters in states around the United States, in 2011. The organization helps raise awareness about deportation cases and immigration policy. (Photographs by Stephen Pavey.)

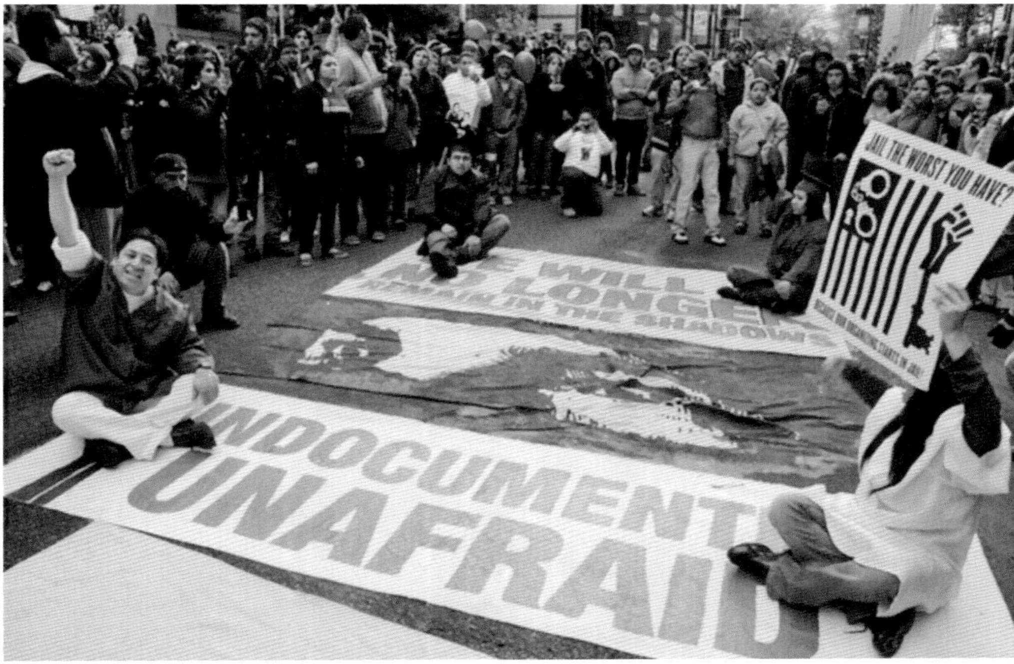
JAIL THE WORST YOU HAVE?
UNAFRAID

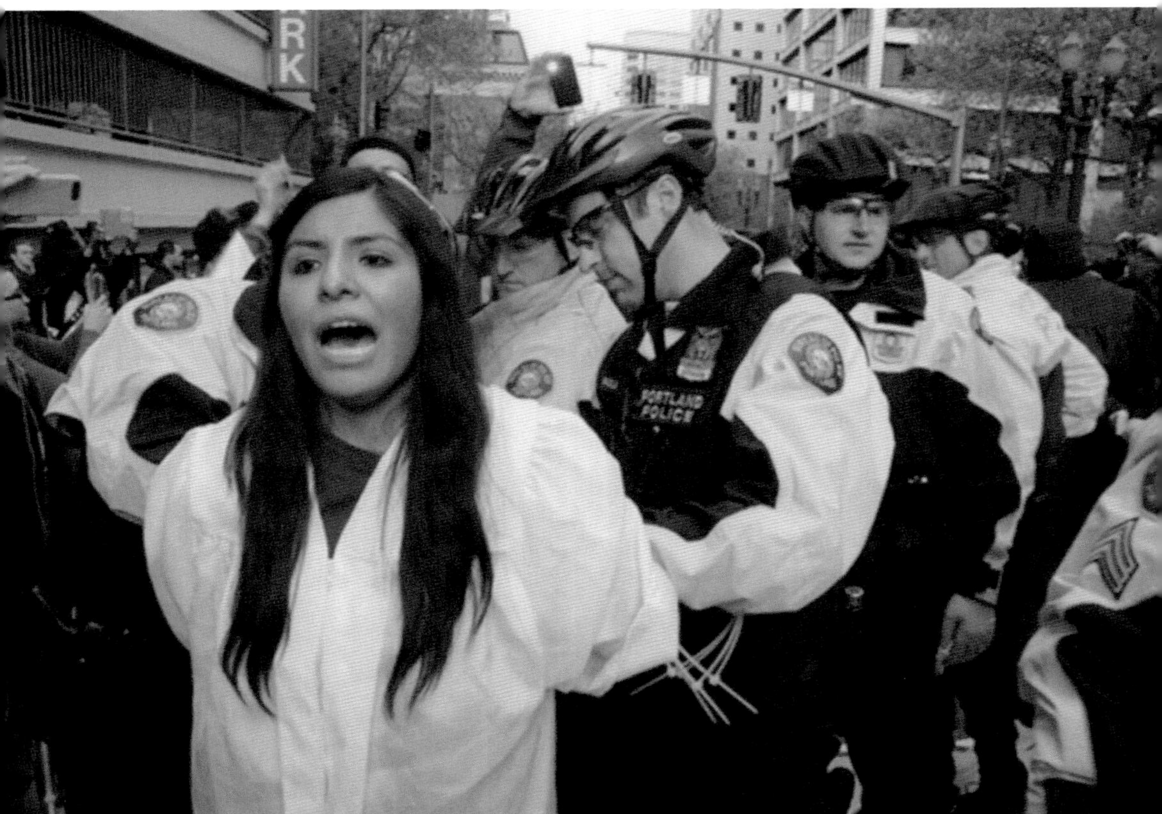
PORTLAND POLICE

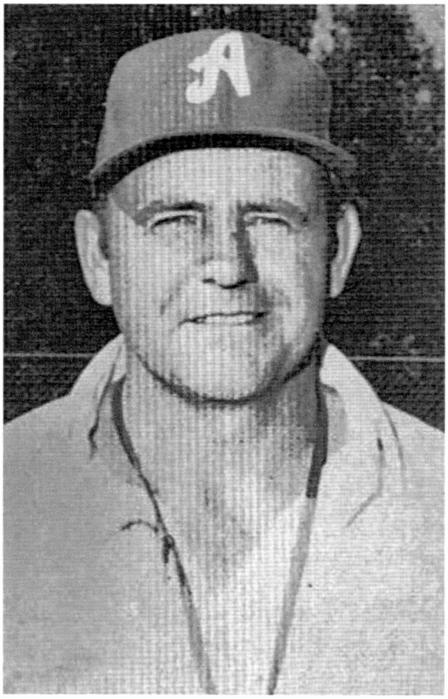

Jim Nagel

Coach Jim Nagel is an Ashland High School football legend. As head coach from 1983 through 2002, Nagel led the Grizzlies to the playoffs 16 consecutive times and a total of five championship game appearances, as well as three state titles. He also served as the school's athletic director from 1991 through 2004. An Ashland resident for over 30 years, Nagel joined the Southern Oregon University coaching staff as an offensive assistant in 2013. (Left, courtesy of Ashland High School; below, courtesy of Jim Nagel.)

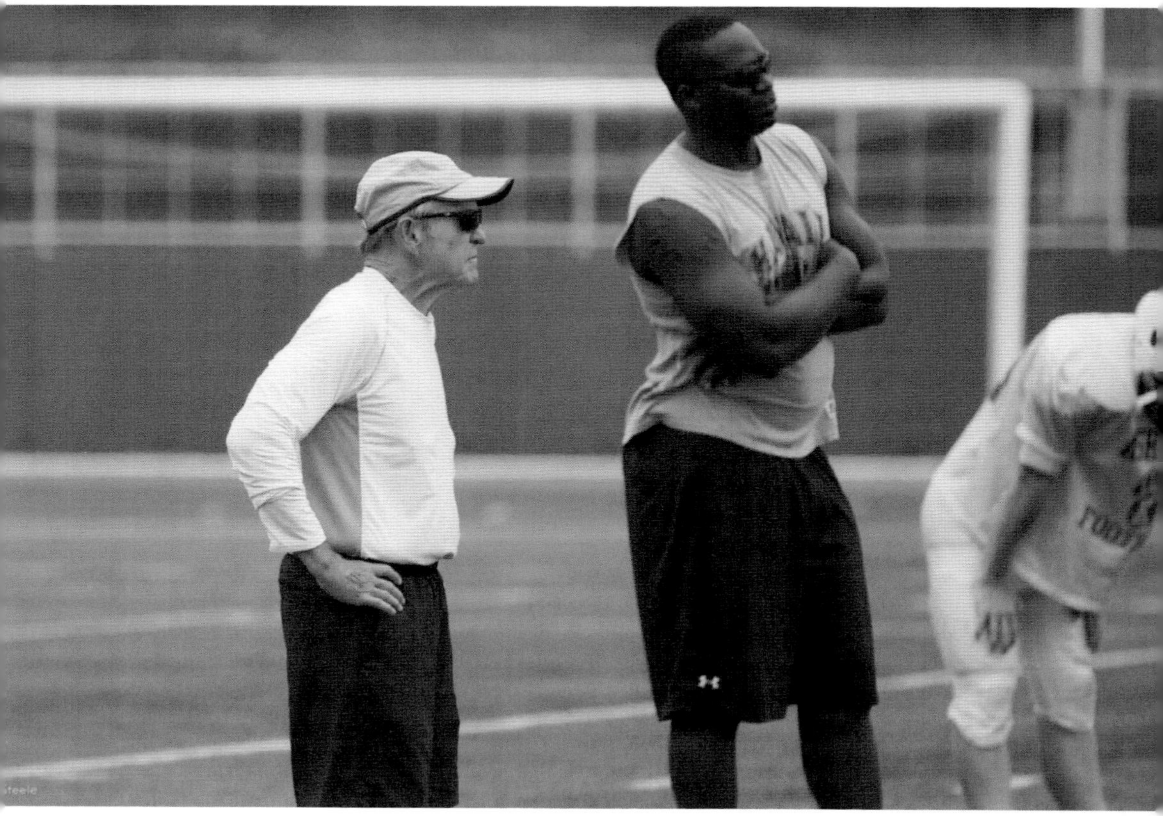

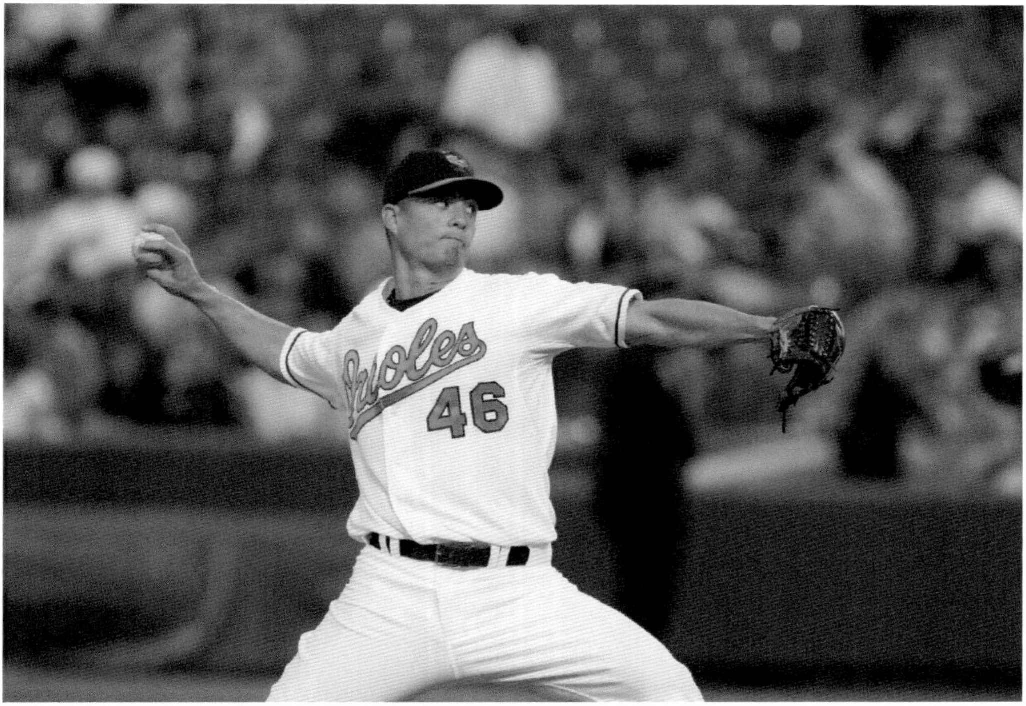

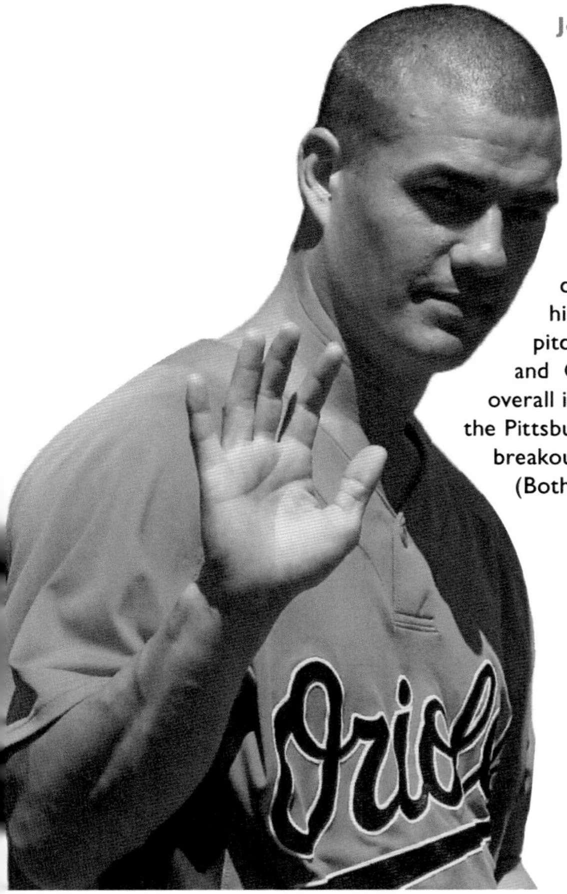

Jeremy Guthrie

A 1997 Ashland High School graduate and Stanford University alumnus, Jeremy Guthrie is a professional pitcher for the Kansas City Royals. He was a standout pitcher for the Grizzlies in high school and helped lead Stanford to the 2001 College World Series. During his senior year for the Grizzlies, he was named the most valuable player in baseball, football, and basketball and was class valedictorian. In addition to the Royals, during his tenure in Major League Baseball, Guthrie has pitched for the Cleveland Indians, Baltimore Orioles, and Colorado Rockies. Guthrie was selected 22nd overall in the 2002 MLB draft. He was drafted in 2001 by the Pittsburgh Pirates but elected to return to college. His breakout year as a MLB pitcher was in 2007 for the Indians. (Both, by Keith Allison under Creative Commons.)

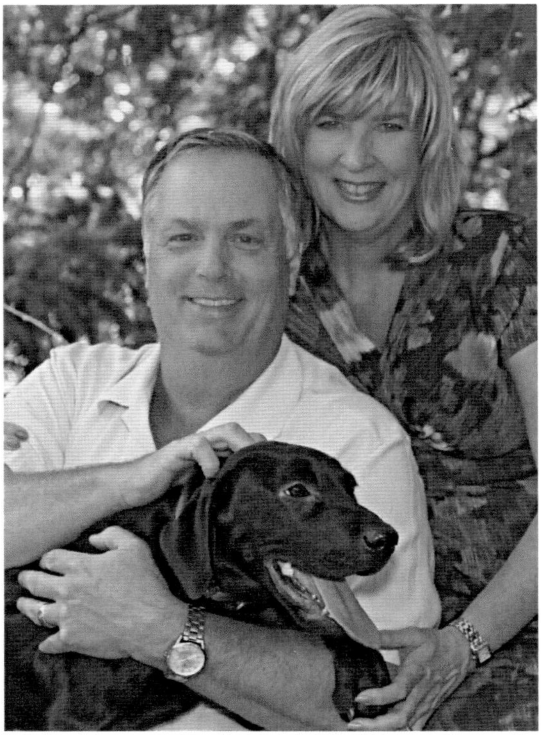

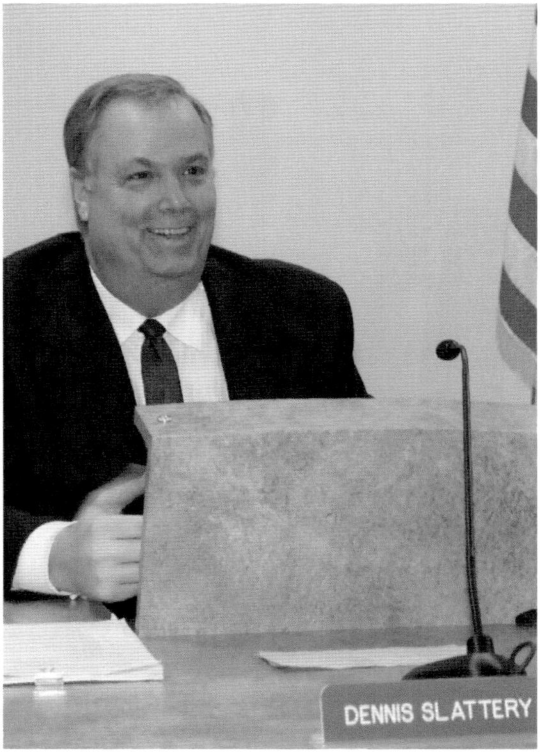

Dennis Slattery

A longtime Ashland resident and tireless community leader, Dennis Slattery is an associate professor in the School of Business at Southern Oregon University and was elected to the Ashland City Council in November 2010. Slattery served one four-year term with the council, opting out of a reelection campaign in 2014 in order to focus his attention on SOU. He moved to Ashland from Alaska in 1977 after serving in the US Navy to attend Southern Oregon State College, where he went on to earn a bachelor's degree and master's degree. Working for nearly 15 years in Ashland's hotel industry during the late 1970s and through the 1980s, Slattery saw himself steadily promoted from a housekeeping role into a top managerial position before committing himself to a career in public accounting and eventually teaching. He has been an SOU faculty member since 2003 and comes from a family with a rich teaching history. In addition to his successful careers in Ashland, Slattery has never failed to put just as much effort into making the community a better place for everyone who calls Ashland home. He has served on the Ashland Chamber of Commerce board of directors and twice was elected president of the chamber. He is currently a member of the university's faculty senate and has also served on the Southern Oregon Regional Economic Development Board and for numerous other area nonprofit organizations and community groups. He is married to Ashland Chamber of Commerce executive director Sandra Slattery. (Both, courtesy of Dennis Slattery.)

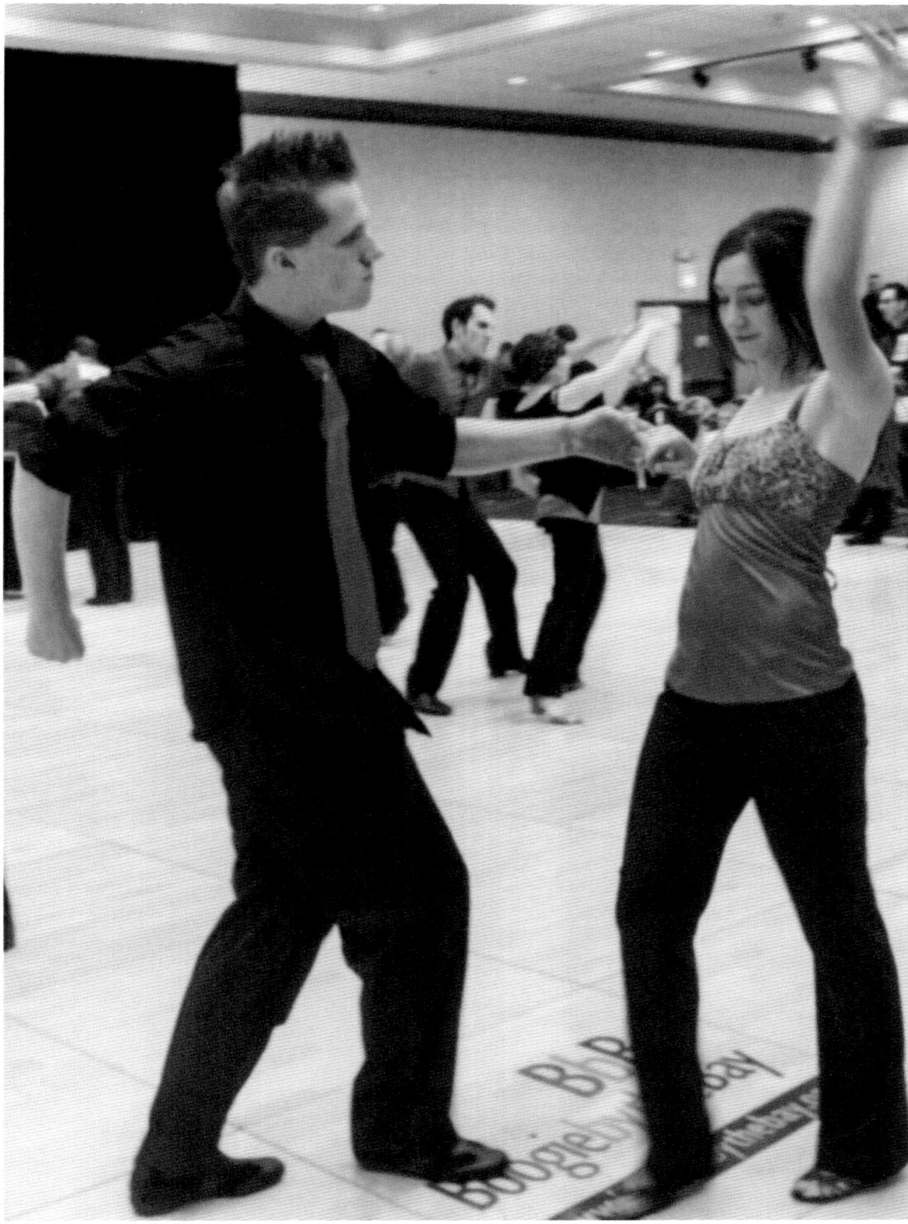

Andrew Vogel

Ashland High School graduate of 2012 and competition-winning West Coast Swing dancer Andrew Vogel was sitting in the driver's seat of his car waiting for a tow when a distracted driver veered across two lanes and slammed into the driver's side of Vogel's vehicle. The near-fatal car crash on October 10, 2011, put Vogel in the intensive care unit of the hospital and left him barely able to sit up in a chair after coming out of a weeklong coma. During his stay in the hospital, Vogel was revived twice with a defibrillator and doctors were not sure if he would ever dance again. Vogel went on to make a full recovery and has since competed in and won dance competitions up and down the West Coast. (Courtesy of Andrew Vogel.)

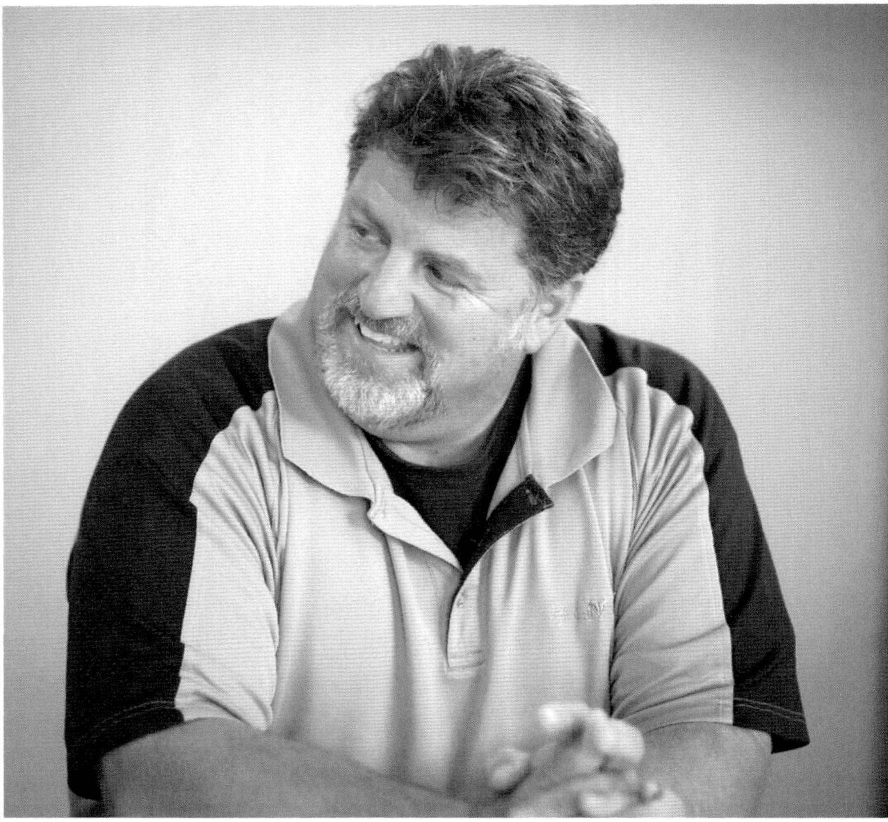

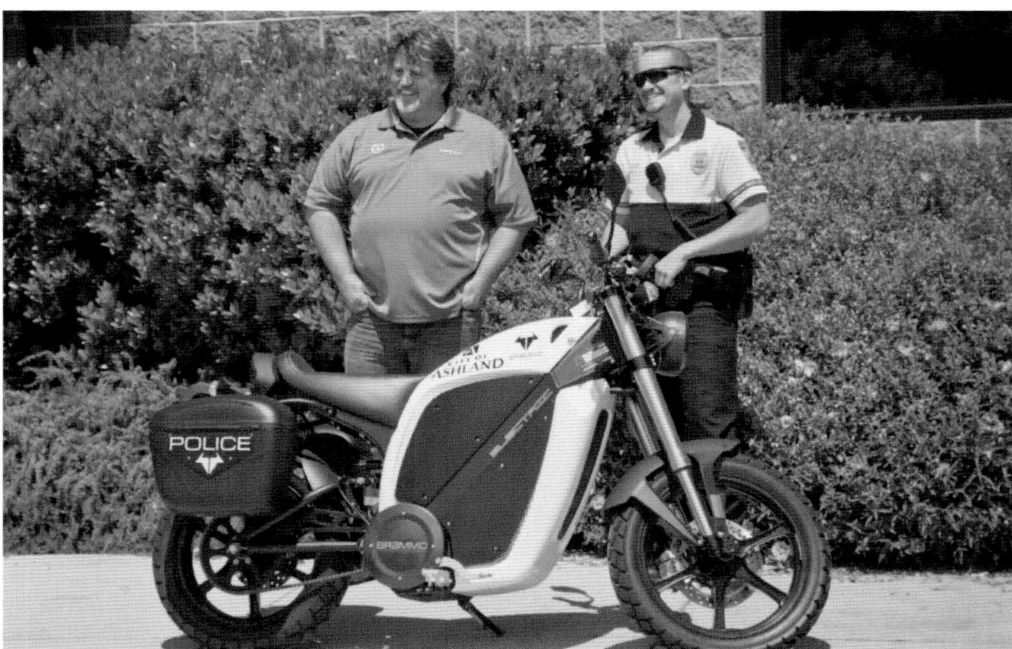
ASHLAND
POLICE

Craig Bramscher (BELOW AND OPPOSITE PAGE)
Brammo Inc. boss Craig Bramscher does not plan on slowing down anytime soon. His company is silently muscling into the forefront of the electric vehicle and motorcycle world and earning multiple industry accolades in the process. Brammo's Enertia electric motorcycle was named the best electric bike in 2012, topping Oakland, California–based Electric Motorsport Native Cycles' S model. A year earlier, the company signed a $13 million investment deal with Polaris Industries Inc. to develop electric vehicle battery technology. Bramscher announced last year his plans to move Brammo's headquarters outside Ashland to nearby Talent, a move that he says will enable the company to more affordably expand its operation in southern Oregon. Initially focused on designing a comfortable sports car for a large-framed man like himself but then shifting toward electric vehicle manufacturing, Bramscher founded Brammo from his garage in 2002. (All, courtesy of Brammo Inc.)

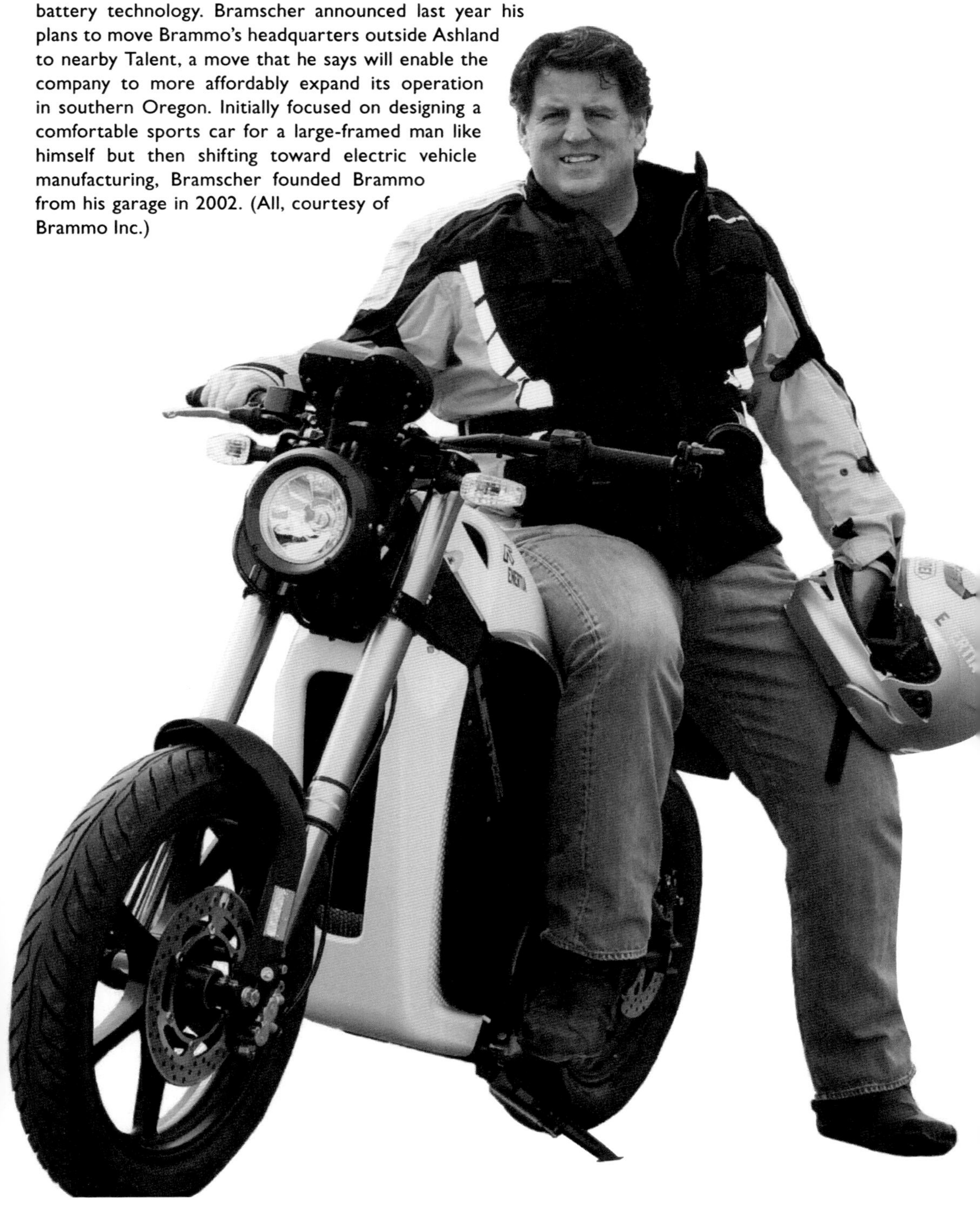

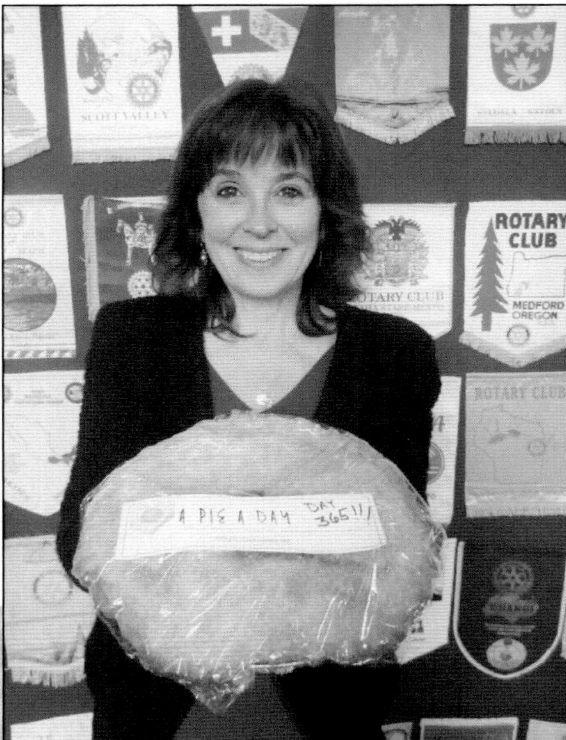

Karen Amarotico

Karen Amarotico, who owns and operates her own catering business in Ashland, baked a pie a day for 365 days in 2011 and 2012 and then handed them out to friends, family, and strangers. She had to bake pies in advance and delivered a few after dark, but they've all found a home, mostly around Ashland. Amarotico baked and delivered a birthday pie for one 89-year-old Ashland man who hit her with his car while she was bicycling, breaking her rib. The man's face dropped when he realized who she was, she remembers. Amarotico baked her first pie when she was 10, and even though she dropped it while taking it out of the oven, her passion for the kitchen has been a constant ever since. (Both, courtesy of Karen Amarotico.)

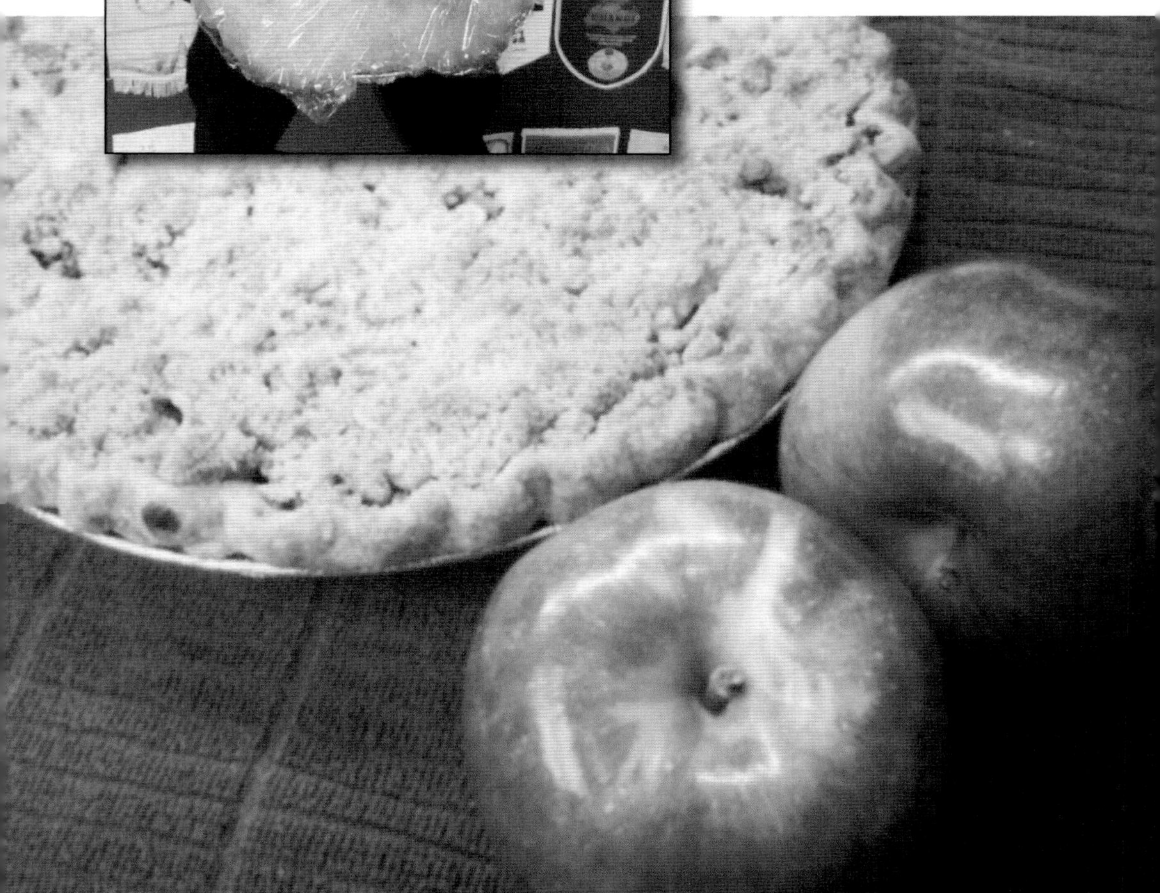

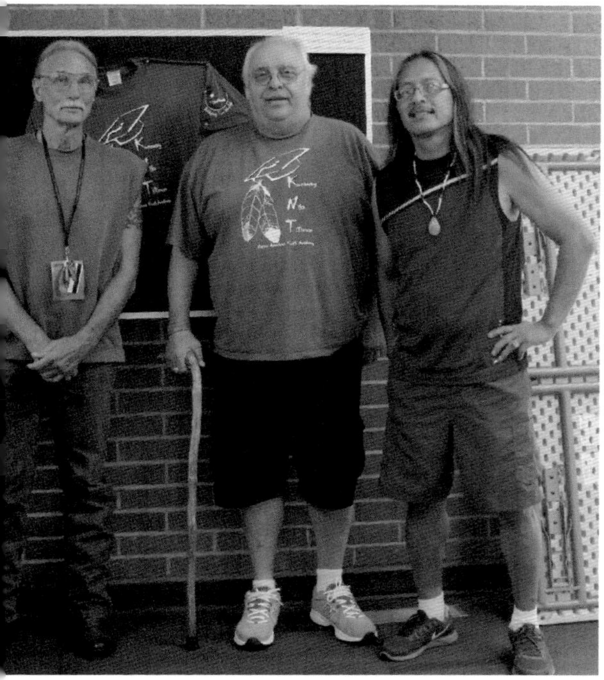

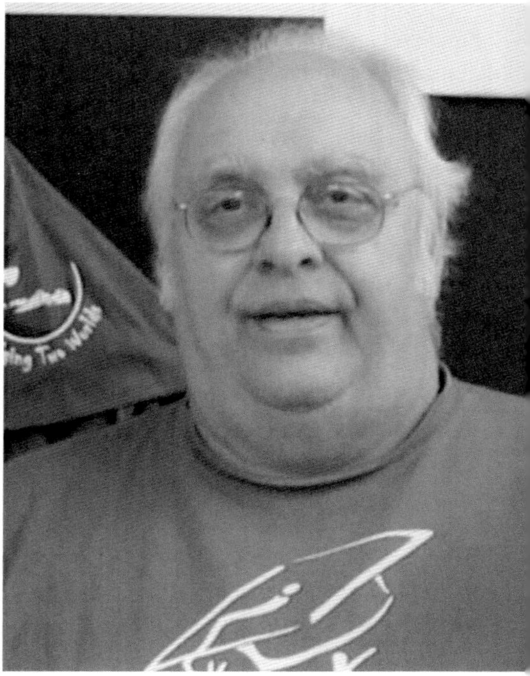

David West

A member of the Citizen Potawatomi Nation, David West is the Native American Studies coordinator at Southern Oregon University and a professor there. In addition to providing oversight for the Native American Student Union at SOU, West is also the program director of Konaway Nika Tillicum, a one-of-a-kind academy and retreat dedicated to providing positive reinforcement for participating Native American youth. Annually, West participates in and helps to organize Ashland's Spring Powwow, and is a member of the Oregon Indian Education Association, the National Indian Education Association, and the National Congress of American Indians. (Both, courtesy of David West.)

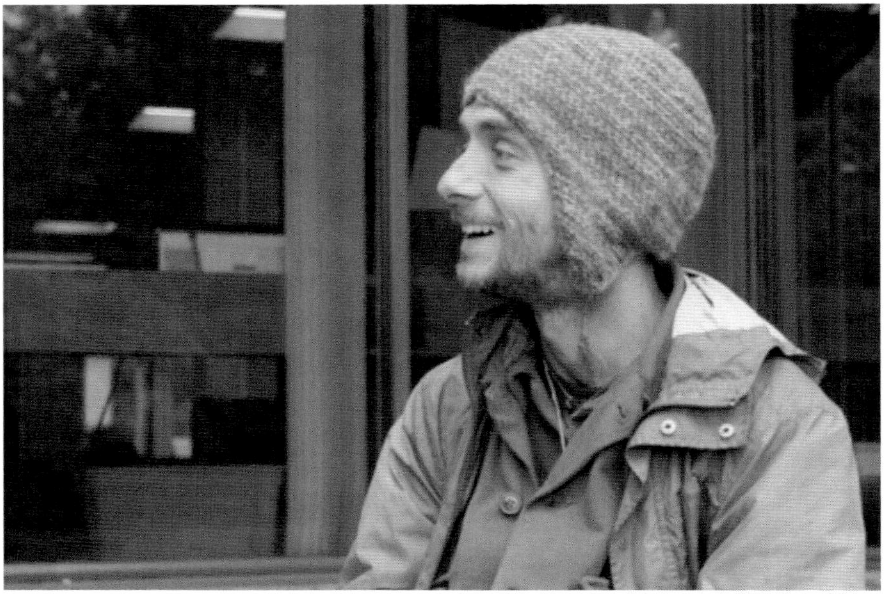

Aaron Fletcher

Ashland has developed a notorious reputation for attracting the homeless, the home free, and vagabonds from all walks of life. Aaron Fletcher, who prefers the term "home free," is unique among them. Now in his early 30s, the Kansas City, Missouri, native made the choice to live home free a little over a decade ago, traveled to Ashland, and decided to stay. During his time as an Ashlander, Fletcher has established a reputation of giving back more to society than he takes. For those in need of a place to stay or instruction in wild and edible plants, jewelry making, or other trades, Fletcher began to help lay the groundwork for the organizations Ashland Homefree Hostel and Ashland Free School in 2012. He has also developed and hands out a pocket resource guide to those living without a place of residence in Ashland. (Both, author photographs.)

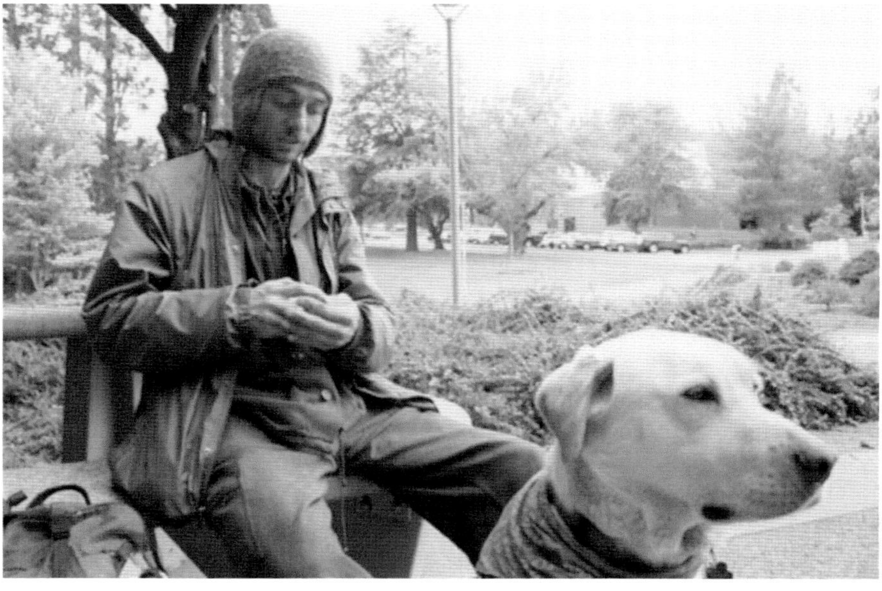

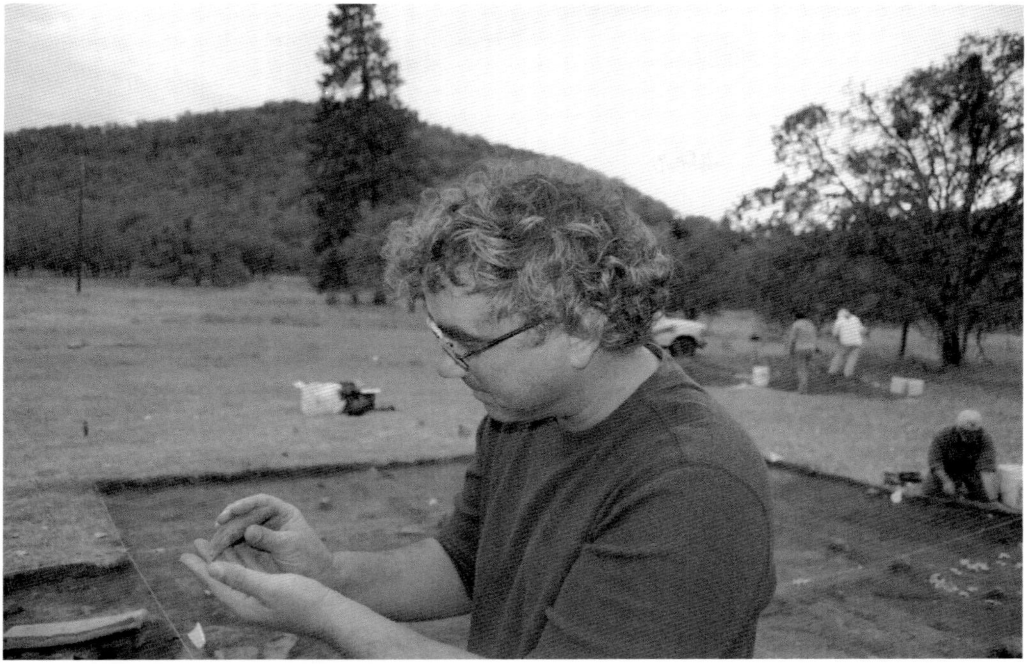

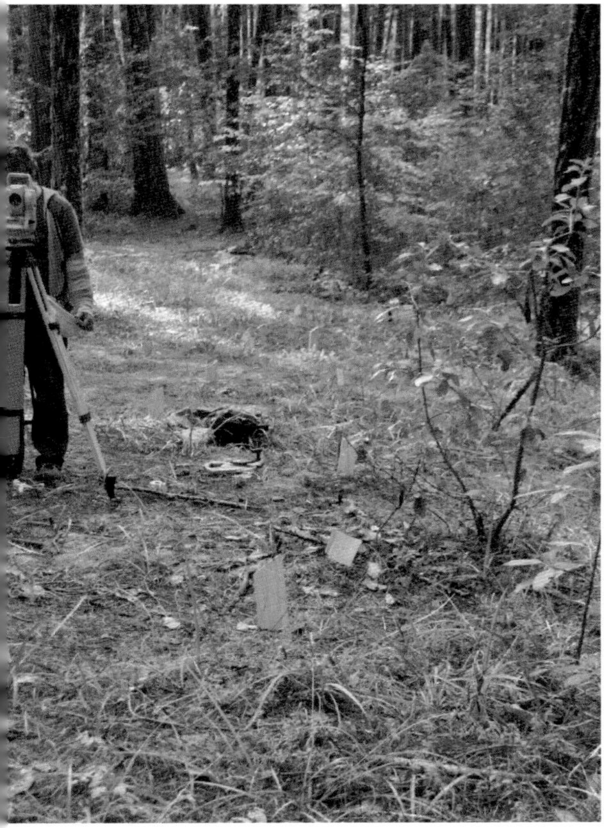

Mark Tveskov
In 2002, Mark Tveskov, associate professor of anthropology and director of Southern Oregon University's anthropology laboratory, led an archaeological survey along Ashland Creek near downtown that uncovered remnants of an ancient fireplace, glass beads, and pieces of stone tools from early Ashland settlers, as well as several stone flakes and arrowheads left by Shasta Native Americans who lived along the banks of Ashland Creek in their village K'wakhakha. His archaeological work around Ashland and throughout southern Oregon has contributed greatly to the ability of today's anthropologists and historians to map areas that were frequented by early settlers and Native Americans before them. (Both, courtesy of Mark Tveskov.)

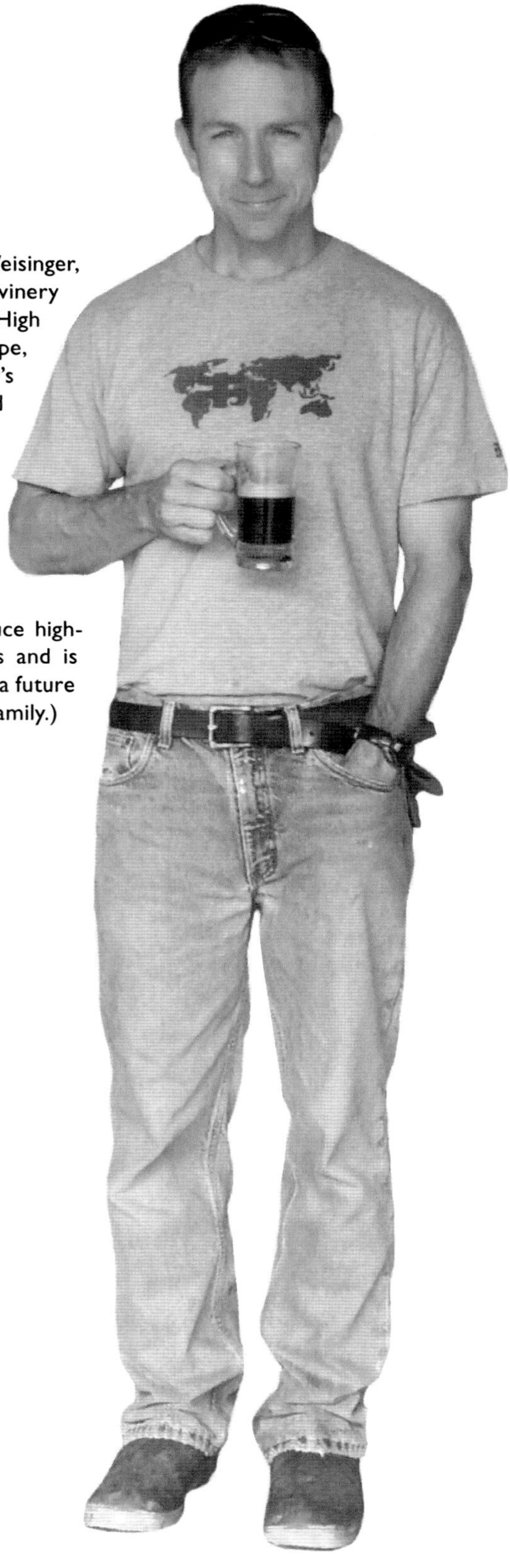

Eric Weisinger
The son of Weisinger Family Winery founder John Weisinger, Eric Weisinger started making wine at his family's winery in 1998. Following his graduation from Ashland High School in 1987, he departed for a trip to Europe, where he and his father traveled southern Germany's wine country and portions of Italy tasting wines and looking into winemaking equipment with the idea of moving forward with John Weisinger's dream of founding a winery in Ashland. Eric has gone on to become a leading wine consultant in southern Oregon after studying viticulture and winemaking firsthand at wineries in New Zealand, California, and Australia. As head winemaker and manager of Weisinger Family Winery, he continues to produce high-quality wines pressed from locally grown grapes and is pushing his family's renowned Ashland winery into a future destined for success. (Courtesy of the Weisinger family.)

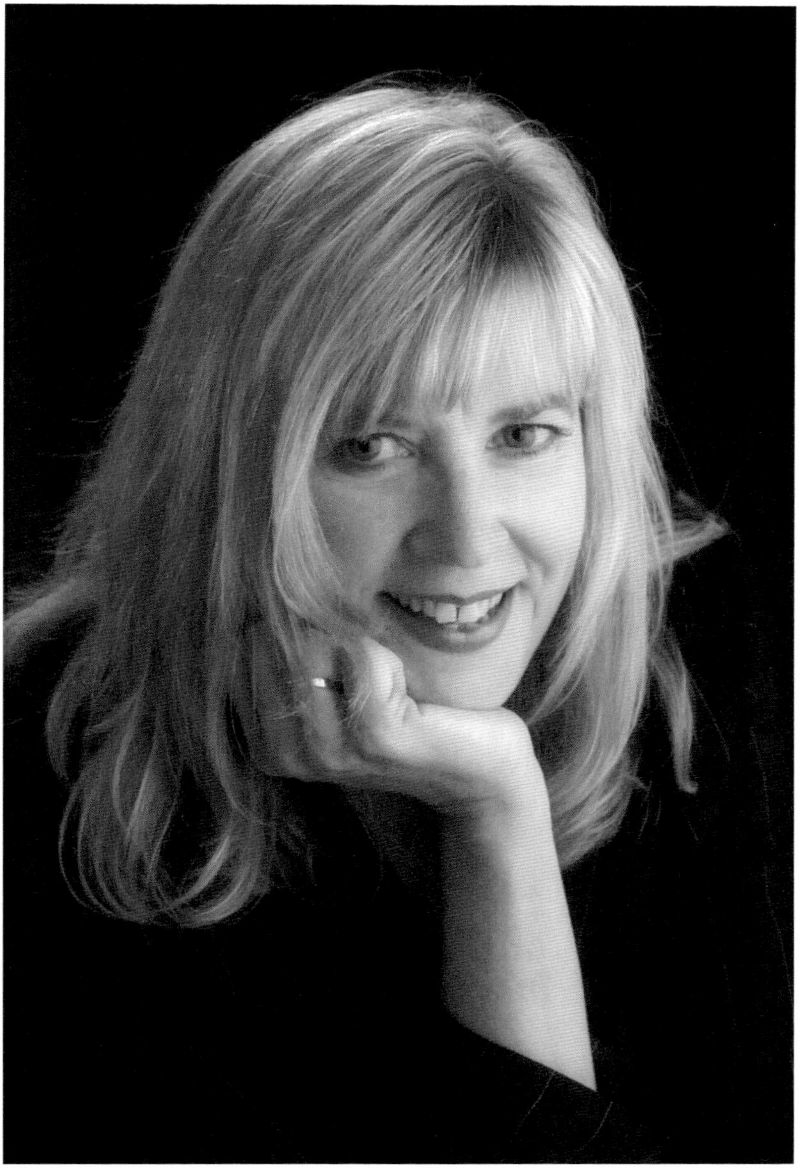

Sandra Slattery
Sandra Slattery has been an employee of the Ashland Chamber of Commerce since 1979, and executive director of the organization since 1985. She has worked on many tourism projects that have served as examples to other communities around the country in addition to acting as a consultant and speaking at state and international conferences. Under her leadership, the chamber has won numerous awards for its success in advancing Ashland's business community and commitment to innovative programs. She is a founding member and former president of the Southern Oregon Visitors Association, past president of the Southern Oregon Historical Society, and current president of the Ashland Community Hospital Foundation, among numerous other community roles. Sandra is married to Dennis Slattery, SOU accounting professor, current Ashland city councilman, and active community member. (Courtesy of Sandra Slattery.)

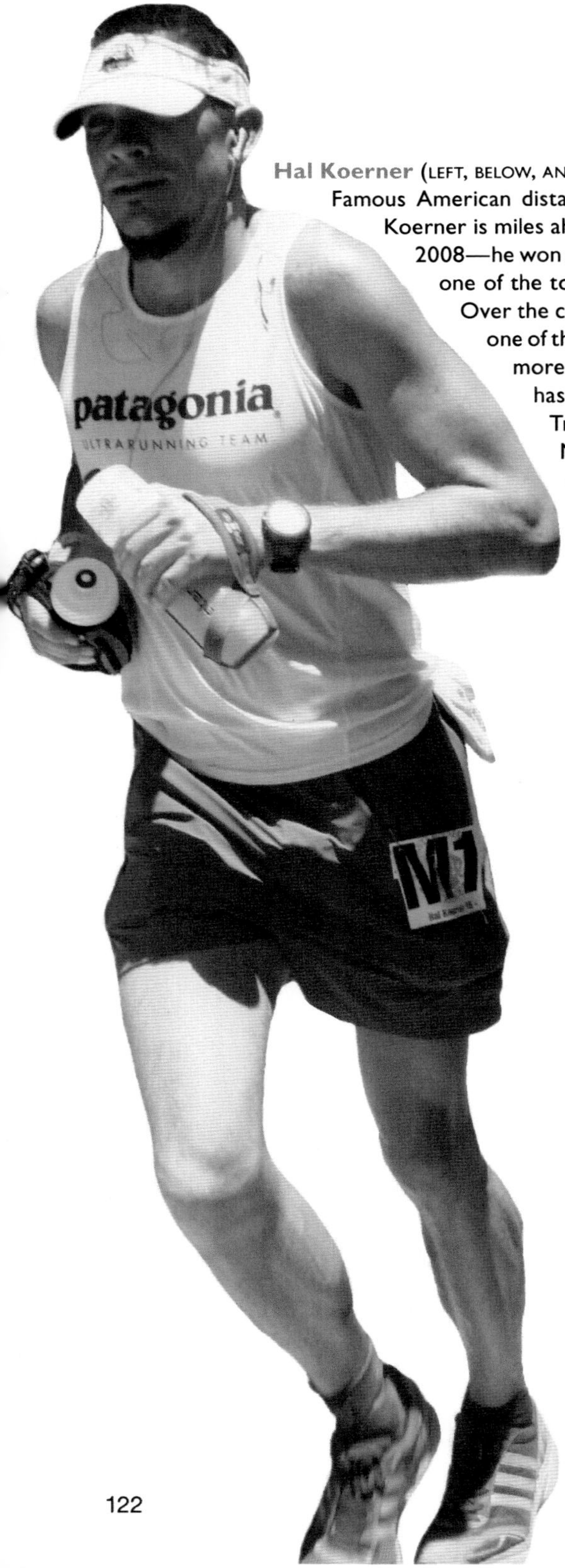

Hal Koerner (LEFT, BELOW, AND OPPOSITE PAGE)
Famous American distance runner and owner of Rogue Valley Runners, Hal Koerner is miles ahead of the pack. In 2007 and 2009—it was cancelled in 2008—he won the Western States Endurance Run, which is considered one of the toughest ultra-marathon endurance runs in the country. Over the course of the last decade, he has continually been named one of the top 10 ultra-runners in North America and completed more than 100 ultra-marathons in his life. Locally, Koerner has played a lead role in organizing and directing the Tar 'N' Trail 6 Mile, Pompadour Half Marathon, Lithia Loop Trail Marathon, and Pine to Palm 100 Mile Endurance Run. (Opposite page, author photograph; below, courtesy of John Fowler; left, courtesy of Kurt Bertilson.)

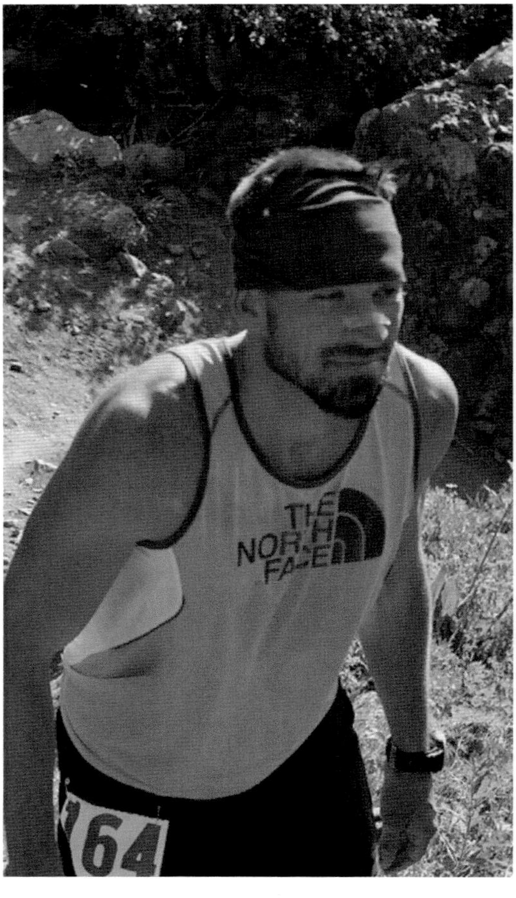

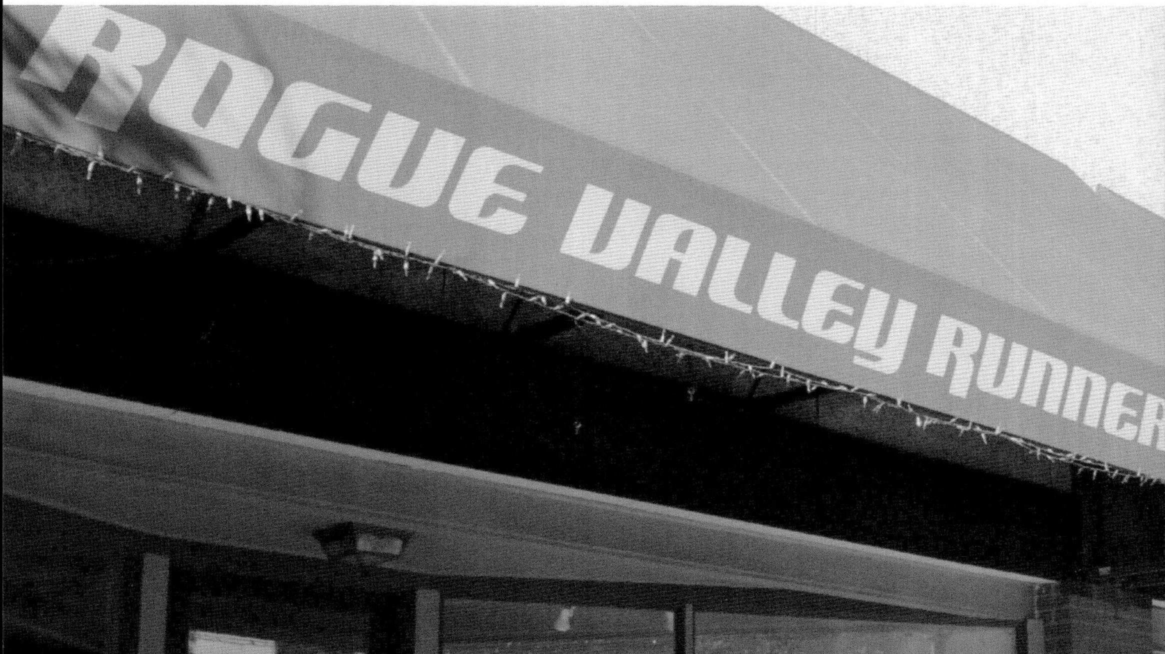
ROGUE VALLEY RUNNER
ROGUE VALLEY RUNNERS

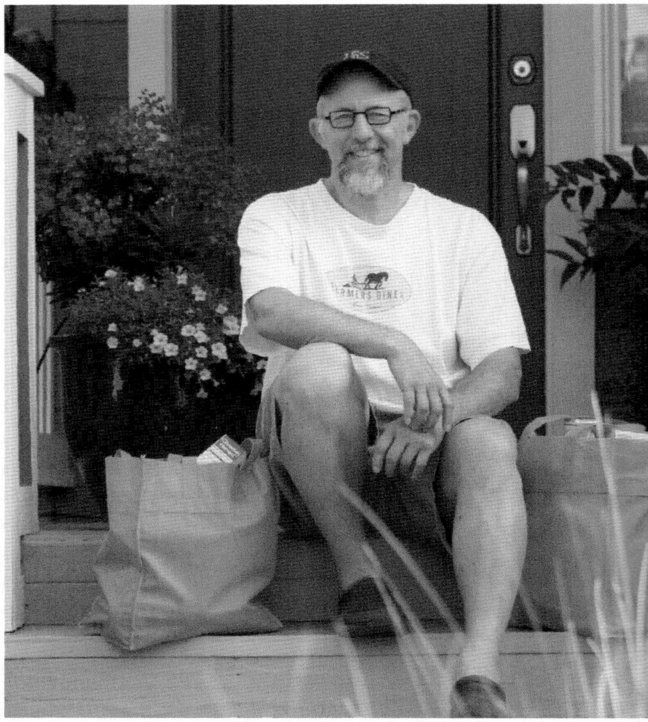

John Javna

John Javna was a fundamental leader in the creation of the Ashland Food Project in 2009. Javna was a part of a small group of Ashlanders who founded the door-to-door food donation pickup organization with the intent of bolstering and steadying the supply of food to local food banks. The plan worked, and the Ashland Food Project model has spurred similar Food Projects across southern Oregon and the nation. The organization received high praise from Oregon governor John Kitzhaber in 2012 and is continually expanding with the participation of more residents. That year, it was reported that about a quarter of Ashland's population participated in the program. John and his wife, Sharon, are also co-founders of ScienceWorks Hands-On Museum in Ashland. (Both, courtesy of John Javna.)

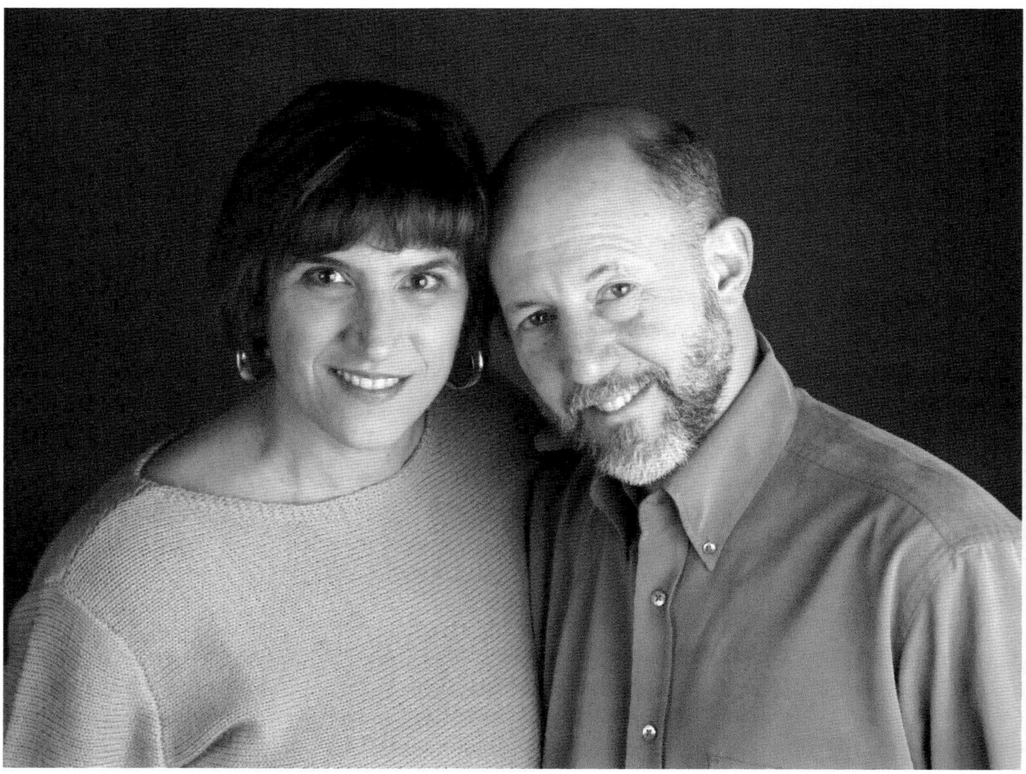

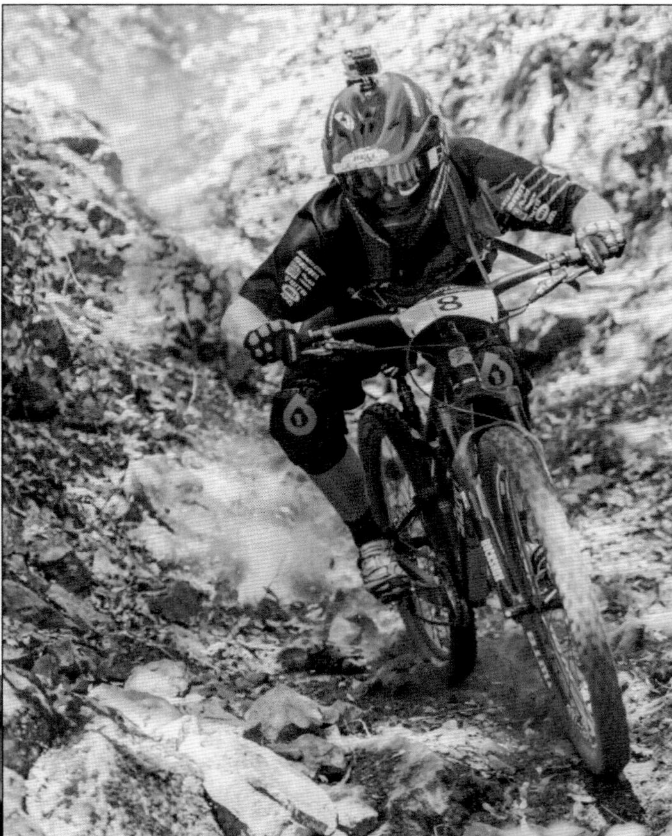

Nathan Riddle
Nathan Riddle is a professional downhill and endurance mountain bike racer, as well as a teacher at the United Bicycle Institute in Ashland. Biking since he was five years old and racing since 20, Riddle has worked in the biking industry and competed in mountain bike events for several years. He has won numerous races locally and across the state over the last decade and lives with his family in Ashland. Although Riddle trains on the trail winding above Ashland's watershed religiously, he adheres to a strict policy of family first, racing second. (Courtesy of Nathan Riddle.)

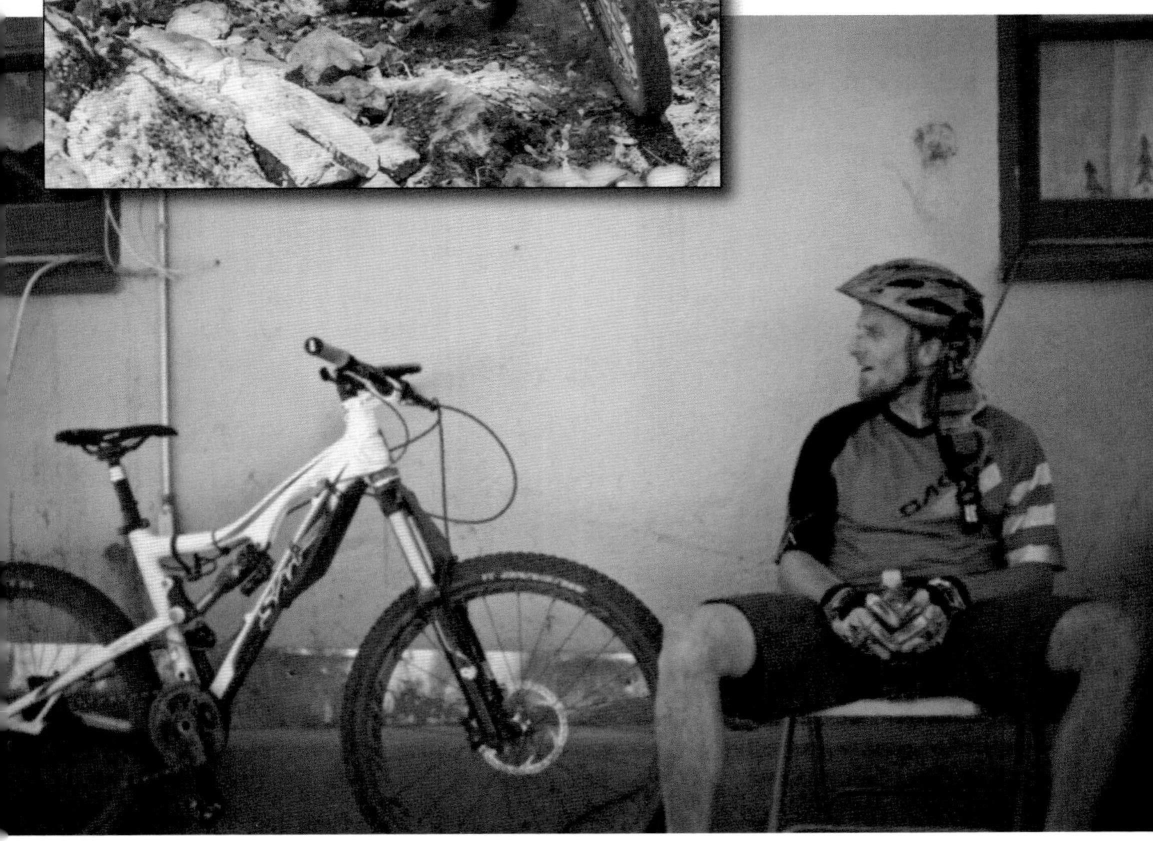

ABOUT THE ASHLAND HISTORICAL SOCIETY

The author would like to thank especially the Southern Oregon Historical Society, whose research library and historical archives contributed greatly to the completion of *Legendary Locals of Ashland*. A nonprofit organization, the Southern Oregon Historical Society was established in 1946 and is located in Medford, Oregon, at 106 North Central Avenue. For more information visit www.sohs.org.